THE NEW AGE DOG

THE NEW AGE DOG

Liz Palika

RENAISSANCE BOOKS
Los Angeles

Acknowledgment is made to the following
for permission to reprint previously published material:

Excerpt from *The Animal Connection: A Guide to Intuitive Communication with Your Pet*, Judy Meyer, copyright © 2000 Judy Meyer, Penguin Putnam, Inc.

Excerpt from *Animal Grace*, Mary Lou Randour, copyright © 2000 Mary Lou Randour, New World Library.

Excerpt from *The Complete Idiot's Guide to Awakening Your Spirituality*, Jonathan Robinson, copyright © 2000 Jonathan Robinson, Alpha Books/Macmillan USA.

Excerpt from *Kinship with All Life*, J. Allen Boone, copyright © 1954 by Harper & Brothers, renewed © 1982 by Daniel U. Boone Jr. and Lois Boone Ragsdale.

Excerpt from *The Natural Dog*, page 167, Mary L. Brennan, D.V.M., and Norma Eckroate, copyright © 1994 Mary L. Brennan and Norma Eckroate, Penguin Books.

Library of Congress Cataloging-in-Publication Data
Palika, Liz
   The new age dog / Liz Palika.
      p. cm.
   ISBN: 1-58063-201-7
   1. Dogs—Behavior. 2. Dogs—Health. 3. Human–animal communication. I. Title.
SF433.P35 2001
636.7'001'9—dc21   2001019722

10 9 8 7 6 5 4 3 2 1

Design by Jesús Arellano

Published by Renaissance Books
Distributed by St. Martin's Press
Manufactured in the United States of America
First edition

CONTENTS

INTRODUCTION

You've never read a book like this one before! You've probably read a lot of books about New Age activities, and it's likely you've read a lot about dogs. And the dog books you've looked at may have contained information about dog care, behavior, or even alternative health care; but they haven't contained everything this book includes. This book takes a look at everything "new" in our relationship with our dogs, from behavior and body language to reincarnation.

What's so New Age about dog behavior and body language? Consider that in the last one hundred years of our relationship with our dogs, training and behavior have consisted of telling dogs what to do. We did the telling and the dogs had to figure out what to do and how to do it. They've done a remarkably good job. In the last decade, however, people who love dogs have said, "Wait a minute! There has to be a better way!" Today, we are trying to understand our dogs, what makes them tick, what their body language says, and how they think. This approach is leading us into a new type of relationship; a New Age, if you will, of people trying to understand dogs rather than vice versa.

In addition to modern approaches to training and communication, you'll find suggestions for uses of herbal remedies, nutritional supplements, and homeopathy for your dog. You may already know the power that crystals, talismans, and color have for you, but how about their affect on your dog? You'll discover what astrology and numerology have to say about your dog and your relationship with him. And this is just the tip of the iceberg; there is much, much more.

When people and dogs first joined forces, the world was a much simpler place—surviving was a full-time activity. Early cave drawings often show a hunter with a dog by his side. The dog was a companion, a watchdog, and a fellow hunter. Today our focus is widely dispersed—try to summarize in a sentence why you do what you do each day—and we seem to easily lose touch with the simpler, more natural parts of our lives.

Your dog, however, can help you regain that simpler life. When you sit outside under a tree, with the wind blowing in your face and your arm around your dog, breathe deeply of the fresh air. Smell the flowers blooming and listen to the birds singing. Turn off the cell phone, ignore the traffic in the background, and instead, focus on that feeling of oneness with your dog and the world around you.

That's what having a dog in your life is all about.

Enjoy the book!

Part 1

YOUR RELATIONSHIP WITH YOUR DOG

Why did you get a dog? If you're like most of us, you wanted a friend who wouldn't argue with you, who wouldn't question your decisions or talk back to you. You wanted a companion who would be there for you and a protector who would use his eyes and ears to watch over you. Our dogs can certainly do all of those things, however, the relationship we have with our dogs is based on many different things including our ability to communicate with them. When communication and understanding increase, the relationship grows by leaps and bounds.

Chapter 1 will help you understand how you (as a human) communicate as well as how your dog communicates. I'll look at verbal communications as well as body language and facial expressions. I'll show you how to use this knowledge and will give you a chance to practice it. After all, clear communication is necessary for the exploring you and your dog will do together.

In chapter 2, I'll take a look at behavior modification, what it is and how it works. Behavior modification works both ways; you may want to change your own actions as well as your dog's. I'll put your new communication skills to work here, too.

In chapter 3, I will talk about some less common communication skills, including visualizations and nonverbal communication. And I'll teach you how to communicate with your dog in a very different but wonderful way.

Spirituality is the focus of chapter 4. According to the beliefs of many organized religions, animals do not have souls. Yet many dog owners feel a spiritual bond with their canine companion. I'll talk about the origin of such beliefs and why people feel the way they do. I'll show you how to increase your own spiritual awareness and how to incorporate your dog into your own beliefs.

Your journey begins here. Let's go exploring!

EVERYTHING BEGINS WITH COMMUNICATION

Jim was having a difficult time getting his Golden Retriever, Betsy, to behave. According to Jim, she seemed to lack self-control and to ignore everything he said. When he enrolled in my dog training class, he was at his wit's end. "I've always wanted a dog," he said, "And I've watched my friends' Golden Retrievers for years, but Betsy isn't like the dogs I've seen. They always seemed so calm, gentle, and responsive."

Jim was making a few mistakes, the first of which was comparing his seven-month-old puppy with his friends' adult dogs. Adult Golden Retrievers are calmer than puppies, and I'm sure if he asked, his friends would admit their dogs had not always been so mellow.

Jim was also having trouble communicating with Betsy. As a naturally soft-spoken man, his verbal communications confused Betsy. Jim's verbal corrections were much like his commands. Often Jim's body language conflicted with his verbal commands and corrections.

He needed help learning how to communicate with Betsy so she understood what he wanted from her.

In the not-so-distant past, dog trainers would have told Jim how to force Betsy to behave. Today, however, Jim is learning why Betsy is behaving the way she is, what mistakes Jim is making in communicating with her, and how he can mend their relationship. The end result will be wonderful; Jim and Betsy will understand and trust each other. Instead of an antagonistic relationship, they will have a symbiotic relationship and no one can ask for more than that.

THE MAGIC OF COMMUNICATION

Your relationship with your dog is based on communication. This can take many forms, including words, tone of voice, facial expressions, and body language. All of these things tell an educated dog (a dog who has learned to interpret people) what it is that is expected of him, but communication works both ways; the dog isn't the only one who must be educated. Communication is effective only when the dog's owner knows that his words, tone of voice, facial expressions, and body language are his communication tools. In addition, the wise owner also learns to see, read, and understand his dog's verbalizations, expressions, and body language.

I learned the hard way many years ago how important my body language and expressions were to my dog and how closely my dog watched me. My German Shepherd, Michi, and I were competing in obedience trials. During one competition, we were doing very well (so well that I expected to win) right up to the last exercise. This exercise was the recall (come). I had Michi sit at one side of the ring, and, as per the judge's instruction, told him to "Wait" as I walked across the ring.

On the judge's command, I said, "Michi, come!" but my dog didn't move. I waited, getting angrier and more embarrassed by the moment. Michi knew this command and did it well all the time; there was no excuse for him to sit there and stare at me without coming.

Finally, after what seemed to be an eternity, the judge walked over to me and said, "You do realize, don't you, that this was your mistake?"

I didn't think that was right at all and began to protest, however, the judge raised a finger to stop me and said, "What did you just do to your dog?"

I thought about it and said, "I called him to come."

The judge said, "No, you didn't. You just ordered him to come in a very angry tone of voice. Plus you were scowling and leaning torward him—very aggressively I might add—with your hands clenched at your sides." He let that sink in for a moment and then continued in a softer tone of voice, "You and your dog were doing very well. In fact, up until now you probably would have placed first or second. Why did you get so angry at him? He hadn't made any mistakes at all."

As I stewed over this information, the judge excused us from the ring and I walked over to retrieve my now worried dog. As Michi and I sat down on the grass outside the ring, I thought about what the judge had said and tried to remember my own actions. Up until that exercise, we had been doing well and I knew it. I am very competitive, though, and going into that last exercise I tensed up, knowing that if we did this exercise correctly we would probably win. This tenseness probably caused the change in my body language. I was afraid we might make a mistake, and I took that tension out on Michi, ordering him to come in a harsh tone of voice, instead of calling him in a non-threatening tone. Michi, hearing the harsh tone of voice and seeing

the change in my body language, assumed that he had done something wrong (even though he didn't know what that might be) and
that I was angry. Confused, he decided it was safer to sit still and do
nothing.

Losing that competition did more for me than winning ever
would have. Winning would have added another ribbon to our
already crowded walls but losing taught me to pay attention to my
voice—both what I say to my dogs and how I say it. This, in turn,
led me to pay more attention to nonverbal communication as
well. What were my facial expressions conveying to Michi? What
did my body language tell him? Michi's momentary misfortune
turned into something very positive for him and for all the dogs
that followed him because I realized with that lesson that everything is based on communication. Without clear communication,
there is no understanding. Without understanding, there is no
relationship, and the relationship I have with my dogs is everything to me.

COMMUNICATION TECHNIQUES

*Although you probably don't think about it much, you are always
using several methods to communicate.*

- *Tone of voice: How you say things*
- *Spoken words: The things you say*
- *Facial expressions: The positions and expressions you make
  with your eyes, eyebrows, mouth, and face*
- *Body language: Your posture, bearing, body position, and
  movements*

UNDERSTANDING VERBAL COMMUNICATION

If you have ever lost your voice (even temporarily), you know how important verbal communication is to us as a species. We talk about everything, and everyone around us is speaking, too. We listen to the radio while we drive our cars and fill our living rooms with voices from the television. We are constantly surrounded by verbal communication.

Our Tone of Voice

Tone of voice refers to the loudness of our voice as well as how the words are spoken. As kids, when we heard the ice cream truck coming down the street and we yelled, "Ice cream!" that tone of voice could easily be referred to as happy and expectant. It was high pitched, excited, and the words were spoken quickly.

Our verbalizations do have a lot of inconsistencies; however, the tone of voice we use in some of our verbalizations can be categorized with some accuracy.

LOVE—This is usually expressed in a soft tone of voice, usually quietly but sometimes shouted to the skies.

HAPPINESS—This is normally expressed using a "normal" to slightly higher than normal tone of voice with a lilt or laugh in it. Laughter, however, is something totally different, and each individual has his or her own laugh.

QUESTIONS—These are usually asked in a voice that goes higher in tone toward the end of the sentence.

DEMANDS—Orders are usually stated in a loud voice. Interestingly, men will usually use a deeper than normal tone of voice when making a demand, and women usually use a higher than normal tone for the same purpose.

FRUSTRATION—The voice usually becomes louder with the extent of the frustration; often deeper in tone with men and higher in tone with women. When people are frustrated, they often speak more rapidly than usual.

ANGER—Men often express anger in a deep, quiet voice; women often express anger with a higher pitched tone of voice, but this can vary among individuals. Angry words are usually spoken more quickly than normal.

FEAR—This is usually expressed in a higher pitched tone of voice, both for men and women. Sometimes, fearful people whisper or speak quietly depending upon the situation.

What we do unconsciously and what our dogs must learn to do is to listen for the variances in tone from the normal tone of voice. By listening to these variances in tone, we (and our dogs) can learn to gauge the emotions of the speaker.

Our Spoken Words

The specific words we speak can affect the tone of voice we use. For example, in my dog training classes I have found that dogs often live up to their names simply because of the tone of voice that their owners use when saying those names.

For example, say the word *killer*. It comes out pretty serious, doesn't it? If a Rottweiler or even a Chihuahua is named Killer, that name would always be said using a serious tone of voice, and that dog would look upon life quite seriously—perhaps too seriously.

Let's look at it from another direction. Say the word *bubbles*. That always sounds kind of silly. If you changed Killer's name to Bubbles, it would change the dog's entire outlook on life because he would be addressed by his owners in an entirely different tone of voice. Instead of his owners looking at him and saying "Killer" in a deep, serious tone of voice, they would look at him and say "Bubbles" with laughter in their voice. What a weight they would take off that dog's shoulders.

We change the tone of voice that we use for different words all the time. Therefore, although the actual words that we speak to our dogs are important, they are important both because of their meaning to our dog and because of the meaning that we put on them as well.

Canine Verbal Communication

Before we can expect our dogs to understand our verbal communication, we need to understand theirs. After all, we cannot ask our dogs to change their method of communication, but we can make changes to our own so that understanding between the two species occurs more easily.

Dogs do not use verbal communication alone to communicate; it is always used in conjunction with body language and facial expression. Again, this is just like us; we do the same thing although we are not always consciously aware of it, but I'll talk more about that later in this chapter. Just remember that verbalizations do not occur alone.

HAPPINESS—Happiness is usually expressed with higher than normal-pitched barks, usually quick and sharp. Some dogs chitter when they are happy.

AFFECTION OR LOVE—Most dogs murmur or groan when they're feeling affectionate. When your dog is cuddled up with you and you're rubbing behind his ears, he's apt to groan, sigh, or murmur.

PLAYFULNESS—Play is solicited with high-pitched barks, usually single barks.

WORRY OR FEAR—These emotions are often expressed with a series of high-pitched barks or high-pitched whines.

ALERTNESS OR WATCHFULNESS—Alertness is expressed as a single bark in the dog's normal voice.

DOMINANCE, AGGRESSION, OR DEFENSIVENESS—These feelings are expressed as low growls that sound like they're coming from the dog's chest.

DISTRESS—Distress is usually expressed with a plaintive howl.

When we understand canine verbal tones and when those tones are used, we can make communication easier between our two species. For example, when puppies are playing with their litter-mates, if one puppy bites another using too much force, the puppy being bitten will yelp. That high-pitched yelp means, "Ouch! That hurt!" If that same rowdy puppy bites his mom, she will growl at him, telling him, "Mind your manners! You're not allowed to bite me!" To deter nipping, we can use both of those verbalizations to our advantage.

TRY THIS

If your dog, during play, gets too rough, you can respond with a high-pitched, "Ouch!" followed by a deep, growling, "Be easy!" Your dog will understand that you are first saying that his behavior was too rough and hurt you, and second, that you won't allow that behavior to continue.

Establish a Vocabulary

Years ago, canine experts felt that our dogs had a very limited intelligence and ability to learn, so people taught their dogs the five basic commands—heel, sit, down, stay, and come—and that was about it. Dog owners today, however, are not confined by that thinking. We know that our dogs are much smarter and more perceptive than we can even imagine, and their ability to learn is hampered only by our ability to teach them. Therefore, establishing a mutual vocabulary is important for your growing relationship.

Because understanding an ongoing spoken conversation is too much to expect (even for our intelligent dogs), you will want to establish a vocabulary for your dog. By making a list of spoken words (or phrases) and their meanings, you can ensure that you and all other family members are using the same vocabulary when talking to your dog. Not only will this consistency help your dog learn, but it will eliminate a lot of misunderstandings.

How large your dog's vocabulary will be depends upon many factors. What do you do with your dog? My dogs and I participate in quite a few different activities, and many of those have words or phrases for specific actions. We're involved in dog therapy work, and we frequently visit the elderly. For this purpose, the dogs have commands such as:

- "Go say hi!" which means get close enough so that the person can touch you.
- "Paws up," which means lift your feet to the rail of the walker, arm of the wheelchair, or bed rail.
- "Turn around," which means face the opposite direction.
- "Step over," which means lift your paws over that obstacle.
- "Leave it," which means ignore that crumb, food, or pill on the floor.

We also have commands for other activities, including obedience, herding, carting, flyball, and other dog sports. And I have specific commands for around the house. Dax gets the newspapers every morning so she knows the command, "Get the papers!" I have turtles and tortoises in the backyard, and the dogs help me find them each morning when I go out to count noses so they know the command, "Find the turtle!"

To begin making your vocabulary list, start with your dog's basic obedience commands. Does he know "Sit"? "Down"? "Heel"? "Stay"? How about "Come"? What words do you use around the house? Do you tell him, "Get out of the way." when he's underfoot? How about, "Go lay down." Make a list of those words you use when out on a walk, when you're playing with your dog, and when he's riding in the car with you.

Once you've made up a list of all the words your dog already knows, think about new words you would like to teach him. What would be fun? Teach him the names of his toys. Teach him your spouse's name and your kids' names. Don't underestimate how many words your dog can learn. He probably already understands more than you think anyway. There is almost no limit to how many words your dog can understand; you're limited only by your skills as a teacher.

KINDER, GENTLER TRAINING

Teaching your dog does not necessarily mean yanking him about with the leash. Instead, teaching your dog is easy and painless if you follow these steps.

1. *Show your dog what it is you want him to do.*
2. *Say the name or word or command.*
3. *Help your dog do what it is you are asking him to do.*
4. *Praise and reward him for it.*
5. *When he does it simply in response to your command (without your help), really reward him!*
6. *When he makes a mistake, let him know using your tone of voice and body language.*

The Problem with Verbal Communication

Although verbal communication is important to the relationship we have with our dog, especially when we need to control his behavior, there is a problem with it. We have a tendency to talk too much, and when we do, our dogs stop listening.

Remember that people talk on the television, on the radio, and on CDs. Our dogs hear our neighbors talking and hear us as we talk to each other and ourselves. When there is too much talking that our dogs don't understand, they just tune us out and let the gibberish go right on by them. Then, when we try to get our dog's attention and find that he's not listening, we have a tendency to get angry, "Sweetie, listen! Why aren't you paying attention?"

I enjoy that old refrain, "Silence is golden." Often at home, I will turn off the television, radio, and music and let the house be totally quiet for two or three hours at a time; sometimes even longer. This gives my dogs and myself a break from the constant noise around us. Then, when I talk to my dogs, their ears go up; they focus on me and are ready to listen.

TRY THIS

One day when the house is quiet, try whispering to your dog. Say his name in a whisper and praise him when he turns to look at you. When you've got his attention, whisper a few other words to him and reward him with praise and a treat. You will find your dog concentrating more to hear you when you whisper.

Another type of misunderstanding occurs when our dogs aren't quite sure what we're talking about. Imagine that your dog is out in the front yard with you, and he decides he wants to go play with your neighbor's child. You tell him, "Sweetie, no!" What does he think? You want him to think that he's not supposed to leave the yard without permission, but he may think that he isn't supposed to play with the child; maybe the kid is the trouble. Or that he isn't supposed to step off the driveway where he was standing when you said no. Or that perhaps he was too close to your car so maybe the car is in trouble, or is the cause of the trouble. As you can see, verbalizations can cause some incredible misunderstandings.

DON'T UNDERESTIMATE YOUR DOG'S ABILITIES

Your dog's understanding of what you're expressing is not limited solely to what you actually say. Many dogs (probably most dogs) also hear what isn't said. Whether you call it ESP or psychic communication, our dogs understand more than we really know. But I'll talk about that at length in chapter 3.

UNDERSTANDING FACIAL EXPRESSIONS

Facial expressions are a vital part of communication and go hand in hand (or paw in paw) with verbal communication. We move our lips to smile, grimace, laugh, or sneer, and we move our eyebrows, wrinkle our nose, and so much more. So many of our facial expressions are done unconsciously that it's almost impossible to control them at all. People who can master the proverbial "poker face"—showing no expression—are very rare.

Some of our facial expressions can also cause confusion. We smile when we're happy, but dogs bare their teeth when snarling, a threatening gesture. Although dogs who grow up with people are familiar with our smile and understand it, wild canines (such as wolves and coyotes) do not and often take it as a threatening expression.

> ### TRY THIS
>
> *Stand in front of a mirror and try to say something meaningful without using any facial expressions. Tell your dog, "What a good dog!" and sound like you mean it. What facial expressions did you make? You may have been able to control a few motions but I bet some snuck through.*

We also cause some miscommunication with our eyes. When we talk to someone, we usually make eye contact with that person, looking directly at them. In our particular species, we understand direct eye contact to be synonymous with sincerity. Dogs, however, generally perceive direct eye contact as dominance. The dog who is feeling very dominant and is willing to challenge the pack order is the one who will stand tall, face the other dog straight on, and make direct eye contact. You may be able to have direct eye contact with your own dog, who understands you and is willing to let you be dominant, but a strange dog could take your stare as a challenge. This simple misunderstanding between species could stimulate aggressive behavior.

Canine Facial Expressions

For both dogs and humans, facial expressions are an important part of conveying thoughts, reactions, and emotions. Dogs, however, have a disadvantage in this area because their faces are not nearly as mobile as ours are. One interesting theory is that the colors and markings on many dogs' faces are there for the purpose of emphasizing facial expressions.

Doberman Pinschers, Rottweilers, Australian Shepherds, Bernese Mountain Dogs, and others with tri-color markings (usually black, brown, and white) have built-in facial expression. The copper or brown markings on their cheeks bring emphasis to the mouth, so that when the dog uses his mouth, it is highlighted and a snarl looks bigger than it is. The copper or brown markings above the eyes do the same thing; they highlight eye movements and expressions.

Siberian Huskies and Malamutes have darker or lighter markings around their eyes and ears. The markings help exaggerate expressions and also make the expressions stand out against a snowy background.

Many breeds have a very dark muzzle. German Shepherds, Boxers, as well as many Mastiffs and Great Danes have coloring on their muzzle that is darker than the rest of their facial coloring. The dark muzzle emphasizes the whiteness of the dog's teeth. Not only does this make the dog's teeth look bigger and more forbidding when he snarls, but they look bigger and more forbidding when the dog is relaxed and simply has his mouth open to pant.

Notably, some of our dogs also have a disadvantage in communication as a result of their physical form. There have been so many breeds developed with different facial characteristics that facial expressions can vary from one breed to another. For example, upright, forward-facing ears signal alertness in German Shepherds, Akitas, Malamutes, Siberian Huskies, and other breeds with upright ears. Labrador Retrievers, Beagles, and Basset Hounds, however, can't use that same signal; they must express alertness in a different way. Their ears can twitch forward but certainly cannot stand up. This can make communication a little confusing.

With all of the breed differences, most dogs do have some similar facial expressions.

A NEW TAKE ON CROPPING

Doberman Pinschers, Boxers, and many other breeds are born with ears that do not stand up. They normally hang down; however, it is acceptable in many of these breeds to have the ears cropped (cut) and taped so that they will stand erect—much like a German Shepherd's ears.

The change in the dog's ear carriage affects communication— both with other dogs and with people. A dog with upright ears is perceived to be alert, watchful, and potentially reactive, whereas a dog with hanging ears is accepted as much more relaxed. These observations are exactly why the ears were cropped in the beginning; people wanted a dog (or breed) who was perceived to be more watchful, more protective, more aggressive, and more alert, and the cropped ear emphasized that look.

In many countries today, it is illegal to crop ears, and more and more dogs are being allowed to retain their natural look. Not only is this kinder to the dogs involved, but it will eventually enhance communication between both dogs and people.

RELAXED, HAPPY, COMFORTABLE—The dog's forehead will be smooth, his mouth closed or partially opened in a gentle pant, and the tongue will be relaxed. Eyes will be relaxed, even partially closed. Ears will be hanging loosely or be up but not forward.

PLAYFUL—He will make soft eye contact, looking at the dog or person that he wants to play with, but not challenging. The eyes will be wide open, the ears relaxed but forward, the mouth partially opened, and there might be a relaxed pant. He may salivate in excitement.

EXCITED—Look for the playful characteristics with greater intensity. The tongue may flick in and out, he will pant, and he may salivate. If the ears are upright naturally, they'll be in an alert position; if they're hanging, they will be forward.

WATCHFUL AND ALERT—Everything will move forward; the ears will be forward, erect, and tense if they stand up. The eyes will be open and alert. The mouth is usually open and the dog may pant slightly. The nose is sniffing.

WORRIED—He will look quickly at his cause of worry, but then will look away. He may look down. His ears will be back. His tongue may flick in and out, either to lick his own nose or to lick the cause of his worry (an appeasement gesture).

FRIGHTENED—His lips will be pulled back, creasing the corners. His ears will be back and flat to his skull. He will lower his head and look away from what is frightening him.

AGGRESSIVE—He will snarl, baring the front teeth including the canines. His lips will be curled and the nose will be wrinkled. His expression will have a severe look. He will make direct, hard eye contact. The ears will be as far forward as possible.

Understanding these facial expressions can help us communicate better with our dog, both by reading him better and by using some of these expressions ourselves. Granted, our ears won't stand erect and it's hard to flatten them to our skull, but we can copy some of the ways dogs communicate with their faces.

WHEN YOUR DOG YAWNS

Have you ever been upset at your dog—for any reason—and had him look away from you and yawn? You might have gotten angry, "Don't look away from me. I'm not boring you am I?" That yawn wasn't boredom—your dog was giving you a calming signal—he was saying, "Relax." Yawning in times of stress is the dog's way of trying to calm things down a little. After all, in the dog's world, stress can lead to a fight where both members could potentially get hurt quite badly. If stress can be relieved with no loss of face or status, it should be.

UNDERSTANDING BODY LANGUAGE

Our words, tone of voice, and facial expressions work in conjunction with our body language. None stands alone when we try and communicate—either with other people or with our dogs. In fact, body language is so instinctive, we often don't realize that we are using it or observing it.

Businesses often hold seminars for their leaders and salespeople so that they can better understand their own body language and the body language of the people they are dealing with. Many first impressions are made (positively or negatively) on the basis of a person's body language while being introduced.

Because dogs' use of verbalization is not as expansive as ours is, body language and facial expressions are their primary means of communication. Therefore, to communicate well with our dogs, we have to use our own body language consciously, and we need to understand what our dogs are telling us with theirs.

Our Body Language

There are many aspects of body language you consciously recognize. When someone crosses his arms over his chest, you immediately feel that that person is shutting you out. This is a very defensive and very protective posture. You feel the same thing when someone backs away from you—even one or two steps—when you're talking to him. There are, however, other body language nuances you may not be as familiar with; here are a few that can affect your relationship with your dog, or with other dogs.

STANDING TALL, FACING FORWARD—This is a dominant position and is fine with your own dog who accepts and understands your position. This, however, can be frightening to a strange, timid dog and a challenge to a strange, dominant dog.

STANDING RIGID, STIFF, OR TENSE—This, too, can be taken as a dominant position. To a dog, it is even one step closer to dominance aggression.

TURNING AWAY—Shifting your body away from a dog is seen as a submissive action. This is good when you're trying to alleviate tension or stress, or to stop a possible dominance challenge with a strange dog. It's not usually a good idea with your own dog if your dog likes to think of himself as in charge.

MAKING EXCESSIVE HAND MOTIONS—Have you ever seen a dog communicate by waving his front paws in the air? Dogs are often confused by people who talk with numerous hand gestures. When getting to know a dog, try to keep your hands still. Your dog, of course, will learn to ignore the excess motions.

LAYING ON THE GROUND OR FLOOR—Placing yourself very low and then allowing your dog to stand above you may seem very innocent but it's not. The dog who is above the other is the dominant dog.

These examples are just a few of the messages we send to our dogs all the time. I'll discuss how we can use our body language to its best advantage later in this chapter.

TRY THIS

Lie on the floor and call your dog. What does she do? If she lies down in front of you and tries to get her head under yours, wonderful. She accepts you as her leader. If she thinks this is great and stands above your head or shoulder, you need to work on some leadership exercises. She's letting you know that you're not really the boss.

Canine Body Language

Dogs have a wonderfully rich body language vocabulary—especially when compared to our own. We are so used to speaking on the telephone and communicating with only our voice that we've lost some of our body language skills. Our dogs, though, depend on body language cues to help them communicate. Many of their expressions, movements, and postures are so subtle that even people who research canine body language probably miss a number of them; however, many dog owners who have learned to watch their dogs do learn their own dog's specific expressions. After all, the more you know, the better your ability to communicate.

SPACE INVASION

All animals (including canines and humans) have a need for personal space. Some, especially those often hunted as prey, prefer a large personal space while others are satisfied with a smaller personal space. Some people need more space than others. When talking to someone, have you felt uncomfortable because that person seemed to be right in your face? That person needs less space than you do.

In nature, a wild animal will move away when that space is invaded. Think of a circular bubble surrounding the animal. When that bubble is pushed upon, the animal moves away until the bubble can relax and form a circle again. If the animal cannot move away and that personal space is intruded upon, however, the animal's body language will immediately tense up and will remain tense until the personal space can be re-established.

Here are some basic cues:

HAPPY AND CALM—The entire body is relaxed, including the tail. The head is positioned neither high nor low; the mouth may be open slightly but is held loosely. The tail is down and relaxed, not tucked.

EXCITED AND PLAYFUL—The dog may playbow, lowering the front end to the ground. The tail will wag. The dog may bounce up and down from standing to the playbow and back up again.

INTERESTED AND ALERT—The head will be raised and the body will lean forward a little. A front paw may be raised, as if in anticipation of moving forward. The tail will be in a medium-height position; it may wag a little but not a lot. The speed of the wagging will increase with the degree of interest.

EXCITED AND ANTICIPATORY—The dog may bounce up and down, may try to jump up on you, and will quiver in readiness. The tail will be wagging.

STALKING, HUNTING, HERDING—The dog will slightly lower the front end (not as far as the playbow, however) and will slink toward the object of his attention. His entire body will be tense, even the tail. The head will be lower than the shoulders.

SUBMISSIVE—A submissive dog tries to appear smaller than the dominant dog or person. He will crouch, lay on his back, or lower his head. The tail will be down or even tucked between the back legs.

DOMINANT—The dominant dog stands tall and positions himself above the other dog (or person!). He may stand on the tips of his toes. He will often put his front paw or chin on the shoulder of the other dog.

PROTECTIVE—The legs will be planted firmly, head will be high or just slightly lowered. The body will face forward, and the tail may be rigid. As action increases, the dog will lean forward toward the problem.

AGGRESSIVE—The hackles will be up; the dog's head will be up, the tail up and still. The dog will stand tall and will lean forward. As tension mounts, the dog will slightly spread his back feet to give himself better leverage.

Obviously we cannot duplicate all of our dogs' body language signals. We don't have four feet, we don't have hackles to raise and lower, and a tail wouldn't fit comfortably in our jeans! Nonetheless, simply understanding our dogs' body language will go a long way toward solving some misunderstandings. When we can look at our dog and say to ourselves, "Wow, she's a little defensive today" or "Molly wants to play." our communication with our dogs will be greatly improved.

THE AMBIGUOUS WAGGING TAIL

A wagging tail doesn't always indicate that a dog is happy, although most dog owners seem to think so. Instead, a wagging tail signifies stress or strong emotion. Granted, that strong emotion might be happiness, but it can also be fear, anticipation, hunger, even aggression. To decide exactly what the wagging tail means, it must be read in conjunction with the rest of the dog's body language.

Your Dog's Sense of Smell

The sense of smell is very important to dogs, and they use their sense of smell while they communicate with each other. Not only does each dog have his own scent, but he can leave that scent to mark territory as he moves through an area, and the dogs that follow know he's been there. "Aha! Thor was here before the dew dried on the grass, and then King was here when the sun was hot."

Individual scents also tell the other dogs how healthy a particular dog is, how well he's eating, and how vigorous he is. A sick dog or an underfed dog will have a different scent than a dog who is healthy and well fed. In addition, dogs excrete sexual hormones (or pheromones) through the urine and tell the scent reader whether or not that particular dog is ready to breed.

Unfortunately, our pitiful noses are lucky to smell a clean, healthy dog, never mind smell individual messages contained in canine scents. Therefore, although the use of scents is very important to our dogs, it's not a means of communication we can participate in.

EASING SOME MISUNDERSTANDINGS

We spend a lot of time with our dogs, and probably think we know them fairly well. But if we really want to take our communication to the next level, we must remember that how we communicate ideas is very different.

In my dog training classes, I often ask dog owners what emotion or idea their dog is trying to convey to them at that moment. In more than 50 percent of the cases, the dog owner is wrong. I can read their dogs because I've learned to do so, but these dog owners haven't watched their dogs closely enough to understand their dog's attempt to communicate. When a dog is trying to convey something to his owner, and the owner doesn't understand, or misunderstands, the dog feels an incredible amount of frustration. This frustration often leads to misbehavior or problem behavior, often simply because the dog doesn't know what else to do.

The best way to learn to understand your dog's body language is to watch him. Look at specific body parts and movements in a variety of situations. When you meet a strange dog on your walk, what does your dog do with his head? How does he hold it? How does he position his tail? His feet? When does he raise his hackles? What happens when you meet a friendly neighbor? What does he do when your kids come home from school? What does his body language look like when you feed him?

TRY THIS

The next time your dog tries to get your attention and you don't understand what he is trying to convey, tell your dog, "Show me." The first few times you do this, your dog will not understand what the words mean, so just begin walking toward your dog or follow him. Encourage him, "Show me." Touch his bowl, "Is this it?" and wait for a reaction. If that doesn't get a reaction, keep moving around. When you find what it is he is trying to tell you, his behavior will show it. It will be a big reaction, "Yes! She understands!"

Ideally you should be able to predict what your dog's body language will look like in any given situation. You should be able to tell when he's happy, upset, ready to dash off, or ready to play. When you know him well enough to do that, you will be well on your way to mutual understanding. When you can predict what your dog will do by watching his body language and his postures, you can then control your dog's actions better (for example, if you allow him to play off leash in a dog park). Best of all, though, you will simply understand him better. Then you need to learn to think about, control, and use your own body language to help him understand you better.

Obviously, watching your own body language is difficult because you use it subconsciously, but you can actively increase your awareness of it. When you are talking to a friend, interacting with a salesclerk, or arguing with your teenage son—just stop and think for a second about the messages you may be conveying with your body language. What are you doing with your hands and arms? Where are they? How is your body positioned? Are you leaning back, forward, or turning away? Is your head thrust forward or turned away? So much of the message you convey to other people is through your body language, not just your voice.

Think about your body language when you're interacting with your dog. When you're happy, how do you greet him? What do you do when you're unhappy? How does your dog react to you in different situations? What is your body language telling him in those situations?

When working with Betsy, Jim had an easy time focusing on his body language. Before he retired, he had served many years in local politics and was aware of the importance and significance of body language. When he transferred that knowledge to his relationship with his dog, there were fewer misunderstandings.

Jim's verbal skills took some time, though, because Jim was naturally soft-spoken. He loved Betsy, didn't believe in yelling, and didn't want to speak harshly to her. However, when he understood that he didn't have to speak loudly—yelling never works—just more firmly and authoritatively (when she made an intentional mistake), he was able to comply and Betsy reacted in a positive manner.

Jim's goal is to have a dog as a good friend. He wants Betsy to understand his needs, listen to his instructions, and be a good companion. Jim, as a widower and retiree, needs Betsy—probably more than he would ever admit—and when Betsy was more of a problem than a friend, he was frustrated. By improving their communication, however, their friendship has grown enormously. It won't be long before Betsy is the companion Jim's been dreaming of.

Chapter 2

BEHAVIOR MODIFICATION FOR YOU AND YOUR DOG

Jessica is an Australian Shepherd, a black tri with lovely copper markings on her cheeks and eyebrows. She is from working lines (she was bred on a working cattle ranch) and she has a strong desire to please. She is the type of dog who gives you the impression that she would literally give her life for her owner.

Jessica's owner, Mike, knows how dedicated Jessica is to him but is still incredibly frustrated by his dog. "Every time I try to show her something or teach her something," he said, "she yelps like a hurt puppy. I'm not hurting her so why does she cry like that? I'm embarrassed and it makes me look like a bad dog owner."

Jessica is a very intelligent, very sensitive dog who doesn't need much training or guidance. If she can understand what Mike wants her to do, she'll do it. Mike, however, is a very dominant, very physical dog owner and is used to working with dogs who need a lot of supervision and heavy training. Jessica's temperament is clashing with Mike's expectations of her, and as a result, this relationship is threatened and both are frustrated.

To save the relationship, Mike needs to look at himself, as a dog owner, and see what he can change—at least in relation to Jessica—he also needs to learn how to help her because right now Jessica doesn't trust him.

Dog owners today do not want to order their dogs around in military fashion; they want to be able to talk to their dogs. They want their dogs to understand what is wanted and to cooperate willingly. Although this is a wonderful goal, dog owners must also understand that dogs are much like us; dogs wish to please us but they also want to please themselves. Individual breed characteristics as well as their individual personalities will affect how much our dogs want to please us. Some breeds and dogs want to please us especially if it also coincides with their own wants and needs. Other breeds of dogs don't care much about pleasing us; their own individual needs come first.

BREED-BASED BEHAVIOR

As dogs were domesticated, they were gradually introduced to a variety of different occupations. Some breeds helped with the hunt, others herded, some killed vermin, and others protected their people. Some of these jobs required the dogs to take directions from people, while other occupations required the dog to think for himself or follow his instincts. Today, many breeds continue to follow these occupations. Terriers are still awesome ratters and need no education from us in this activity. A breed's original occupation has much to do with the breed's desire (or lack of desire) to follow our directions.

Therefore our goal is to understand our dogs, understand ourselves as dog owners, and learn how to change both our behavior (when needed) and our dogs'. By doing this, we can help create that symbiotic relationship we're striving for.

LEARNING TO BE A GOOD HOST

If the dog is barking at the front door when a guest comes over, and the owner tries to quiet the dog by yanking at him, dragging him away from the door, and then isolating him in the backyard, the dog learns that someone coming to the door is a very negative thing. The dog's behavior will continue to deteriorate because of this negative association, and ultimately, the dog may even bite a guest.

WHAT IS BEHAVIOR MODIFICATION?

Behavior modification has recently become an all-encompassing term—a catchall phrase—to apply to anything that changes behavior, especially regarding dogs. Many dog trainers call their work behavior modification while some behaviorists say that training is training and behavior modification is something totally different.

We can simplify the discussion by saying that behavior is how a dog responds to stimuli (to things in the world around him). Those responses may be in the dog's attitude, manners, or actions.

The same definition can be applied to people. A person's behavior is how that individual responds to stimuli, or the world around him.

Behavior modification is the process of changing those responses. Generally, we regard behavior modification as changing bad or unwanted behaviors into good or desirable behaviors. Many times, however, dog owners unwittingly teach their dogs bad habits or behaviors using behavior modification techniques.

An alternative to the scenario described on the previous page might look like this: The owner snaps the dog's leash on his collar when the door bell rings, and then makes the dog sit when the guest comes in. When the dog barks, the owner says, "Quiet. That's enough." When the dog is quiet, he is praised for being quiet. When the dog is under control and is quiet, the guest is encouraged to pet him.

In this situation, the dog is using his obedience skills and is learning good manners. He is also learning to associate guests with affection and is increasing his comfort with new people. He is still in the house with the family and guests and is not isolated outside suffering from social deprivation.

Behavior modification is then, to us, a recognition first of both our responses and our dog's responses to stimuli, and then our ability to change those responses. Although this sounds somewhat complicated, it really isn't.

Behaviors Happen for a Reason

Our actions and our responses to our dog's actions and behaviors contribute significantly to how our dog will act in a particular situation. After all, to the dog, there is no problem associated with barking at guests. Guests are trespassers, and you should be warned that trespassers are at your home. The same applies to many other canine behaviors that we consider problems (from a dog's perspective, a shoe on the floor is no different from a chew toy). The following are explanations for some common unwanted behaviors. (Don't worry, I'll address ways to correct these behaviors later in this chapter.)

TRY THIS

Is there something your dog is doing on a regular basis that you would like to change? Ask yourself these questions and see if you can come up with an answer.

- *When (time or situation) does your dog behave in the way you don't like?*
- *What is your response to this action?*
- *From your dog's point of view (not yours!), what does your action tell him?*
- *What can you do to change your dog's reaction to the stimulus that begins his action or behavior?*

JUMPING ON PEOPLE—Dogs jump up on people to greet them face-to-face and to lick their faces as a puppy does to an adult or a submissive dog does to a more dominant dog. Dominant dogs jump up on people to make themselves appear bigger and more dominant. Height and position are very important to dogs.

DIGGING—In hot weather, dogs dig to create a cool place to relax, and in cold weather dogs dig down for the warmth of the earth. Dogs dig to bury special toys and bones as well as to find new treasures, such as gophers, moles, and rodents. They will also dig because of boredom, frustration, and loneliness.

BARKING—Barking is a dog's way of speaking. The message may be important, such as there are people trespassing here, or it may signify boredom. It is natural communication.

DESTRUCTIVE CHEWING—Puppies chew because it's pleasurable. Chewing the corner off a cushion and then shaking it so the stuffing comes flying out is great fun. They also chew to relieve the pain of teething. As they grow older, the habit of chewing can relieve boredom and frustration.

There are many environmental factors that cause problem behaviors. Some of these include:

FENCES AND GATES—These very necessary barricades restrict the dog's ability to investigate, roam, and explore. Some dogs know they are safe behind a fence and will "fence-fight" behind one. Their bravado disappears abruptly when the gate is opened.

TETHERS AND CHAINS—Not only do these restrict the dog's freedom but they also leave him open to trespassers, invaders, and tormenters. These types of restraints may not be uncommon, but they should be avoided at all costs. Many behavior problems (including aggression) result from dogs being tied up, tethered, or chained.

OTHER DOGS—Barking dogs, trespassing stray dogs, loose neighborhood dogs, intact male dogs, and bitches in season can all can cause your properly restrained, fenced-in dog to start acting crazy.

ANIMAL WILDLIFE—Wildlife can either be a threat (such as a bear, puma, or coyote), or it can be prey (such as a squirrel or rodent). Wild animals can also be a source of disease and can cause a normally well-behaved dog to bark, dig, escape from the yard, or kill the animal.

PEOPLE—People can be viewed as trespassers when coming onto your property or when walking past. Sadly, some people (particularly children) may torment your dog.

NOISES—A dog that is sensitive to sound may react fearfully to loud noises such as the garbage truck, motorcycles, thunder, low-flying airplanes, or construction. Some dogs stop thinking when reacting to loud noises and will do anything to get away, including escaping from the yard or jumping through a closed window.

You also cause a number of your dog's problem behaviors although you probably don't want to admit it. Your individual personality, mannerisms, and habits affect the way you relate to your dog. I'll take a look at this in more detail later in this chapter, but for right now just keep in mind that your dog's behavior is also affected by *your* behavior!

Of course, your dog's health impacts his behavior. A dog with a bladder or urinary tract infection may urinate on the carpet, while a dog with an upset tummy may have loose stools. A dog who is teething will chew on anything and everything. Many factors can affect your dog's conduct, so if a problem occurs suddenly, have your vet examine your dog. When a dog is sick, behavior modification techniques are inappropriate.

Changes in the home can also affect your dog's actions. Guests in the home; a new baby; a child leaving home for school, camp, or college; or a move to a new house can result in a host of new (and often unwanted) behaviors. You may find yourself playing detective, trying to figure out what has happened to cause a change in your dog's behavior. Although this is sometimes quite difficult, it's nonetheless an important task. Obviously, you must know the cause of a problem before you can eliminate it or work at preventing it.

Whenever you examine your dog's behavior, you must keep in mind that your dog has some basic needs and desires. As intelligent social animals, dogs need companionship and mental stimulation to thrive. Dogs that are kept alone in the backyard for hours every day with nothing to occupy their minds often develop behavior problems. Before trying to "solve" problem behaviors, make sure the dog's needs for companionship and social interaction are being met. It's no surprise that well-behaved dogs are the ones who spend a lot of time playing, interacting with, and just hanging out with their owners. They're the happiest.

IT ISN'T *ALL* TRAINING

Observers of all things canine have recently made some interesting connections between a dog's physical state and his conduct, including:

- *Food—Many dry kibbled dog foods are very high in carbohydrates. Carbohydrates metabolize to glucose, causing—in some dogs—a type of sugar high. If your dog appears hyperactive and unable to control himself, you might want to change his diet to a food higher in meat. I'll discuss diet more in chapter 6.*
- *Exercise—Healthy dogs need good aerobic exercise each and every day.*
- *Play—Play is good exercise but it's also needed for good mental health. Take time to play with your dog; it's good for both of you.*

CHANGING YOUR DOG'S BEHAVIOR

Your dog learns in many different ways. When he stuck his nose in a flower and a bee stung him, he learned to avoid that particular type of flower and buzzing insects. Or, depending upon his personality, he learned to hunt down and kill buzzing insects. When you decide to change something about your dog's behavior, you will be teaching your dog. You'll probably be changing something in your own behavior, and perhaps making some changes in his environment.

How do you accomplish all this? Well, there are a number of different ways. First of all, you must remember that your dog is learning all the time. A learning opportunity occurs every time you do something with him in the house, in the car, outside playing, or on a walk. He may learn that a particular neighbor likes to pet him and scratches in just the right spot behind his ears, or he may learn that the dog in the yard three houses down from you growls at him when he walks past. He has probably already learned what makes you laugh and what gets your attention. Your dog is always learning something new.

The most common ways or methods in which learning occurs follow:

HABITUATION—This type of learning refers to what happens when your dog gets used to things in the world around him. When he first sees a sheet on a clothesline blowing in the wind it may startle him; however, after he's seen it two or three times, or after you've walked him up to it and said, "See, silly, this isn't scary," he has become habituated to it.

CLASSICAL CONDITIONING—If you get out the box of dog treats, does your dog come running? That is classical conditioning. He has learned that the sound of the dog treats means he will get a treat. He has put the two factors together.

OPERANT CONDITIONING—Have you seen, either at your local county fair or on television, the chicken who plays a tiny toy piano for food? The chicken pecks at the keys of the piano, and when she hits the correct key, food drops down into a slot. The chicken's behavior is a result of operant conditioning.

WHERE PAVLOV FITS IN

Ivan Petrovich Pavlov was a Noble Peace Prize–winning Russian scientist who will always be remembered for his experiments with dog behavior—particularly classical conditioning. Pavlov blew meat powder into a dog's mouth causing the dog to salivate. The amount of salivation was measured. Then he began to ring a bell just prior to the introduction of the meat powder. After several trials he found that salivation would begin when the bell was rung; the dog had made the association between the bell and the meat powder.

Training a Behavior

To train your dog to engage in a particular behavior, break the behavior down into small components and reward your dog for succeeding with each component. For example, you can train your dog to let you know when he has to go outside to relieve himself. Perhaps he stares at the door when he needs to go outside, but you can't always see him staring at the door so you want him to give you another signal. Because barking can mean so many things, and you want a signal that isn't confusing, you'll want to teach him a different, specific behavior. Let's teach him to ring a bell when he needs to go outside.

Go to the local craft store and get two or three medium bells—perhaps an inch or two around—and some heavy twine, ribbon, or leather strips with which to hang them. Once the bells are fastened to the strips, hang them over the doorknob or handle so that the bells are at your dog's nose height. Fasten them securely.

With some really good soft treats in one hand, take your dog over to the bells. Rub some of the treat on the bell and encourage him to lick it. When the bell jingles, praise him and give him a treat. Repeat this until he's doing it eagerly; then stop for this training session.

Repeat the first step when you begin your next training session so that you know your dog has retained the lesson. Then have him ring the bells, open the door, give him his treat, and praise him outside. Repeat this several times and stop.

Repeat the previous step when you begin your next training session. Then, as you go back in the house and close the door, ask your dog, "Do you have to go outside?" or whatever phrase you used to housetrain your dog. Have him ring the bells; then take him outside to the place where he normally relieves himself. Praise and treat him there.

As you can see, this training involved several steps, each working toward your eventual goal of having the dog give you a signal to let you know he needs to go outside. It's important that you don't go on to the next step in training until your dog understands and will reliably perform the step previously taught. If you rush your dog through the steps, it is very unlikely that he will learn the behavior. Take your time and make sure your dog understands.

You can train a variety of different new behaviors using the same type of training technique. Just think of the steps you will need to teach your dog. Keep the steps very small, reward each one enthusiastically, and be patient.

Positive Reinforcements

Dogs do things for a reason, just as we do. A positive reinforcement for us might be our paycheck, a smile from a co-worker, recognition from the boss, or a bonus at the end of the year; a positive reinforcement for your dog must be something that will keep him excited about what it is you want him to do.

When training your dog, keep in mind that he has no idea why you may want him to do something, and he may not be able to see or understand the benefit of that training. That's why you will use positive reinforcements.

A positive reinforcement is anything that your dog likes that will help motivate him to repeat a particular action or will keep him working for you. Treats and toys are good positive reinforcements so long as they are treats and toys your dog likes. If your dog doesn't care for a particular treat, it's obviously not going to work as a motivator.

Petting is also a good positive reinforcement if your dog is physically close to you when the positive reinforcement is needed. A scratch behind the ear, a pat on the side, or a scratch at the base of the tail will all reward good behavior.

Your voice is also a good positive reinforcement and one that is quite flexible. You can tell your dog, "Yeah! Good boy!" both when he's close to you and when he's a distance away. Your voice must be happy when you praise him. Be sure to use words he's learned mean good things.

The timing of positive reinforcement is of ultimate importance, especially when you first begin working with your dog. He must know that he's doing something right as he's doing it; therefore the praise must happen at the moment the dog does something correctly. To use a very simple example, when you tell your dog, "Benny, sit," and his rear end touches the ground, praise him, "Good to sit."

As you teach your dog something new, your positive reinforcement can act as a lure, and then it can also act as the reward.

When your dog understands what you want him to do, the positive reinforcement can be given somewhat sporadically. Instead of giving him a treat every time he sits, give him the treat when he sits very quickly, or in a nice position. The random rewards cause your dog to think more about what he's doing, "Hmmm . . . I wonder when she's going to give me the treat? I wonder what I need to do to get a treat?"

TRY THIS

With your dog close to you, speak to him in a happy tone of voice, using the words you normally use to praise him. Is his tail wagging? If he doesn't have a long tail, is the stub of his tail wagging? Talk to him until you get his tail and whole rear end wagging with happiness. NOW he knows what those words mean.

Negative Reinforcements

Many dog owners think that negative reinforcement is bad and that it is damaging to the dog's spirit or psyche. Those dog owners are confusing negative reinforcement with punishment.

If you come home from work and find the trash can dumped over and trash all over the yard, you will want to do something to your dog. Your first reaction may be to grab him by the collar, drag him over to the trash can, shake him, and yell, "Bad dog! Shame on you! Look what you did!" That is punishment.

Punishment like this—punishment that occurs after the unwanted behavior—is rarely effective. It may deter your dog for a short period of time but the behavior will come back.

Negative reinforcements, however, are not the same as punishment. Negative reinforcements can be as simple as withholding a positive reinforcement, or can be an interruption that stops behavior as it's happening.

TEACHING SPECIAL WORDS

To teach your dog that a particular word or phrase is important, trigger an association between the phrase and a reward. For example, if you want "Good dog." to mean "Yes. That's right. Good job." then you have to teach your dog that. Start with some really good treats in one hand. Ask your dog to sit in front of you, and when he does, tell him "Good dog!" in a happy, thrilled tone of voice and immediately pop a good treat in his mouth. Repeat this five or six times and quit for this session. Repeat it later. Within a few sessions, your dog will be convinced that "Good dog." is an awesome phrase, and you can use it in your training to let him know he's done something right.

If you are in the kitchen and see your dog sniff toward the trash can, you can interrupt him, "No! Get away from there." That is negative reinforcement. It is not going to break your dog's spirit or hurt him psychologically; it is simply stopping bad behavior before it happens.

With your dog close to you, make a noise to get his attention. Smile at him, using a lot of facial expressions. He will probably react positively.

Then try to diminish your facial expressions, leaving only your eyes to express your happiness. Your dog may be confused, but he'll probably continue watching and may continue to wag his tail.

Then, changing only your eye expression (with no or as few facial expressions as possible) look at your dog with a hard stare. Does he see it? Did he stop wagging his tail?

This hard eye expression can be very effective. When you see your dog about to get into trouble, clear your throat, and when he looks at you, give him "the eye."

IT TAKES TWO TO TANGO

I started teaching dog training classes many years ago because I liked dogs. I felt that if I could increase understanding between a dog and his owner, and make the relationship a good one, I could potentially keep the dog and owner together. The owner would not give the dog away, and the dog would not be euthanized because of problem behaviors. I still feel that way. However, one aspect of my classes was not anticipated.

As a new teacher, I didn't realize that I would have to study the people in my classes as much as I do the dogs! Although they are called "dog training classes," probably 80 percent of my teaching is actually directed at the dog's owner. Not only does the dog's owner need to understand his dog, but he also needs to understand himself and that's usually the harder lesson to learn.

I have found that with dog owners there are several different attitudes that often create problem dogs. Although the following profiles are generalizations, many owners have found them to be useful. Look at these profiles, honestly. Do you see yourself here? You might want to ask your spouse or a good friend to identify you in this list (after first promising not to get angry if you don't agree with her decision).

AMBIVALENT—These dog owners aren't even sure they want a dog, never mind want to do anything with the dog. These dogs usually feel rejected and isolated.

ANTHROPOMORPHIC—This group of dog owners believes that dogs are the same as people, feel the same as people, and have the same intellectual capabilities as people. These dogs usually try hard to please but are often overwhelmed.

DOMINANT/PHYSICAL—These dog owners believe in "spare the rod and spoil the child (or dog)" and use physical force or punishment to make sure their dogs aren't spoiled. I find that dogs respond poorly to either type of treatment.

DOMINANT/VERBAL—These owners want instant obedience, respect, and submission from their dogs and use loud, harsh, or stern tones to try to accomplish it.

LOGICAL—These dog owners prefer to use "common sense" methods of training rather than psychological "mumbo-jumbo"; even though "common sense" to people has little meaning to dogs. These dogs blunder their way through but are often confused.

NAÏVE—These dog owners know nothing (or very little) about dogs and often follow everyone's advice even when that advice conflicts. Their dogs are often very, very confused.

PERMISSIVE—These owners want the dog to love them and work for them out of love; they wish to avoid any form of discipline or correction. Dogs belonging to this type of owner usually regard their owner as weak and incapable of leadership.

RIGID—Inflexible owners are unwilling to change; the dog must do all the changing. My experience is that nothing in class will be accomplished when owners have a rigid attitude. Their dogs are often incredibly frustrated.

I've found that people who fit into the dominant categories (both verbal and physical) have a tendency to blame problem behaviors on someone or something other than themselves. The problems are the dog's fault, or a previous trainer's fault. These people rarely see themselves as the cause of the problems. If you see yourself in this category, the first thing you need to do is realize that there are many causes for problem behavior and you *are* a part of it—even if you don't think so now.

People who are naïve and permissive will often try to explain the problem away. They usually talk too much, and there is always a reason, an excuse, or a story behind every problem. When training their dogs, these people often try to cajole their dogs into obedience, "Come on, Ben, you can do it. Come on, please . . ." They excuse their dog's behavior, "He's always better at home than he is in dog training class." "He's distracted tonight but he usually does it well." If you see yourself in this category, half of the battle is won. Try to control how much you say to your dog; speak in clear phrases (not sentences), and do not beg the dog to do anything. Simply tell the dog and help him do it. If you have a submissive dog, you'll probably be able to work things out. A more dominant dog will look upon your pleading and begging as weak and could try and take control. You will have to seriously change your image of yourself, your dog's perception of you, and how you approach his training.

The logical, anthropomorphic, and rigid personalities are usually calm, cool, and collected. These owners think a lot—sometimes too much—and often have done a lot of research but not much practice. If you see yourself in this category, you need to step away from your research and pay more attention to your dog. Instead of trying to think logically, let yourself feel something for the dog and from the dog. If you aren't sure whether this is the right category for you and your dog, hand the dog's leash to a friend. Have your friend practice your dog's commands. You will see your dog's entire attitude change— within a few minutes he will be happy and bouncy—yet when you take the leash back, he will revert back to his normal attitude with you. That's a key that the problem lies within you, not your dog.

The ambivalent people try to draw attention away from the problem although it is very much there. If you're ambivalent about even having a dog, that's the first decision that should be faced. Is this dog right for you? Is any dog right for you? Is any pet at all right for you? Address this issue first. Then, if the dog is still part of the family, you can face the dog's behavior problems.

Many dog owners see themselves in several categories. You might be naïve and anthropomorphic with a touch of permissive or domi- nant/physical, dominant/verbal, and rigid. You may not clearly have any of these attitudes, but have just a few tendencies within one or two particular categories. No category is good or bad, or preferred or not preferred; a balance is the ideal.

Personally, I see myself in several categories. I am very logical, with strong logical traits. Yet I have anthropomorphic tendencies even though they conflict with my logical side. I also have a tendency to be too permissive even though I am also dominant/verbal. In other words, I'm a logical person, who very much makes her dogs a part of her family. I like to be permissive with my dogs, yet when I want them to do something, I want them to do it without arguing, squabbling, or ignoring me.

No matter what category (or categories) you see yourself in, what is important to realize is that you are the only one with the power to make any changes. If your dog has a behavior (or two or three) you would like changed, you must first be able to look at yourself and see if you're part of the problem.

Changing Our Own Behavior

Jessica's owner, Mike, is an excellent example of someone with a dominant attitude with both physical and verbal traits. He is a strong-willed, authoritative, physically strong, and loud person, but he also cares deeply about his family and his animals, including Jessica.

Jessica is and always has been willing to work for Mike; however, when his dominant, authoritative approach becomes too much for her, she yelps—and that drives him nuts. When Mike realized that he could use Jessica's yelps as a cue that he was being too rough with her (physically, verbally, or emotionally) and that he should back off, he was able to begin to control his own behavior. For example, if he wanted her to do something, and she didn't, he would normally grab her by the collar—which invariably caused her to yelp. With his new understanding, he could let go of her collar (or not grab it in the first place), take a deep breath (to gather himself and control himself), and tell her quietly what it was he wanted her to do. By controlling his own behavior, he was able to stop Jessica's yelping. Because Jessica's yelping is a fear and stress reaction, he is also lessening her stress. Feeling less stressed, she is better able to attend to him.

Although the big, strong, dominant man and the sensitive, willing dog will always be opposites, they are now at least able to work together productively, with more trust and significantly less tension. With practice and patience, they can even be good friends.

TRY THIS

Have a seat in a comfortable chair and close your eyes. Think of a behavior your dog does that you would like to change. Picture in your mind the dog performing that behavior. Where are you? Are you nearby? Are you a part of the behavior? What do you do? What do you say? How does your dog react?

Now, think of that behavior again but remove yourself from the scene. What happens? Will the dog be unable to complete the behavior because you aren't there? Or will the behavior still happen? If it does, what can you do to change your reaction to the behavior and as a result change the dog's behavior?

SPECIFIC BEHAVIOR PROBLEMS

As I've mentioned, there are a variety of reasons why certain behavior problems may occur. With all of them, look at yourself first to make sure you aren't part of the problem or that you aren't making the problem worse. With this caveat, I'd like to address why some of the more common problem behaviors occur and what you can do about them.

Aggression—Territorial

A territorial dog is protecting his family and property. It's very natural for many breeds, especially the herding and working breeds. In addition, it's very easy for an owner to reinforce this trait simply by reacting to the dog's first protective tendencies. Obedience training emphasizing you as the dog's leader will help control aggressive territorial responses. You must convey to the dog that you are not weak and unable to protect yourself. Instead, you want your dog to understand that you are strong and will call for his help if it's needed, but otherwise he is to allow you to decide when protection is required. You will probably need a professional trainer's help to achieve good control over this dog. To manage this problem and others, see Appendix B: Remedies for Your Dog, for more information and ideas.

Aggression—Fear-induced

Fear-induced aggression can be inherited, it can be taught by over-protective owners, or it can be caused by a lack of socialization during puppyhood. The first step toward controlling this behavior is to make sure you aren't rewarding it. When your dog reacts fearfully, do not soothe him or coddle him; your dog sees those behaviors as praise. "Aha. I was right to be afraid." Instead, ignore the reaction (if you can), interrupt it, or correct it. You will also need to do some careful socialization to see if you can accustom the dog to the things or people that he responds to fearfully. To diminish his fear-induced aggression, working with a professional behaviorist is a good idea.

Play Biting or Nonaggressive Biting

All puppies bite. When they're in the litter they bite each other, and in the process they learn how to control it. If they bite too hard, a littermate will yelp and the biter learns to be a little easier next time. Puppies who are taken from their litters too young (before eight to nine weeks of age) are often biters. They haven't had enough time with mom and littermates to learn this lesson. You must prevent the bites from happening by removing your hand, stopping the play before the puppy gets overstimulated, or by putting a toy in the puppy's mouth. If a puppy bites, correct the puppy immediately by grabbing the scruff of the neck (so that you can physically stop the bite) and verbally correcting the puppy, "NO! No bite! That's not allowed!" If you must, close his mouth with your other hand.

GAMES TO AVOID

Don't play tug of war or wrestle with your puppy. Both of these games teach the puppy to use aggressive behavior and his strength against you.

Jumping Up on You

Your dog jumps up to lick your face, either submissively as a puppy would or to establish dominance by being bigger and taller. Teach your dog to sit rather than jump up. Don't knee him in the chest; that will only break his ribs. Don't grab his paws; that will cause him to become shy about his feet. Instead, teach him to sit. If he sits when he greets you, he cannot jump up on you at the same time. Use your hands on him to help him sit and to keep him in that position. Do not ask him to sit without having your hands on him until you know without a doubt that he can do it. ("Getting it right" every time is self-reinforcing.)

Jumping on Other People

When a dog jumps on people, it is usually a friendly greeting. But some people don't want to be jumped on, and for the elderly, it can be dangerous. Use your leash to control your dog and make him sit. If people are coming to your house, put the leash on him when the doorbell rings, make him behave himself, and don't let your guests pet him until he's sitting still. When you're out in public with your dog, do the same thing. Make him sit and don't let people pet him until he is sitting still.

Barking

The list of causes for excessive barking is a very long one. Anxiety, loneliness, boredom, and excitement are some of the more common causes. When these problems are addressed, the problem barking should diminish. More exercise, new toys, less time alone, or more quiet time—depending upon the exact reason for the barking—may begin to solve your problem. In addition, an obedience trainer can teach you to give (and your dog to follow) commands, including "No bark!" or "Quiet!" But note that using these types of commands should be ancillary to rooting out the cause of the problem.

Destructive Chewing

As with unwanted barking, destructive chewing can be caused by any number of things. A lack of exercise is almost always a contributing factor, as is boredom and a lack of training. Destructive chewers must first be prevented from chewing, which means that when they aren't supervised, they should be kept either in a kennel crate or in a dog run. Never leave the destructive chewer alone with full run of the house. Each time he chews on a forbidden item, each time he destroys something just reinforces in his mind that he can. Instead, keep him safe and away from those things. Then when you are able to supervise him, teach him to play and chew on his toys, praising him whenever he makes the right decision and picks up his toy on his own.

The Landscape Artist

The dog that is digging up the lawn, uprooting plants, and destroying the garden is probably bored, underexercised, and lonely. You can begin to address this problem by increasing his exercise, making sure you have a good playtime every day, and emphasizing his basic obedience training. Then you will need to build your dog a run. A dog run will prevent him from getting into trouble when you can't supervise him. When you're home, you can let him out of the run for time with you in the house or for supervised playtime in the backyard.

Running Away

This problem is always associated with a poor response to the come command. Begin by reteaching the come, using a sound stimulus (such as shaking a box of doggy treats) and food treats. Shake the box of treats as you call him and show him that when he comes to you he will get a treat—a good treat. Repeat this several times each training session and continue the training for several months. Yes, *months!*

Running away is a hard habit to break, and you must totally change how your dog thinks about coming back to you when you call him.

Dashing Through the Door or Gate

Running past you out the door can usually be resolved by teaching your dog to sit and stay at the door or gate. Always practice this with your dog on a leash and hold on to the leash so that he doesn't get away from you should he decide to dash. Once he understands the sit and stay, make him sit when you get to the door or gate. Then give him permission to walk through.

REVERSING BAD HABITS

To alleviate unwanted behaviors:

1. *Look inward at yourself; how are you making this problem worse?*

2. *Practice your dog's obedience training daily.*

3. *Do not allow your dog to sleep on your bed; he must have his own place. On your bed he thinks he's your equal.*

4. *You must always eat first—even if it's just an apple—because the leader of the pack eats first and best.*

5. *You always go first—through doors and entranceways and gates—and give your dog permission to follow you.*

6. *Have your dog work for everything he wants—treats, toys, and petting—even if you simply have him sit. Don't give him anything for free.*

7. *Don't be embarrassed to ask for professional help from a trainer or behaviorist if you need it.*

NO QUICK FIXES

As you've seen throughout this chapter, there are no quick fixes for problem behavior. Just as there is no one reason for problem behavior, there is no one cure. If you look inward at yourself and honestly recognize how you're assisting (we won't say causing) your dog's problems, however, and if you work with patience and consistency toward solving or controlling those problems, you are more likely to succeed.

Chapter 3

TAKING COMMUNICATION ONE STEP FURTHER

Many years ago, a dog of mine, Bear, developed separation anxiety. Bear, an Australian Shepherd, was about one year old and was at that time an only dog. We had lost our old German Shepherd, Michi, to kidney failure just a month or so earlier.

Bear was expressing his separation anxiety by trying to stop me from leaving the house. As I picked up my car keys, he would put himself between me and the front door, trying to block my way. In all other respects, Bear was a well-mannered dog, especially for a one-year-old puppy. I was at a loss as to what was causing this behavior. I wondered if it was related to the loss of Michi, but because his anxiety began about a month after Michi's death (not right away) I was unsure about the connection.

My efforts to train, correct, or comfort Bear made no impression on him. In desperation, I contacted dog trainer friends of mine, and although I tried many of their suggestions, none made any difference. Bear's anxiety continued to increase until he was absolutely frantic when I tried to leave the house. Finally a friend recommended I take Bear to see Samantha Khury, an animal communicator, who would ask Bear what was wrong and help him handle it.

My initial reaction was to take this suggestion and toss it out with the garbage—it seemed a little far out to me—but I was at my wit's end; my dog was suffering. My dire situation, reinforced by my experiences of shared thoughts with my sister (ESP if you will), led me to call Samantha.

When I made the appointment, she asked me for my first name and my dog's name. That was it. When Bear and I showed up for the appointment, she asked why we were there, and I told her Bear had separation anxiety when I left the house. She didn't ask for anything else, just told me to leave Bear with her and to come back in forty-five minutes.

When I came back, Bear jumped in my lap, excited and wiggly. Samantha asked me, "Who was the black and red German Shepherd who passed away a couple months ago? Bear misses him but didn't tell me his name."

My chin hit my chest. How could she have known about Michi? How did she know when he died and that he was black and red? I didn't tell her that nor could she have researched it—I never told her my last name.

She continued by telling me that Bear was worried because he blamed my silver car for Michi's death. Wow! I drove my white pickup to that meeting; the silver car was parked at home. How did she know I even had a silver car? How could she have known that when I took Michi to the vet when he died, I took him in the silver car? Samantha said that Bear blamed the silver car for Michi's death; and that when I left the house, he was afraid the silver car might do the same thing to me—that I might never come home again.

Needless to say, I was blown away. Although my logical, practical, common-sense side said that this type of communication was something out of science fiction, there was no way that she could have learned this information unless she could actually communicate with Bear.

Oh, and by the way, when we traded in that silver car, Bear's anxiety totally disappeared. Samantha was right.

WHAT IS PSYCHIC ABILITY?

The brain is incredibly complex and powerful. Although researchers are mapping parts of the brain, seeing—with their powerful tools—the electrical activity in certain parts of the brain when we use it, there are still vast parts of the brain that have unknown uses.

THE SKINNY ON *PSYCHIC*

The word psychic *is often thought to refer to someone who can foretell the future; however, the more correct usage of the word actually refers to powers of the brain. According to* Webster's New World Dictionary, psychic *means beyond natural or known physical processes; apparently sensitive to supernatural processes.*

Many people assume that psychic powers (powers of the brain) are only for the world of science fiction and fantasy, but as Samantha

Khury proved to me, there are many people—including you and me—who can use those powers.

Most people attribute "strange" incidents to such things as intuition, coincidence, or just plain happenstance as my sister and I did for many years. On numerous occasions, I would think of my sister, hear the phone ring, and it would be her, usually asking me, "You wanted to talk to me?" We always joked about it, but we never *really* talked about it—probably because talking about it would venture into uncharted territory where we weren't very comfortable.

After Bear's session with Samantha, however, I did want to talk about it so I made an appointment with Samantha for just myself. As it turned out, I didn't ask much; she answered most of my questions before I even asked them. Yes, my sister and I had a telepathic bond that would only grow stronger as we grew older. Distance wouldn't have an affect on it; the bond would continue to grow even if one of us moved away.

Samantha also confirmed my feeling that I had an ability to connect with animals. I have always been able to work with dogs in my dog training classes that other people couldn't manage. From childhood on, I could also handle reptiles—including snakes—that would bite other people. It was fascinating to listen to her talk; she is a remarkable, talented woman.

Many people have discovered that they have some psychic talents or abilities. And many people feel that everyone has some ability, that it is only a matter of finding where that talent lies.

It is also thought that all animals have some kind of psychic awareness and the ability to communicate. It may be relatively easy to think that our dogs have some psychic abilities (after all, they *are* special.) as well as horses, cats, and other treasured pets. But what about vultures, or cockroaches? Well, according to the majority of animal communicators, just about everything on this earth has some awareness and ability to communicate.

The belief that animals have an awareness of self and the ability to communicate is not new. In many Native American tribes, the medicine man (or woman) or the shaman would regularly make contact with the animals in the world around him. He might ask for help for a good hunt, ask where hunting was good, ask for healing for a tribal member, or even just for guidance in making a decision. This ability was regarded as very special and to be treasured, not scoffed at or ridiculed.

Unfortunately, not everyone is a believer, and I can still understand the doubts of skeptics. For a long time, I actively dismissed my own thoughts about psychic abilities—I felt that this was a door best left closed. Certainly, most of us have been trained to accept only those things that can be seen, weighed, or measured. Because psychic abilities don't fit within the parameters of scientific, logical thought, they are derided, rejected as coincidences or outright lies. I'm afraid that until we have equipment that can actually "prove" the existence of a psychic episode, psychic abilities will continue to be ridiculed.

MY CLOSE ENCOUNTER

I can remember roaming the Connecticut woods close by our home as a child. I would stop at a natural spring to drink. One day I went nose to nose with a poisonous water snake, a species known to be aggressive. I remember thinking (not speaking), "Please don't bite me. I won't hurt you." And he didn't. He moved away and I took a drink.

THE PURPOSES AND PLEASURES OF COMMUNICATING WITH ANIMALS

One obvious benefit of telepathic communication is that you can use it to clear up any other communication problems you have with your dog. Best of all, though, it will open an entirely new world to you. You will be able to understand how your dog views the world around him, and it's nothing like the way you see it.

In my dog training classes, people repeatedly have told me, "I wish I knew why my dog did that." The lack of communication with their pets results in considerable frustration for most dog owners. After all, if we knew why the dog chewed up the sofa, dumped over the trash can, or clawed up the screen, we would have more hope of fixing the problem. It was simple for me to resolve Bear's separation anxiety once I knew its source.

Some dog owners would like to communicate with their pets just so they could understand them better. Karen, who shares her home with a Dalmatian mix named Molly, said, "I love to watch Molly, especially when we're out for a walk or at the park. She is so aware of everything around her. I just wish I knew what she was thinking as she observes the world."

Other owners want to know that their pet is happy. Steve, who lives with a Border Collie, Chuck, said, "I feel bad that Chuck doesn't get to actually work. After all, his instinctive and natural job is to herd sheep. I try to keep him busy, but I often wonder if I'm doing the wrong thing by keeping a working Border Collie in the city."

Although the communication skills I mentioned in chapter 1 and the behavior and training skills I discussed in chapter 2 will all help you in your relationship with your dog, they can still leave you wanting more. That "more" is a deeper understanding of who your dog really is, what he thinks about, and how he sees the world around him.

Some dog owners really want to know, too, what their dog thinks of them. Other dog owners aren't so sure that this would be useful information. Steve said, "I want to know whether or not Chuck is happy, but I'm not so sure I want to know what he thinks of me. Like most Border Collies, Chuck is very smart and I'd hate to find out he thinks I'm dumb. That would really change our relationship." Steve shook his head, "And I don't think it would be for the better."

Steve has a real worry. If he finds out his dog doesn't think too highly of him, he's afraid it would damage their relationship, but he probably doesn't have anything to worry about. If he communicates with Chuck, either personally or through an animal communicator, he should be up front with his dog and simply tell him, "Don't tell me how you feel about me, especially my intelligence." After all, Chuck probably already knows Steve is worried.

PROFESSIONAL ANIMAL COMMUNICATORS

Samantha Khury is a professional animal communicator. She has worked with many different people, animal species, and organizations and has an excellent reputation among her peers. She isn't alone, though; there are many animal communicators available to help you and your dog. Appendix D: Resources in the back of this book lists several well-known, respected communicators who are available for consultations.

Many of us are leery of being ripped off, and to many people, anything that uses the word *psychic* just screams "fake". Unfortunately, there are fakes and quacks in this field just as there are in any other profession. My friends and I hired a communicator for a small group consultation. The communicator (she should go nameless here) was horrible. The only good information she gave us was what she gleaned from leading questions. Everything else she said was dreadfully inaccurate; she couldn't even get the dogs' personalities correct. Needless to say we were very disappointed; however, it was partially our fault. We had gotten her name from an advertisement and had not asked for any references.

Having learned the hard way, my best advice is: Before you hire any animal communicator get some referrals and references. Who recommended the communicator to you? What was their experience like? Can you talk to someone else who has used her services? Assume that the referrals the communicator gives you will be from people who were very satisfied with her services. In light of this, ask for references from colleagues, too.

Many animal communicators also give seminars, and attendance is usually much less expensive than an individual session. Going to a seminar is a great way to familiarize yourself with a communicator's style and abilities. Then, if you feel comfortable with her, you can schedule an individual session.

YOU CAN BE AN ANIMAL COMMUNICATOR

If you're like most people, you'd rather communicate with your dog yourself than have someone else do it. An animal communicator is much like a translator, and working with one can hamper the flow of the conversation. Besides, direct communication builds a strong, intimate bond between you and your dog.

Most communicators say they were aware of their skill as a very young child. In fact, many believe that all young children have the ability to communicate with the world around them. Do you remember squatting in the backyard talking to a caterpillar? I do. I also remember talking to our cats. In fact, some of my earliest memories are of talking away to my cat, Bootsie, as she lay next to me on my bed. Today, I can't remember what Bootsie said, but I do remember that she did talk to me.

A NATURAL UNDERSTANDING

My six-year-old Australian Shepherd, Dax, went nuts—almost literally—when she met my nephew Adam. She first saw Adam when he was just a week old and acted as if she had been waiting her whole life for this child. She wiggled, bounced around, cried, licked him, and protected him from all strangers, even those who just wanted to ooh and ahh at him. Through his first year of life, she rarely saw him more than once or twice each month, but the bond between the two of them was as strong as if they lived together. Once Adam could walk, he started each visit to my house with a mad dash to Dax. It was clear to me that they were communicating with each other. At times, Dax would approach Adam, her nose just about touching his, and they would look deeply into each other's eyes. Adam, a very active little boy, would be very still. Thirty seconds or so later, it was over and they looked away. Each time this happened my sister (Adam's mother) and I both got goose bumps. I wish I knew what was being said, but these were obviously private conversations.

Apparently, as we grow up in this scientific, logical world, most children either lose the ability to communicate telepathically or are discouraged from developing it. Nonetheless, some people retain their psychic abilities, although often they're hidden and dormant. Psychic episodes are labeled "flashes of intuition" or laughed at, "Ha. Just a little ESP." Other intuitive skills, especially those that merge with our other natural abilities—such as my ability to work with animals—simply become a part of who we are and our telepathic moments are not considered "psychic."

Developing Your Skills as a Communicator

Judy Meyer, an animal communicator and author of the book, *The Animal Connection,* says, "The secret to communicating with your animal can be summed up in just two steps: One, talk to them and two, listen to them." She adds, "It's not complicated and it's really that simple." Some people may actually find it to be this simple, but it was a little harder than that for me. I found I was able to communicate better with some of my dogs than with others; apparently our dogs have varying abilities, too.

According to Diane Stein, author of *Natural Healing for Dogs and Cats,* we must recognize animals as the intelligent and spiritual beings that they are before we can begin communicating with them. They are not "dumb" animals. Stein contends that if a person tries to communicate with the attitude of "You're the dog and I'm the boss!" there probably won't be any response. Not only will the dog ignore the communication, but that person probably won't be able to hear anything anyway. If someone tries to communicate with a loving, inquisitive attitude, however, the lines of communication will be wide open.

In the Beginning

Most dog owners go into telepathic communication expecting wonderful things. They will learn the secrets of animal communication and solve the problems of the world—or at least dogdom. But it doesn't begin quite that radically. Most of the time early communications are quite small, maybe a flicker of thought or a glimpse of a visualization. So keep your excitement in check.

Here are a few hints to make your initial attempts easier and more successful:

KEEP IT SIMPLE—As with any other new skill, it's important to begin with easy exercises. Don't try to solve all of your dog's problems, ask philosophical questions, or carry on long, detailed conversations in the beginning. Start with simple concepts, simple questions, and simple visualizations so that you and your dog can develop your skills together.

FIND A QUIET PLACE—Practice communicating at home in a place where there are few distractions and where you are both comfortable. The living room or family room is fine so long as other family members are busy elsewhere and the television and music are turned off. You don't want any disturbances. You may also find a good spot out in your backyard, under a tree, at the beach, or any other place where you can have restful, peaceful, uninterrupted quiet.

YOUR DOG IS WORTH TALKING TO—When you begin your first exercises, think of your dog as an intelligent being. Admittedly, he may not be familiar with quantum physics, but then neither am I, and I consider myself intelligent. Your dog is quite bright with regard to the things important to dogs, including you.

PRACTICE VISUALIZATIONS—As you make contact with your pet, you may speak to him (aloud or silently), but you must also concentrate on visualizations. Although your pet understands some words (and some pets know more words than others), animals tend to communicate with visualizations. For example, if you tell your dog, "Paul will be home from work in a little while." Your visualization may be of Paul's face, then of his form dressed in work clothes walking up to the front door with the sun or shadows behind him showing that some time has passed.

BE SPECIFIC—A general question such as, "How do you feel?" is much too broad a subject. Ask, instead, about the tummy ache your dog might be suffering from or the leg that he twisted while playing the day before.

TIME IS RELATIVE—Animals live in the moment and do not think of time, or the passage of time, or events in the future, as we do. It's not that they are unaware of time—they are aware—it's just not a concrete concept to them.

THINK IN POSITIVE TERMS—When communicating with your dog, try to think in positive terms rather than negative terms, for example, "Sammy, I'm very happy when you chew on your own toys," is more effective than "Don't chew on the furniture."

The First Sending Exercise

It's usually easier for most people to send messages to their pet than it is to receive messages, so your first exercise will be to send a simple message to your dog. In the quiet, peaceful place where you both feel at ease, sit on the floor with your dog. Place two items that your dog knows well in your lap, such as a tennis ball and a squeaky toy, or two different types of dog treats.

Invite your dog to lie or sit right next to you. Some people, as they first develop their communication skills, can make better contact if they are touching their dog, so you might want to snuggle up with him a bit, lay your hand on his side, or have some other kind of gentle physical contact with him.

Put the two different items on the floor in front of you and your dog. Look at them both very carefully; then close your eyes. Visualize one of the objects. Create a very vivid picture in your mind of that object, and then, silently saying your dog's name first, ask him to show you which object you visualized. Open your eyes and see if your dog has received your message. Did he move toward, touch, or sniff the object you visualized?

If you didn't get any response at all, try again. Telepathically, ask your dog, "Sammy, can you help me?"

If your dog doesn't answer, don't despair; keep your mind open. You may have to practice several times; after all, you and your dog are both learning a new skill.

When you do get a response from your dog, control your reaction. If you jump up and down and act like the world is going to end, you may startle your dog and he may not cooperate again. Instead, praise him for helping you, give him a hug, and tell him how special he is. That's enough.

Do not go on to the next exercise until you and your dog have connected on this one. When you can look at one of the two items, visualize it, and your dog can pick out the correct item five times out of five tries, then you can move on.

MEDITATE TO CLEAR YOUR MIND

Many people have a difficult time clearing their mind. If your mind is filled with issues of the day, memories, emotions, or skepticism, you will have a difficult time using your psychic abilities. Not only will those thoughts prevent you from forming clear visualizations, but they will also prevent you from receiving messages from your dog. You can, however, meditate to clear your mind. Sit in a comfortable position in your quiet place. Concentrate on your toes and relax them. Think about your feet and relax them, then your ankles, calves, knees, and so forth, consciously seeing and feeling your body and relaxing all the parts of it. As thoughts enter your mind, simply send them away and go back to feeling and thinking about your body. When your mind is quiet and you feel relaxed, go ahead and use your psychic abilities.

The Second Sending Exercise

This exercise is the same as the first except that you should have several different items. Have some of your dog's toys and some items of your own—your wallet, for example, and your keys.

As with the first exercise, look carefully at one item, memorize it, and then visualize it. Ask your dog (telepathically) to please pick out that particular item and to point to it in some way so that you know he's received your message.

Feel free to tell your dog—verbally, if you wish—that you know this seems like a silly game, but it's important to help you develop your skills. Let your dog know that this game will be a lot more fun once your skills are better.

As the exercises become more difficult, the margin for error grows. Thus, it isn't as critical to attain a perfect rate of success before moving on to different exercises. Instead, when your dog indicates the right item four out of five tries, you can move on to the third exercise.

The Third Sending Exercise

Your third exercise is going to be a little more difficult than the prior ones because you will be practicing it during your daily routine instead of going to your quiet place.

When you and your dog are in the same room together, and your dog is not asleep, think of him, visualize his tail wagging, and send him telepathic praise, "Sammy, good dog. Yeah, I love you." Watch your dog. Did his ears perk up? Did his tail wag? Did he come to you wiggling with happiness? If he did, he got it.

This is a fun exercise to practice, because once you've got the hang of it, you can do it anytime. Don't be in a hurry to send lots of messages and ease into the exercise slowly. Increase the distractions gradually; remember, your dog has to be able to concentrate on you, too, and too many distractions will make that hard to do.

LEARNING TO RECEIVE MESSAGES

As I mentioned earlier, it is usually harder for most people to consciously receive messages than it is to send them. I think the main reason for this is that we prevent ourselves from hearing messages; we put up blocks (consciously or subconsciously) to stop them. For some reason it's okay to try and send messages but to receive them is a little more, shall we say "over the edge". Especially if you admit to it!

Personally, I think many people already "hear" their dogs but don't know it. Part of my ability to work with animals, including the dogs in my dog training class, is based on my skill at "hearing" them. I don't hear words from other peoples' dogs, but I feel emotions and sense things from them. I just "know" the dog.

Many people say they have this ability with their own dog; they just "know" things. This is the first step in receiving telepathic messages.

True communication requires you to receive (and receive as well as you can) as well as send. It's not fair to simply send messages to your dog without hearing or seeing your dog's responses. After all, to discover what your dog thinks is the purpose of telepathic communication.

Because receiving messages is often difficult, you'll want to do everything you can to ensure success. Use your quiet place, make sure family members don't disturb you, and turn off the phone ringer. If it makes it easier for you and decreases distractions, close the curtains over the windows. Make yourself comfortable and open your mind, let thoughts flow through, but don't let them linger. Just relax.

The First Receiving Exercise

Make yourself comfortable, and invite your dog to lie down next to you. For the purpose of communicating, it's best if you and your dog are touching one another. Tell him verbally, out loud, what you are going to do today. "Sammy, you've been able to hear me but I want to hear you." As you say this, you will be forming a mental picture of yourself receiving your dog's message. Your dog will hear your spoken words and will see your visualization. Tell him, too, that you will need his help; he will have to project firmly today because you don't yet know how to hear him.

Have his two favorite toys in your lap as you did in the first sending exercise. Look at them carefully—both of them—and then close your eyes.

Telepathically project to your dog a visualization of his toys and ask him which he would like to play with when the session is over. Ask him to show you rather than move toward the toy. Then relax and let the answer come.

The answer is often quite subtle and soft. You must be relaxed to let it come in. If you find your mind wandering or anticipating your dog's response, just chase those thoughts away and wait for the visualization of one of his toys.

When you see it, don't go berserk. Instead, tell your dog that you saw it as you hug him. Then play with him with that toy for a few minutes. Praise him for helping you and for sending such a strong picture. Good dog!

Repeat this exercise several times over several days, using the same toys at first and then different toys. This type of exercise takes quite a good deal of practice, so don't rush your progress. When you are getting the visualization well, move on to the second exercise.

GO WITH THE FLOW

When you see or hear a message from your dog, you may begin to feel "weird." You may begin to question your sanity. Remember, however, that in many, many cultures, this telepathic ability is regarded as a special gift. It is something to treasure rather than fear. There's no reason to let your emotions or logical thoughts interfere with your communication.

The Second Receiving Exercise

Once you've begun receiving messages from your dog, you will probably need to prove to yourself that you are actually hearing him rather than echoes in your own mind. Here's how to do that.

In your quiet place, get comfortable and invite your dog to get comfortable next to you. Clear your mind, and ask your dog something only he would know, such as: "Where did you hide your big rawhide bone?" "What were you barking at last night?" "Why don't you like the new neighbors?"

After you've asked your question, relax and wait for the answer. It may be a simple answer, such as a visualization of the rawhide bone hidden under the bushes in the backyard or a nighttime view of a raccoon. Your dog, however, may dislike the neighbors for several reasons, and the answer may be a bit complicated. Be patient and allow it to come in.

When you receive the answer, thank your dog and then before you lose details, savor it.

USING TELEPATHIC COMMUNICATION

So, you can communicate telepathically with your dog, what now? Well, first of all, don't misuse your ability. Continue to speak to your dog verbally and to ask him to do his obedience training using verbal commands. Sending and receiving requires effort and concentration—especially in the beginning—and if you misuse it, your dog may decide to ignore you.

You can, however, set up one formal session each day in your quiet place and talk to your dog. This session could be silly stuff, "What's the best smell in the backyard?" or loving stuff, "Where do you like to be rubbed or scratched?" or serious stuff, "Why do you bark in the evening when I ask you not to?"

LET YOUR SENSES SOAR

Allow all your senses to work when communicating with your dog; you shouldn't conceive of received messages as only simple pictures. As you learn to receive messages and your dog gets better at sending them, you will find that the received messages may be quite complex. Along with the visualization itself, you may see colors surrounding it like a frame. Your dog's feelings will be there, too, so don't be surprised by feeling emotions. There may even be odors (after all, scent is your dog's strongest sense), although humans aren't generally very adept at receiving them. No matter how complicated the message seems initially, just let it enter your mind. You can think about it later.

Your dog might not always wish to cooperate. If you go to your quiet place and he takes off out the doggy door, he's made the decision that he doesn't want to talk today or at this moment. Respect his choice.

Additionally, if your dog looks away from you during a session, moves out of arm's reach, or refuses to answer a question, he's communicating in a different way. Something about your question, tone of voice, or line of reasoning is bothering him. Stop, think about what you're asking, and consider alternative approaches to the issue before you ask again.

Don't make all of your sessions question and answer inquisitions. Your dog won't enjoy that and may decide to stop cooperating. Instead, make a point to hold a two-way conversation. Comment on the rabbits outside of the fence, and then let your dog make a comment about them, too. Tell him a relative he likes is coming to visit and wait for his response. You can learn just as much about your dog this way as you can by asking questions.

Help with Obedience Training

Although many dogs participate in their obedience training sessions willingly, and continue to respect those exercises, some dogs don't. A rebellious, defiant, or stubborn dog can make training very difficult and potentially threaten the relationship between dog and owner.

Your communication with your dog can help you explain to your dog why these exercises are important. "Sammy, I ask you to sit at the front door and wait for my permission to go outside so that I can protect you from danger. If you dash outside when a car is coming, you could be hit." Even the most rebellious dog will usually comply when he understands why certain behavior is requested.

On the other hand, if your dog sees a problem in your training, he can help you correct it. "That collar you use hurts my neck, especially when you yank on it. I don't need to be yanked; just show me what you want."

You can also ask your dog what motivates him the most. Are there some special treats he really likes—a squeaky toy or a favorite ball? By knowing ahead of time what rewards he considers extra special, you can use them to maximize the benefit of your training sessions.

Working with Behavior Problems

As I discussed in chapter 2, behaviors happen for a reason. Your dog digs, barks, chews, or escapes from the yard for a reason. Bear developed his separation anxiety for a reason. Chapter 2 showed you how to work with and try to control behavior problems, but sometimes the most thoughtful and consistent behavior modification techniques just don't take hold. When you have developed psychic communication with your dog, you can try to talk with him about specific behavior problems.

When raising the subject of problem behaviors with your dog, do so very carefully so that he doesn't end all communication. Don't accuse him of stuff, "Why are you such a bad dog? I've never had a dog as destructive as you are." Not only will this threaten your ability to ever communicate with your dog again, it will probably affect your entire relationship with him.

Instead, phrase your questions and comments nonjudgmentally: "Sammy, I saw there was a new hole in the lawn this afternoon. Were you hunting for gophers?" Then let your dog take it from there. Once you know why he's digging, you can explain why you value a lawn without holes. In return, offer him a place where he can dig with abandon—perhaps out behind the garage.

Your communications with your dog might also reveal a physical reason for unwanted behavior, such as a bladder infection, a sore leg, or another health problem. You may also learn about events that trouble your dog, such as being teased by neighborhood kids or encounters with a wild animal that regularly visits the yard. Once communication is open, you can learn much from your dog.

Use your communication skills—both verbal and psychic—to give positive reinforcement for good behavior. When Sammy digs in the new place and not in the lawn, reward him. If you ignore the new good behavior, it may disappear. After all, some dogs will work for negative reinforcement just as some kids do. So acknowledge, praise, and reward the good behavior.

Your Dog's Physical Health

One of the most difficult things a dog owner has to face is diagnosing a sick dog. In the natural world, animals will generally conceal illnesses, injuries, and weaknesses for as long as they can. After all, the strong (or those who appear strong) survive. However, our dogs have been domesticated long enough and trust us enough to show us when they are hurt or sick. The challenge for us is to determine exactly what is wrong with our pet.

If you can use your psychic abilities to communicate with your dog, you can ask some specific questions that can help locate health problems. Although your dog cannot tell you the actual diagnosis—he can give you information that is extremely helpful to the vet. For example, he may tell you he hurts in the area surrounding his kidneys, and he's always thirsty. Those tips, along with the results of a blood test, may lead to the identification of kidney disease.

When asking your dog questions about his health, don't use medical terms. Instead, ask whether a particular part of his body hurts, or is sore, or feels different. Very specific questions that are simple in language are more effective than broad questions and medical terminology that your dog doesn't understand.

Then, when you talk to your vet, you can decide how to give him this information. Some vets are very accepting of animal communication; others are not. If you feel that telling your vet, "My dog said . . ." would make him very uncomfortable, then simply tell him, "My dog is sore here."

Give Your Dog a Sense of Purpose

As a dog trainer, I see many dogs, especially of the working and herding breeds, who feel lost. Their instincts tell them that they should be busy working, but as a pet without a job to do, they feel unneeded and alone.

My breed of choice is the Australian Shepherd. These dogs are probably second only to Border Collies in their need to work. If there are no sheep, Aussies will herd kids, cats, the birds in the backyard, or me! Aussies were also bred to be versatile ranch dogs who were asked to perform numerous chores around the ranch in addition to herding sheep. Around the house, they have those same needs, and when those needs aren't satisfied, the dogs are prone to getting into trouble.

I give my dogs a sense of purpose by asking them to work for me. Notice I didn't say, "Order them to work," I said, "Ask them to work." There's a difference. Because I ask instead of order, my dogs are eager and extremely willing to work. Dax brings in both morning newspapers, even the Sunday issue that's as big as she is. Dax also knows how to find turtles, so she helps me count turtle noses in the backyard each morning to make sure no one has escaped. Kes picks up the damp towels and dirty laundry in the bathroom and drops it in the hamper. She is the lizard finder and lets me know if one of the pet lizards has escaped from a cage. Riker is the one who picks up the dog toys and puts them back in the toy box. I will occasionally ask the dogs to do something else, too, depending on my needs.

I usually ask the dogs verbally but will reinforce the request with a psychic sentence or two. Saying verbally, "Riker, put the toys away, please" followed by a psychic, "Paul will be home soon, and we don't want him to trip on a toy as he walks in." When the job is done, I will praise him both aloud and telepathically.

My dogs have other jobs, too, including protecting the house and cars, and warning me of trespassers. What jobs you wish to give your dogs will depend upon your needs.

Here are a few suggestions:

- Listen to and respond to obedience training and commands
- Become or remain housetrained
- Help around the house—learn how to perform a chore or two
- Protect the house, car, and family
- Respect other dogs' and peoples' possessions

Add to your dog's list anything else that is important to you. Teach your dog using the training techniques you learned in chapter 2 and reinforce them psychically. When you are initially teaching something, for example, use the training techniques but also visualize your dog doing what you ask. By sending a visualization to your dog, he will have a good understanding of the lesson, and his training will progress quickly. You can also reward him psychically, too!

EXPLORE THE POSSIBILITIES

Where you take your new psychic communication skills from here depends on you. What interests you? What have you been wanting to know?

You can, if you take the sessions slowly (so that you don't bore him), ask your dog how he feels about his life, you, your family, and the world around him. You could learn a lot and will undoubtedly be fascinated by his outlook on life.

You might also want to ask some philosophical questions. A friend of mine is fascinated by reincarnation and was sure that she and her dog had been together in previous lifetimes. So she asked her dog, "Have we been together before?" She was startled by the answer because not only did her dog say yes, but her dog also said yes, they had been together several times!

You began developing this skill so that you could better understand your dog, so enjoy it. Enjoy your abilities and enjoy the growing closeness you and your dog share.

Chapter 4

SPIRITUALITY AND YOUR DOG

Gene had never owned a dog before Al wandered up his driveway. "My mom liked cats and disliked dogs," he said. "And although as an adult I've thought about getting a dog, I just never wanted one enough to do anything about it." He rubbed Al's ears as the dog leaned up against his leg, "When Al came up my driveway, it was as if he was sent to me. I really, really needed him." Gene was facing a lot of stress in his life at that time—his wife had just passed away; he missed her terribly and was very unhappy living alone. In addition, his job was quite demanding.

When he showed up at Gene's, Al, a mixed breed dog with some shepherd in his ancestry, had been on his own for a while. He was thin; his paws were torn up and he had a sad, dry coat that needed a bath. Gene bathed the dog, took him to the veterinarian's office for a checkup and vaccinations, and then the two spent time getting to know each other.

They hung out together at the house, went for long walks, hiked in the local mountains and went swimming in the ocean. Gene found that Al liked to ride in the car so Gene put a seat cover over the leather passenger seat in his car, and the two went for long rides up the coast.

Gene said, "This is going to sound really corny but it's as if I've known Al all my life and he's known me. We immediately clicked or got in sync with each other or something. I feel like it's almost spiritual." He laughed self-consciously, "A spiritual relationship with a dog. I have gone over the edge, haven't I? But it's what I feel!"

A SPIRITUAL CONNECTION?

Gene isn't the only dog owner who claims to have a spiritual relationship with his dog; many, many dog owners feel that deep bond. However, trying to explain to someone else what that spiritual bond is can be very difficult. Not only is the word *spirituality* hard to define, but explaining that feeling—that deep inner belief—can also be very difficult.

Moreover, for many people, spirituality is directly associated with an organized religion, many of which, in turn, hold that dogs and other animals are not spiritual beings. The whole subject gets quite complicated.

An individual's feelings about spirituality are often affected by his or her own religious background. Depending upon the religion in which you were raised or practice as an adult, when you think of spirituality you may think of cathedrals, altars, angels, crosses, or Jesus. Your thoughts or ideas about spirituality can also be affected by your opinion (positive or negative) of a particular religion. Some people claim to have no belief in spirituality because they have had a bad experience in an organized religion.

To other people, spirituality is associated with yoga, prayer, or meditation. It may be linked in your mind to the earth and the world around you—to nature—and the spirits surrounding you. Spirituality may mean listening to yourself—your inner voice—or your feelings. Regardless of what you believe (or think you may believe), the topic of spirituality is multifaceted with many questions and few concrete answers.

In this chapter, I'll explore the subject of spirituality—particularly as it relates to the human/canine connection—and then I'll show you how you can achieve a spiritual relationship with your dog.

A SPIRITUAL IMAGE

One way I like to look at spirituality is to think of the entire subject as a bicycle wheel. The tire around the outside represents all of the people looking for meaning, looking for answers. Each spoke is a path leading to the center axle or hub representing spirituality. And each path is composed of different ideas, beliefs, or religions. There may be many different ways of finding spirituality, or of looking at it, but they all lead to the same thing: a sense of inner peace and joy. That is really what spirituality is all about; it's finding your own peace—in yourself—and being happy about it.

A LOOK AT THE PAST

It has long been thought that dogs and people have shared a companionship for between twelve and twenty-five thousand years. New research and new ways of dating archeological artifacts, however, indicate that the relationship may actually be much older than that.

OUR PETS' INNER BEING

Diane Stein, author of Natural Healing for Dogs and Cats, *writes: "Pets are as spiritual as people, if not more so. Dogs and cats have a oneness with earth and nature that few humans experience."*

A complex of shelters dating back to the Paleolithic Age—125,000 years ago—has been found in La Grotte du Lazaret, France. Interestingly, wolf skulls have been discovered at the entrance to each shelter. In what way were wolves involved in these people's lives? Was it a physical relationship? Were they connected in some spiritual way?

Most ancient societies practiced spirituality in some manner. We don't know the significance of the wolf skulls at the entrance to each shelter, but they obviously meant something special to these people. Perhaps the wolves were there to warn away trespassers or to guard against evil spirits. We don't know. We do know, however, from archeological sites and from surviving artifacts that spirituality itself was important to many ancient societies.

It's often hard, however, to see where dogs fit into this ancient spirituality. Sculptures, paintings, and other artwork were fragile and few have survived. Those that did survive often portrayed leaders and people of social prominence, not the people or animals of daily life. However, some very old artwork of dogs does exist. In addition, there are ancient stories (myths, legends, and folklore) in which dogs serve as characters, and these can give us ideas about how dogs were regarded. By understanding the past and seeing where our beliefs originated, we can better understand our own feelings today.

EASTERN THOUGHTS

The Ainu people of Japan believe that dogs have the ability to detect ghosts. Perhaps they're right.

Ancient Greece and Rome

If Greek mythology tells us anything about the ancient Greeks, it's that they sure liked their dogs. For example, Xanthippus, the father of Pericles, was so fond of his dog that they were buried together when Xanthippus died. Alexander the Great named a city Peritas in memory of his dog, who accompanied him on his military campaigns. Ancient writings all speak of Alexander's dedication and affection for both his dog and his horse.

You may recall Odysseus' faithful hound Argos, of Homer's *Odyssey*. Argos was the first to recognize Odysseus upon his return from his many years of travel. Argos, quite an elderly dog by that time, was elated to see his master and began wagging his tail. Odysseus yearned to go to Argos to greet him, but knew that if he did so, his identity, which he was trying to keep secret, would be revealed. Sadly, as Odysseus turned away, Argos died. We can tell that Homer had a wonderful knowledge of dog behavior from his descriptions of Argos and also from his descriptions of the sheep dogs belonging to Eumaeus, the swine herder.

The Greek gods are often depicted in stories and artwork with dogs, usually Greyhound or sighthound-type dogs. The goddess of wealth, Hecate, is always accompanied by a dog and the protector of the hunt, Pollux, must of course have his hunting hounds.

Like the Greeks, the Romans viewed their dogs with great affection, and Roman folklore features many stories of dogs' loyalty and courage.

Ancient Egypt

Dogs were treasured companions in Egypt. The ancestors of today's Greyhounds were used in hunting and kept as companions. In fact, the birth of one of these dogs was celebrated and was second in importance only to the birth of a son.

When a dog owner passed away, his dogs were mummified and buried with him to keep him company and protect him in the afterlife. The walls of Egyptian tombs were often decorated with images of Greyhound-type dogs.

THE CANINE GOD

The Egyptian god, Anubis, was depicted to look something like a hound-type dog or a jackal. Anubis' job was to accompany souls of the deceased to their final resting place. He was often portrayed with a human body and a dog- or jackal-type head.

European Legends

Ancient stories and folklore that tell of the devotion of dogs for their people are found throughout Europe. One of the most famous stories concerns the Welsh Prince Llewellyn's faithful hound, Gelert. The dog was left at home with Llewellyn's son, Owain. When Llewellyn arrived home, he found blood on the dog's face and Owain missing. Enraged, Llewellyn killed the dog, only to find his son safe next to the body of a slain wolf. In honor of his devoted dog, Llewellyn had a statue erected in his memory.

Ancient China

Many ancient Chinese statues and pieces of artwork depict dogs favorably. In fact, written records from more than four thousand years ago reveal that dog trainers in China were held in high regard.

The Fu dog that resembles a stylized Pekinese was regarded as good luck. Clothes were often embroidered with a Fu dog made of silk thread. The wearer of these clothes was then guaranteed to find good fortune and happiness.

THE MORE THINGS CHANGE

Sadly, some ancient cultures used dogs as sacrificial objects. We may deplore this practice, but we sacrifice dogs every day in shelters all across the country.

Native Americans

Dogs were very much a part of many Native American cultures. The dogs varied in type, form, and occupation depending upon where they lived and with what tribe. Some were scavengers, while others were hunting companions. Some dogs pulled travois and others carried packs.

In some Native American mythologies, dogs represented both birth (or rebirth) and death. Like Anubis, they also escorted the newly dead to their afterlife. In Alaska, the Aleutian people believed that the First Father descended from Heaven in canine form. In other tribes, it is said that the First Woman had ten children sired by a dog.

Many other Native American tribes kept dogs, as they did horses, but did not include dogs in their mythologies or belief systems. More often, wild animals such as the wolf, the deer, the buffalo, or the bear were featured as religious symbols.

THE TALE OF FOUR EYES

The Seneca people of eastern North America tell the tale of a hunter who was good to his four dogs. He fed them well and allowed them into his lodge. One day as he and his dogs were out hunting, they were chased by a great bear, a monster bear. Four Eyes, a small white dog with a spot over each eye, spoke to the hunter, "My friend, run away and we will try and stop the bear for you." The man hesitated, but realizing his spear wouldn't stop the bear, he ran away quickly. Then he heard horrible battle sounds from behind him and knew that his dogs were faring badly. Soon, Four Eyes appeared to him again and said, "My friend, my companions are dead but I will try and stop the bear from chasing you. In return, take care of my mate and our expected pups." As his dog disappeared, he heard more sounds of battle, but the bear never caught up with him. At home, he took Four Eyes' mate into his lodge and soon she gave birth to puppies, one of which was marked just like his father with a spot over each eye. When the puppies' eyes opened at two weeks of age, that puppy looked up at the hunter in a wise and knowing way.

Western Religions

Religion is a system—either personal or organized—that is grounded in the belief that there is a creator of the universe or one or more supernatural powers. Any discussion of spirituality must consider religion because religion and spirituality are one and the same to many people.

The great trilogy of Western religions—Islam (which I'll categorize as Western for the sake of convenience), Christianity, and Judaism—rarely mention the dog in their teachings. When they do, the statements are not generally favorable. The Old Testament contains about thirty references to dogs; and all but two references are negative. I Samuel 17:43 says, "And the Philistine said unto David, Am I a dog, that thou comest to me with staves?" Apparently beating a dog with sticks was normal or commonly accepted behavior! Ancient Jewish tradition did not allow images of animals, and thus there are no statues or other Jewish artworks of dogs.

Similarly, references to dogs in the New Testament are not very positive. For example:

- Matthew 7:6—"Do not give what is holy to the dogs; nor cast your pearls before swine, lest they trample them under their feet, and turn and tear you to pieces."
- Matthew 15:26—"But He answered and said, "It is not good to take the children's bread and throw it to the little dogs."
- Philippians 3:2—"Beware of dogs, beware of evil workers, beware of mutilation!"
- Revelation 22:15—"But outsiders are dogs and sorcerers and sexually immoral and murderers and idolaters, and whoever loves and practices a lie."

A PLEASANT EXCEPTION

The only breed of dog mentioned by name in the Bible is the Greyhound. Proverbs 30:29-31, King James Version, says, "There be three things do well, yea, Which are comely in going; A lion, which is strongest among beasts and turneth not away from any; A greyhound; A he-goat also."

AND ANOTHER PLEASANT EXCEPTION

The nomadic Bedouin people have for centuries been devoted Muslims. According to Islamic belief, dogs are unclean and Muslims should, therefore, avoid contact with them. But the Bedouins consider their beloved Salukis to be a gift from Allah to his children, rather than dogs, and so contact with their Salukis is permissible.

Eastern Philosophies

As you probably know, Eastern philosophies are quite diverse in their beliefs. Nonetheless, some recurring themes are found among them. For example, Eastern belief systems are not generally centered upon the belief in a creator of the universe or one supernatural power, unlike the major Western religions. And as a rule, Eastern philosophies share a belief in the wholeness or oneness of life and that all life should be respected. They also tend to advocate a practice of nonviolence.

Hindus, for example, believe that all life is sacred and holy. A well-known demonstration of this belief is seen in cow veneration. Cows represent the non-human world to Hindus. It is not surprising that in contrast to the dogma of many Western religions, Hindu doctrine holds that animals have souls and that the soul of every living thing in this world will eventually achieve peace and liberation.

A truly remarkable Eastern philosophy is that of the Jains. A Jain may not practice any profession in which he may harm living things. That means no Jain will serve in the military, work as a butcher, or even participate in agriculture. Jain believers will not even harm an insect.

A goal of Buddhists is to attain an awareness of our oneness with the universe. Kindness and compassion to all sentient beings, according to Buddhist beliefs, are highly valued qualities. This is observed by Sylvia Boorstein in her book *That's Funny, You Don't Look Buddhist.* Boorstein writes that the Buddhist metta meditation uses a set of resolves or wishes for the well-being of all living things: "May all beings be safe. May all beings be healthy. May all beings be happy. May all beings live with ease."

Similarly, Taoists view nature as sacred and celebrate its many manifestations. Taoists perceive humans to be very much a part of nature, as all life, and indeed all the elements are fundamentally interwoven in one pattern.

Although the Eastern philosophies do not really focus on dogs specifically, they have a special reverence for all living creatures. From an Eastern perspective (broadly speaking), your dog and you have a spiritual connection that is absolute, created and sustained through your greater spiritual connection with all life.

A Growing Relationship

This very brief look at the history of dogs and people shows us that although dogs have been our companions for thousands of years, our relationships with them have been both very different from and also very similar to the relationships we strive for today. At times we see glimpses of that symbiotic relationship (such as that of Alexander and his dog), and occasionally the dog is seen as a spiritual being (as with the Egyptians). In so many other cases, the dog is simply there, like a piece of furniture. The old adage "familiarity breeds contempt" comes to mind.

We can learn from this history, however. We can see why dogs are treated so poorly even today by some cultures; it is in their history to do so. We can see, too, why some cultures treasure certain breeds; again, it is in their history to do so. Of course, we don't have to follow the paths that were laid down by our ancestors; we can make our own way.

DEVELOPING YOUR OWN SPIRITUALITY

People develop their spirituality in countless different ways, and no one way is right or wrong. To find your own spirituality, you must look inside yourself. It's already there; you just need to discover it and bring it out. You can enhance the process by looking to your dog; he's already a spiritual being and can help you find what is in yourself.

Jonathan Robinson, author of *The Complete Idiot's Guide to Awakening Your Spirituality* describes spirituality as:

- Any practice that helps a person become more loving and peaceful.
- A process by which people connect more deeply with their inner source no matter whether they call that source their higher self, God, the creator, or another name.
- A system by which people become more aware of themselves, their strengths and weaknesses, and the need for guidance from a source beyond their own ego.

• The ability to dive more deeply into the present moment, thereby overcoming ego obstacles that cause unnecessary suffering.

All spiritual growth begins by looking first at yourself with these ideas in mind. Other spiritual practices might include reading, meditating, meeting with people who think as you do or share your interests, or attending religious services. Our daily routine is filled with spiritual moments. When you pause to take pleasure in the brisk wind or a lovely sunset, these can easily be spiritual moments. When your dog looks up at you, makes eye contact, and smiles, that is a spiritual moment shared between the two of you.

Take Time to Meditate

Living as we do in a fast-paced, mechanized, computerized world, it's easy to lose touch with your inner voice. In chapter 3, I showed you how to focus on that inner voice, your intuition, and your psychic skills. Now you will concentrate on that inner voice to bring forth your own spirituality.

Your intuition is your means of knowing something that you cannot support analytically. Things that you know through your intuition, you simply know. When you can quiet your mind and let scientific, analytical thinking move through, then you can hear your intuition, and your psychic mind.

Using the skills you learned in chapter 3, relax in your quiet place, with your dog by your side, and clear your mind. As you clear your mind, keep putting the thought or idea of spirituality there. Think about the related thoughts that arise. When you think about spirituality, what comes to mind? Where does your dog fit in? Don't chase away thoughts that seem wrong or out of place; instead, think about why they appeared. How do they play a part in your definition of spirituality?

While meditating, think about your own beliefs as they are right now. Do you feel comfortable with the idea of a higher power? If so, what form does that higher power take? Do you believe in the Christian definition of God and of Jesus as God's Son? You may believe Christian doctrine, or you may have an entirely different belief system. Whatever beliefs give meaning to your life and to the world around you are fine. A large part of spirituality is a belief that there is a higher power; this higher power—whoever it might be—is a part of what gives you inner peace and joy. So as you meditate, spend some time exploring your own beliefs.

Short, calm, relaxing sessions such as these (one per day seems to work for a lot of people) will help you clarify your beliefs and their origins. These meditative sessions can be a wonderful journey of self-discovery.

SPIRITUALITY IN THE OPEN

Native Americans don't feel that spirituality is found in a building, such as a church. Instead, the whole earth is a temple or place to practice spirituality. Any place you stand, sit, or rest is a sacred place where you can worship at your own pace, in your own time, and in your own language. Using this technique or belief, you may find that your quiet place is in your backyard under some trees, at the beach, or in a secluded place in the wild. Pick a special place where you feel most at peace and where you won't be disturbed or interrupted.

Letting Go of Our Ego

Our ego is that part of our awareness that we use to distinguish ourselves from others. Western society emphasizes a strong ego; we are told to strive to "be someone." Children are told that it's okay to be different and that they shouldn't follow the crowd. That is all fine—it's not wrong for us to have a strong ego—after all, it is important for us to recognize our sense of self. Without an ego, how can we answer the question, "Who am I?" To gain a sense of spiritual awareness, however, you must be able to set aside your ego and recognize that you are merely a small part of a much larger picture, a servant to a much higher force.

A spiritual being chases away all thoughts of superiority to other beings. Mother Teresa never spoke of herself as superior to the people of the streets whom she nurtured and loved. She spoke of those people as her equals, as spiritual beings just like her. Deep spirituality does not come with considering yourself superior, either to other people or to your dog.

One of the easiest ways to chase away your ego is to allow yourself time to be of service to others. You and your dog could participate in a therapy dog program where you visit the sick, the elderly, or the dying. You could spend time at the local animal shelter caring for unwanted and unloved pets. There are a variety of ways you can be of service to your community and at the same time enjoy a feeling of connection where your ego has no role to play.

Be Honest with and about Yourself

To achieve true spiritual awareness, you must be honest with yourself. When you are genuinely honest with yourself, you examine yourself objectively, see your good and bad points, and recognize them both.

EGO BUSTER

While meditating, imagine yourself as a small tree. Feel your roots sink into the dark, damp soil and feel your body grow tall, pulling toward the sky. You are you, an individual. Now expand your vision: You are one of hundreds of thousands of other trees in a forest, just like you, all with roots in the soil, all reaching for the sky. You are a very small part of a very large picture.

You can use your negative feelings to help see yourself as you are. If you recognize that you are being impatient, short-tempered, or intolerant, these negative feelings can help you become more aware of yourself. Be careful when thinking about your negative feelings, however—many people are overly critical of themselves and see problems where they don't exist. (Of course, being overly critical of oneself is negative, too.) Don't allow yourself to fall into that trap.

Think, too, about your dog. You are trying to achieve spiritual awareness with your dog. Don't you think that he knows exactly who and what you are? He does. He probably knows your strengths and flaws better than you do and he still loves you. If your dog can stare your flaws straight in the eye, so can you. So be honest with yourself, see those flaws and weaknesses, and turn them into strengths.

Emphasize Your Positive Qualities

Urging your ego to take a backseat is hard, and being honest with yourself about yourself is even harder. It may be that for you emphasizing your own positive qualities is harder still, but acknowledging your own strengths is certainly not a crime. Wouldn't you advise a friend that he should not ignore his good attributes? Be your own friend and remind yourself of your strengths on a daily basis, and don't forget to take them out and show them to the rest of the world.

A sense of humor, for example, is a great quality to have and to share. Humor allows you to laugh at the world around you as well as yourself. Comedians are popular because they use humor to deflect the trials of life around us. When Kelsey Grammar, as Frasier, commiserates with his brother about his lack of a love life, we can laugh too, and we can commiserate with him. When Jerry Seinfeld, as himself, complains about a cab driver in New York, we can laugh too, because we've probably been in a similar situation. The battles (both big and small) that we face in life aren't nearly as threatening when we can laugh at them.

Curiosity is another wonderful quality. Curiosity is what led you to this book; curiosity is what leads us to explore the unknown. Without curiosity, mankind would still be sitting around a campfire in the dark afraid of things that go bump in the night. If you find yourself jaded and without curiosity, go for a walk with your dog and watch him. He is full of curiosity. His nose is sniffing out scents, he's watching the birds fly by, and he's checking out anything that's changed since your last walk. Let your dog's curiosity rekindle yours!

Sincerity, it seems to me, is vastly underrated today. I'm not a saint, but I do all I can to be sincere and to urge others to be the same way. Deception is often prized in business, but deception is a negative trait that is even more harmful to the deceiver than to the person being deceived. Instead, mean what you say and show it with your words, your facial expressions, and your body language. Show it with your actions. Deception will lead you away from spiritual awareness and will eat away at you. Sincerity, however, is a positive quality to be treasured.

Kindness and compassion are positive qualities that cannot be emphasized enough. Kindness and compassion may be expressed with a single hug to a friend who is having a bad day or by delivering a meal to an elderly shut-in. Include your dog in your kindness—take the time to learn how your dog shows that he needs your attention and give it to him. Certainly, when we think of highly spiritual people, such as Mother Teresa and Mahatma Gandhi, we think of kindness and compassion. And although we needn't devote ourselves entirely to others, kindness and compassion are vital to achieving spirituality.

AN EASTERN VIEW

Mahayana Buddhists believe that compassion is the central virtue on the path to enlightenment. Such compassion is to feel another's suffering as one's own.

Courage is another positive quality but one that is difficult to define. A horse carrying his rider away from danger, running even when hurt, is called courageous. The police dog that dies while protecting his partner is courageous. You can be called courageous if you race into a burning house to save a baby, but you are also courageous if you are honest about yourself and your own strengths and weaknesses. Courage comes in many forms, and often looking inside ourselves is just as courageous (or more so) than an act of heroism. Courage in any form comes from inside, from strength of character and from the heart. It is a strength to be nurtured and cherished.

Give Love and Accept Love

When you think of love, your first image may be that of romance, but of course, you have experienced many types of love, such as the parental love for a child or the love for a treasured friend. Spiritual awareness brings forth another type of love—not just for our canine companion—but an all-encompassing love for all of creation. Because spirituality is essentially inner peace and joy, it brings with it a love for all that surrounds you.

Now before you dismiss this with a "Hah!" with thoughts of the driver who cut you off on the freeway or the burglar who broke into your house, keep in mind that, although you may be angry with these people, each of them deserves love too. It takes considerable effort to turn away anger and hurt and replace it with love. You may have to consciously take hold of your emotions and say to yourself, "My anger is negative and self-destructive. I will let it go." and then do so.

You must also be able to accept love. Many people can freely give their love and friendship but are reluctant recipients. Although accepting love occasionally results in heartbreak and sadness, those emotions can be released, too, and replaced with love. Allowing yourself to accept love from the world multiplies the love you are able to give back.

If you have never yet had a close bond with a dog, you have never experienced the love that a dog can give you. There is nothing like the love a dog has for his owner—nothing. A dog loves absolutely, with no judgments, no restrictions, and no barriers. And dogs give love while asking for little in return. Unfortunately, some people distance themselves from their dog's unconditional love. It feels somehow unnatural or just overpowering. But a dog's love is free and without conditions. Learn to accept your dog's love. After all, you are just as fantastic as he thinks you are.

The Power of the Earth

The Native American blood that runs in my veins is a very small percentage of my heritage; most of my ancestors were from Europe. However, I respect and enjoy the Native American view of the world, particularly with regard to spirituality. Not only do most Native American cultures feel that the earth itself is sacred and that animals have souls, but most also believe that the earth, wind, rain, and sun have power. In addition, they believe that these entities will share that power with the people who believe.

Have you heard people say they need to get out of the city? Perhaps they said they needed to take a vacation and go camping, hiking in the mountains, or fishing. These people may not realize it, but the natural world renews the strength that the cities steal. My father always said that a camping vacation to the mountains and big trees recharged his batteries. He could manage the rigors of daily life so long as he could take a vacation to the mountains once or twice each year.

TRY THIS

To feel the spiritual power of the earth, sun, and wind, take your dog with you and go to a quiet place outside. Sit in the sun and invite your dog to lie down next to you. Relax and let the wind blow through your hair. Clear your mind of everything but the information your other senses bring you: the smell of the earth and the plants, and the feel of the sun and the wind. Enjoy the sight of the trees, sky, and clouds. As you relax, let the power of the earth come into you. Most people say that it feels like their heart is swelling in their chest or that a warmth is spreading throughout their body.

Countless Resources

As you explore spirituality, don't be afraid to ask questions and seek help. Although this chapter is one resource, there are many other sources of information and guidance. You may speak to a pastor at a local church or the rabbi at a local synagogue. Most spiritual leaders are excited to discuss beliefs with anyone, even those not of their congregation.

Talk to other dog owners, especially those who seem to have a particularly close relationship with their dog. People love to talk about their canine companions.

There are many books on the subject of spirituality so check out your local library, bookstore, or the Internet. The subject is vast and as you probably know, quite controversial. For more information, see Appendix D: Resources.

LET YOUR DOG TEACH YOU

Because your goal is to develop a spiritual relationship with your dog, it makes sense to let your dog accompany you and teach you. After all, he is already a spiritual being. Dogs, and all animals, are much more in tune with the world around them than we can ever hope to be. This awareness is very much a part of every animal's spirituality. In her book *Natural Healing for Dogs and Cats*, Diane Stein writes: "We must recognize animals' spiritual nature which is their bond with the Earth Mother."

How your dog can help you depends very much on both you and your dog. Many people say that their dog's companionship is enough to help quiet their thoughts and allow their inner voice to reveal itself. Other people find pleasure in watching their dog, especially as he explores the world around him. You (and your dog) will have to find your own path, but with the skills you've learned, you will.

J. Allen Boone, author of *Kinship with All Life,* was at one time the guardian of the famous German Shepherd movie star, Strongheart. Strongheart was a very intelligent and spiritual dog. Boone, who had never been a dog owner, nor, admittedly, a spiritual person, became Strongheart's student. Boone said, "When I began my dog-trains-man experiment with Strongheart, I was compelled to learn that if I wanted to achieve complete awareness with him, I would have to use something far more penetrating and perceptive than just a couple of eyeballs in my skull!" He continued by saying that he had to stop using his eyes and begin using his heart and mind to "see" Strongheart.

"This type of vision is what I finally had to come to use with Strongheart in order to begin actually seeing him as the spiritual being he was. My association with the biological part of him, while an interesting experience, was getting us nowhere. It was limiting us to those conventional and restricting ruts and routines that humans and dogs have been moving in for centuries. But when I began mentally getting Strongheart and I both out of those ruts, he and I began overflowing our banks (so to speak) and experiencing a type of living I had never before heard of. The more I lifted my concept of Strongheart out of the physical and into the mental, the more we moved toward the spiritual. Thus, with Strongheart's help, I was receiving priceless, primary lessons in the cosmic art of seeing things as they really are."

Be Patient

Spiritual awareness generally takes a good deal of time. You need time to know yourself, time to know your dog, and time to practice your spiritual exercises. In these busy days, it's often hard to find the time to do one more thing, never mind several things. If a spiritual relationship with your dog is important to you, however, you will need to make some time. Thirty minutes for a walk with your dog is great, but even a few minutes here and there are fine for moments of self-reflection. Let your dog accompany you as you work around the house or run errands. He'll enjoy being with you, even if he isn't the focus of your attention.

Why not let some of your daily chores become more spiritual in nature? I'll be the first to admit that washing dishes and dusting the furniture are not particularly inspirational activities, but even daily chores can have a spiritually satisfying element. As you mow the lawn, take the time to smell the fresh cut grass. Enjoy the beauty of your flower garden. As you clean house, enjoy the skill it took to weave the lovely throw blanket hanging on the back of your sofa.

If you have been working with these exercises, don't worry if you don't experience a big difference right away. Although some people find spirituality comes to them in a flash—usually through some kind of special (and often traumatic) event—most people find that spiritual awareness is an on-going adventure.

As you get to know yourself better, and are more honest with yourself, you will feel more inner peace. The same applies to your relationship with your dog. As the two of you get to know each other better, as you spend time together doing things (and doing nothing!), your relationship will deepen. You'll develop a deep feeling of connection with both your dog and with the natural world. Perhaps you will have feelings similar to those expressed by Mary Lou Randour in her book *Animal Grace: Entering a Spiritual Relationship with our Fellow Creatures*. Randour writes: "One day I noticed within myself a quiet tranquility. As I accomplished the tasks of the day—my practice of psychology, personal chores, and animal advocacy—I felt serene, strong, and in possession of a seemingly limitless energy."

Part 2

YOUR DOG'S HEALTH

Although your dog may be a capable friend, companion, and protector, he can't bathe himself, brush himself, or clip his own nails, so he needs your help. In reviewing your dog's physical well-being, I'll take a look at both some old methods that still deserve usage and some new ideas.

Chapter 5 discusses ways to care for your dog's coat and muscles. I'll talk about grooming, massage for your dog, Ttouch™, and even a hot stone massage.

In chapter 6, I'll delve into the controversial topic of a dog's nutritional needs. I'll discuss food quality, preparation, additives, and more. I'll take a look at natural foods, including raw food diets and homecooked meals, as well as food as medicine and food supplements.

Chapter 7 will explore ancient medical techniques. Many of your grandmother's treatments were quite valid and are still worth employing today. I'll discuss some "old wives' tales" and some other old medical techniques, including herbal medicine, acupuncture, and acupressure.

My discussion of canine health will end in chapter 8 with an overview of holistic medicine and homeopathy. What are these methods? You'll learn where they originated and how they work. Are any of these techniques right for you and your dog? If you decide to use these methods, can you work with a traditional veterinarian, or should you change vets?

Our explorations continue.

Chapter 5

GOOD HEALTH FROM THE OUTSIDE IN

One of my favorite chores isn't really a chore at all. Each evening I sit on the living room floor and call my dogs to me. This is the time of day when I give each of my three dogs some individual attention and care. Each dog gets groomed, brushed, combed, and checked for fleas, ticks, burrs, foxtails, and mats. Obviously, I have brushes, combs, and other grooming paraphernalia close by. It's also a good time to check for lumps and bumps, cuts, scrapes, bruises, ear, eye, or other infections, or other potential health problems.

I always start with Dax (to reinforce her status as the oldest dog in the house), and I invite her to lie down between my outstretched legs. She is so enthusiastic that she practically throws herself down; then she rolls over and goes belly up. Dax grins—showing her front teeth—when she's happy and she grins widely during our grooming sessions.

After Dax is thoroughly combed and brushed, she remains lying down in front of me; she knows we're not done yet. After grooming, each dog gets a massage, and this is each dog's favorite part of the evening. In fact, I think they put up with the grooming because they love the massage. While I massage her, I let my fingers really feel her skin and her body so that I can detect any problems that aren't visible above her coat. I pay attention to lumps, bumps, cuts, and any sore spots that make her flinch. By massaging her entire body, I can take care of her better than I could if I just attended to what I could see.

When I'm done with Dax, it's Kes's turn, and she gets combed, brushed, and massaged just like Dax. Then it's Riker's turn. As the youngest, he's always last, but it doesn't seem to bother him; it's always been like that, and I think it's taught him patience. Riker has a very thick coat, and although his coat gives testimony to his wonderful good health, it also creates problems of its own. I have to spend more time grooming his coat, working through the thick undercoat than I do with Dax and Kes.

When Riker was three months old, he broke his right rear leg just above the paw in an accident. It was a bad break although he healed very nicely. Now that he is completely healed, he still enjoys a good massage of that leg, especially after a very busy, tiring day. I don't doubt that it must still ache sometimes, and the massage probably soothes it.

Many dog owners look upon caring for the outside of their dogs as a task to be done only when absolutely necessary. I have seen dogs being brought in to a local grooming salon in horrible condition, with matts and tangles all over their body and infested with fleas and ticks. I know how good I feel after a shower and shampoo; can you imagine going weeks without being clean or brushed? I'm sure those dogs must feel horrible.

Caring for the skin and coat of your dog doesn't have to be a burden; it can be a wonderful experience with your friend. In fact, it's a good excuse to spend time together. Plus, caring for the outside of your dog helps keep the inside of your dog healthy.

MORE THAN JUST GROOMING

Some dog owners seem to think that grooming applies only to Poodles and other breeds that get regular haircuts. Grooming, however, really encompasses all the routine care of your dog's physical body including combing, brushing, bathing, trimming toenails, and everything else that might be needed—even routine mouth and tooth care.

Obviously, dogs with a thick coat, like my young dog, Riker, will need more brushing and dematting than will a short-haired Labrador Retriever. In addition, Poodles, Schnauzers, and Shih Tzus normally visit a professional groomer on a regular basis for a haircut, and an older dog will need more attention to keep his teeth clean than will a young dog. So grooming needs vary. With that in mind, you do need to know the basics of good grooming to keep him feeling and looking good.

There are many books and videos available that will tell you how to groom your dog, so I'll keep this section simple. I'll look at how your grooming chores can be made easier yet still provide your dog with good care.

Combing and Brushing

Combing and brushing your dog pulls out dead (shedding) coat, removes dirt and debris, stimulates the skin, and distributes natural oils throughout the coat. In addition, it stimulates the lymph system, which works with both the immune system and in waste removal in the bloodstream. It's also a great time for you to bond with your dog because when you are gentle your dog will love the grooming.

There are scads of types and styles of grooming combs and brushes available for sale to dog owners. Do you need one of each? Absolutely not. You can keep your dog well groomed quite simply.

If you have a short-haired dog, a soft bristled brush and a few rags are all you need. The soft bristled brush should be used daily to loosen dead hair and get dirt and debris out of the coat. A damp rag wiped over the dog after brushing will pull out any remaining dead (shed) hairs.

A metal comb is the best friend of medium- and long-coated dogs. With a metal comb, you can part your dog's coat and comb through sections at a time, removing tangles, dirt, and debris. When all of the hair has been sectioned and combed, you can then comb through the entire coat.

The key to using these simple tools is to groom the dog daily. If you don't, mats and tangles form, and dirt builds up. You may then need a mat-splitter, rake, or other special grooming tools. Daily attention eliminates the need for onerous, unpleasant grooming sessions.

GETTING OUT STICKY STUFF

If your dog has something sticky in his coat—like gum—use an ice cube to freeze it and then break it out of the coat. Vegetable oil can also be rubbed into something stuck in the coat to loosen it. Of course, only use vegetable oil when you will be immediately bathing the dog afterward!

Bathing, Brushing, and Toenails

It's commonly believed that bathing your dog frequently is bad for him, but this is only true if you bathe your dog often with a very harsh shampoo and are drying out his skin as a result. As therapy dogs, my dogs must be bathed before each visit. This means that they get bathed weekly—sometimes twice weekly—and their coats are shiny and glow with good health.

One of my favorite dog shampoos—especially for dogs with oily skin or smelly skin (or that just get very dirty)—is Joy dishwashing liquid. It cuts through the skin oils very well and rinses out cleanly. It is concentrated, however, so squeeze out a small amount of the soap (a teaspoon for a medium-sized dog) and dilute it with water. Then use this diluted soap to wash your dog. Joy dishwashing liquid is biodegradable and contains no phosphates.

Commercial dog shampoos are available by the hundreds and you may want to use one of these; however, make sure you read the label before using it. Many dog shampoos are labeled "medicated" and may contain sulfur or betadyne to kill bacteria on the skin. Others may contain coal tar, which treats skin problems. Using these ingredients when they aren't needed (when there are no skin problems present) will upset the natural balance of the skin.

Commercial flea shampoos usually contain insecticides that are toxic to fleas. These insecticides may also be toxic to young dogs, old dogs, or dogs with sensitivities or compromised immune systems. Even some herbal shampoos containing pennyroyal or eucalyptus can cause problems in sensitive dogs.

Make sure you read the label carefully and understand all the ingredients. If you don't know what an ingredient is, contact the manufacturer and ask. The labels of many products usually have a telephone number, a Web site, or an e-mail address. Don't be embarrassed to ask questions about a product; it's your responsibility as a wise dog owner to know what a product is before you use it on your dog.

SIMPLE SHAMPOO SAFETY

If you decide to use a new shampoo, test it on your dog before you spread it over his entire body. The day before you plan on bathing your dog, touch your finger to the shampoo, and then rub a small amount on the skin inside one thigh where there isn't too much hair. Blot off the excess shampoo but don't wipe or rinse it off. Watch this spot for any reactions. If your dog's skin does react (redness, itchiness, a rash, or hives), immediately wash off any shampoo residue and don't use that product on your dog.

To rinse all the soap (no matter what kind) from your dog's coat, try a vinegar rinse. Dilute one cup of white vinegar in a gallon of water, pour it over the dog, work it into the coat, and then rinse it out. It works great.

Always brush and comb your dog before bathing him. If you bathe him with tangles, burrs, or foxtails in his coat, the hair will mat and tangle even more. You will probably have to use some sharp scissors to cut those problems out of the coat. If you have to trim anything out of the coat, make sure you place your fingers between the scissors and your dog's skin so that you don't pull up some skin with the hair, and then cut it.

Bathing your dog will loosen any shed or dead hair, so always brush your dog again after he's dry from his bath. And note: Your dog's nails will be nice and soft right after a bath, so that's a great time to trim.

NAIL TRIMMING MADE EASY

If your dog dislikes having his nails trimmed, use a Dremmel tool to smooth them down. This small power tool (either battery-operated or plug in) is used in many crafts and has a spinning shaft that powers different attachments. The stone-grinding attachments wear down dog nails with just a touch. It is much faster than fiddling with the nail, finding the right spot to cut, and then trimming it. To use a Dremmel properly, make sure the hair around the nails is swept back so that the hair isn't pulled by the spinning tool.

Eyes, Ears, and Teeth

Your dog's eyes flush themselves with tears so they don't really need cleaning, but should your dog develop some matter in his eyes (from dust, dirt, or allergens) you can rinse his eyes with saline solution. I keep a bottle of saline solution in my first aid kit so I always have some available. If the matter returns almost immediately, is green or brown, or if there seems to be a lot of it, then your dog needs to visit your veterinarian.

Your dog's ears should be cleaned regularly, at least once per week. Clean the ears more often if your dog gets dirty from work or play. A cotton ball or piece of gauze dampened with witch hazel (with the excess moisture squeezed out) works well. Holding the earflap with one hand, gently clean all the ridges and crevasses of the ear, getting as far into the ear as you can without forcing your fingers into the ear canal. If your dog's ears are dirty, you may have to use two or three cotton balls or pieces of gauze. Note that many dogs with chronic ear problems also suffer from allergies. An allergy test at your veterinarian's office is well worth the cost.

USE YOUR NOSE

Your sense of smell is the best way to detect any problem in your dog's ears. A clean, healthy ear will smell damp but will not have any unpleasant odors. If an infection is brewing, the ear may smell yeasty, moldy, cheesy, or otherwise malodorous.

Your dog's teeth should be cleaned two or three times a week, although a daily cleaning is even better. Regular cleaning will keep plaque from building up. Plaque and tartar on your dog's teeth are quite destructive to his overall health. When these build up over time, periodontal disease can develop, sometimes resulting in serious infection. So keeping teeth clean is very important. A piece of gauze wrapped around one finger, dampened with water, makes a good toothbrush. Touch the dampened gauze to some baking soda and then gently rub the baking soda onto the teeth, making sure to get all the crevasses in the teeth. Make sure, too, to get all the way down to the gum line.

If your dog will allow it, using a Water Pik™ dental care machine will help you keep your dog's teeth sparkling. The Water Pik sends a stream of water through a very small hole in a handheld device. The force of the water dislodges debris on the teeth and is excellent for preventing the buildup of plaque and tartar.

THE JOY OF THE CHEW TOY

Chew toys not only help keep your dog busy, but they'll help to keep his teeth in good condition. If your dog's teeth tend to show a good deal of tartar, make sure he has something hard to chew on. Clean, bleached rawhide bones (the white ones), commercial chew toys, or even a carrot or two will help scrape the tartar off his teeth.

The Genitals and Anal Glands

Female dogs usually keep themselves quite clean. Unless an intact (unspayed) female dog is in season (when she can be quite messy), you will rarely need to perform any special cleaning. If she has a long coat, you may want to trim the hair around the anal region, just to prevent it from getting dirty when she relieves herself.

Males, however, are another story. The hair at the end of the penis sheath should be trimmed regularly. As he urinates and marks territory, this hair will become soaked with urine, and if it isn't trimmed, it could lead to an infection. It smells bad too. Just be careful when you trim the hair; don't cut anything else!

Many male dogs are also prone to developing a discharge in the penis sheath. If you see a discharge at the end of the sheath, especially if it's green or brown, take your dog into the veterinarian's office. He may have you treat the dog with an antibiotic for a period of time, but the vet will also show you how to wash or flush the area to keep it clean.

The anal glands are located on each side of the anus. As the dog defecates, the squeezing of the muscles deposits some scent from these glands onto the feces. This is the dog's "calling card" of scent. If the dog has soft stools, or if the anal glands produce too much of this oily matter, the glands may become too full. This, in turn, can result in inflammation and infection of the glands, causing your dog pain and misery. You can help by expressing some of the extra matter from the glands. To do so, protect your hand with several layers of thick paper towels, and then squeeze the glands. Put one thumb about one-half inch on one side of the anus and your fingers about one-half inch on the other side. Push in slightly, then together (toward the anus), and then slightly (gently) out. You may have to try a couple times to get the hang of it. If the glands are full, the oily material will squirt out onto the paper towels. If you have trouble mastering this technique, or if your dog protests, ask your veterinarian to help you.

If your dog seems to have repeated trouble with his anal glands, add some fiber, such as a teaspoon of bran or some chopped vegetables, to his diet. If the glands are swollen, red, and inflamed, a compress of warm to hot (but not *hot*) water soaked with calendula or red clover tea will relieve some of the inflammation and make them easier to express.

WHEN YOUR DOG DRAGS HIS BUTT

It used to be thought that if a dog dragged his rear end across the ground or floor, he had worms. That may be true in a very few cases, but most of the time this behavior indicates that the dog's anal glands are full. He's trying to release the pressure and discomfort of those full glands.

Flea and Tick Control

I couldn't discuss the health of the outside of your dog without talking about fleas, ticks, and chemicals to control them. Fleas and ticks are very dangerous parasites; they can harm your dog by biting him and taking blood from him. They can also pass along additional parasites (including tapeworms) and numerous diseases. If your dog is to remain in good health, you must keep fleas and ticks off your dog.

Many products are available that are designed to control fleas and ticks. Some are insect growth regulators, some stop the insects from breeding, and some actually kill the insects once they bite your pet. Some of these products also control other problems, including internal parasites, especially heartworms. Talk to your veterinarian if you want more information on this topic; most of these products are available only by prescription.

Many commercially produced pest control products have been tested and found to be very safe, as long as owners read the labels and watch their dog carefully for side effects. Nonetheless, many dog owners are still quite concerned about the safety of using these products on their pets. I, for one, feel that a little skepticism is a good thing. If you want to avoid using commercial products to control fleas and ticks, there are some other techniques you can use. The most important thing is that you do something (instead of nothing) and you do keep the insects off your pet. In addition, work with your veterinarian. You will need to make sure your dog does not become infested with parasites or diseases transmitted by mosquitoes, fleas, and ticks.

Some flea and tick control ideas that you can try include:

- Physically examine your dog every day. Remove and destroy ticks and flea comb your dog.

- Use cedar, eucalyptus, or pennyroyal on the dog's bedding to chase away fleas. These substances can be toxic if ingested, however, so do not use directly on the dog.
- Brewer's yeast, vitamin-B complex, and garlic—when fed as part of the dog's diet—will make some dogs unappetizing to insects. These are worth a try (and are good nutrition by themselves), but this approach doesn't work for all dogs.
- Sprinkle borax on the carpets throughout the house. Borax dries out the adult fleas and their larvae. Replenish the borax each time you shampoo the carpet.

A NATURAL APPROACH

Fleas do not like citrus, so here's a recipe for a spray you can use in the house or on your dog. Take the skins and fruit of several lemons, oranges, or grapefruit (whatever you have available), cut them into quarters, and put them in a large pot. Cover with water and bring to a boil. Let the mixture boil rapidly for several minutes; then turn off the heat and let it steep. When cool, strain off the fruit residue. The liquid can then be put in a sprayer and used directly on your dog or in the house. (I've heard that citrus also repels cats, so don't try this on your feline friends.)

HEALTH PROBLEMS OF THE SKIN AND COAT

Caring for your dog's skin and coat involves more than just grooming. You must look after the outside, obviously, but if the dog isn't healthy inside (either because of poor nutrition or other health problems) that condition will be reflected by a poor coat. I'll talk more about good nutrition in the next chapter, but some other health problems that commonly have a poor coat as a side effect might include any of the following.

ACNE—Acne usually occurs when bacteria build up in or on the skin. Some adolescent dogs are prone to it just as adolescent humans are and this is probably related to hormones in the system. Acne can be treated by keeping the affected skin very clean and washing it often with soap. Note that a washcloth soaked in warm calendula tea can be placed on the acne breakout to soothe the skin and reduce the inflammation.

ALLERGIES—Food allergies, inhalant allergies, and contact allergies can cause a variety of skin and coat conditions. Licking the feet, chewing at the base of the tail, constant scratching, and bald spots are all symptoms of allergies. Allergies can also cause the coat to appear thin and dull as well as increase shedding.

Identifying the particular allergen at work can be difficult. If your pine tree begins shedding vast quantities of yellow pollen on the same day your dog begins scratching himself, well, then you know the source of the allergy. Unfortunately, it's rarely that simple. Instead of playing a guessing game, you are better off spending the money at your veterinarian's office to have some allergy tests run. When the results are in, you will know exactly what your dog is allergic to, and you and your veterinarian can plan a course of action. For example, if your dog is allergic to beef and wheat (two very common food allergies), you can modify your dog's diet. (Make sure you remember to read the labels on dog treats, too.)

SOOTHING IRRITATED SKIN

Australian tea tree oil, also sold as Melaleuca alternifolia *and* Melaleuca, *is very soothing to allergic, red, or irritated skin. The oil can be applied directly to the affected skin or can be diluted with water in a mister and sprayed on the skin and coat. Gently rub into the skin and leave it on. Repeat as needed.*

COAT DRYNESS—If your dog's hair coat is dry, dull-looking, and brittle, there is a problem. No matter what type of coat your dog has, it should be supple and shiny. A common cause for a dull coat is an improper diet. Good nutrition is the foundation for good health, including a healthy coat. (See chapter 6 for lots more on nutrition.) Some shampoos are not suitable for dogs, and you may be washing the sheen out of your dog's coat. Shampoos made for people are much too harsh for dogs, as are, surprisingly enough, many of the medicated shampoos made for dogs. As you begin treating the dry coat, try using Joy dishwashing liquid for several baths. It is much milder than most shampoos.

A BOOST FOR LACKLUSTER COATS

To get your dog's coat to shine, you may want to add some fatty acids to your dog's diet. Some flaxseed oils or fish oil capsules from your local health food store are both good nutrition and good for the coat.

DANDRUFF—Dogs are constantly replacing skin cells. As new skin cells are produced, old ones flake off. Normally this process isn't highly visible because the cells are small and the dander falls out of the coat; however, when the process is accelerated, large flakes of skin are shed and you see dandruff. Apparent dandruff is a symptom that something is probably wrong in the dog's system. The dog may have parasites, hormonal imbalances, or even disease. A visit to the vet's office to eliminate these or other problems is in order. Do *not* use dandruff shampoos made for people; these are much too harsh to use all over your dog's body.

DEALING WITH DANDRUFF

If your dog gets a clean bill of health from the vet, you can treat dandruff in several ways. First, make sure your dog's eating a good diet. Add some flaxseed or fish oils to his diet. Shampoo him well with Joy; then give him a vinegar rinse, finishing with a clear water rinse.

HOT SPOTS—If your dog scratches and then develops a weepy sore on his skin, he has just produced a hot spot. Once the skin is damaged, bacteria take hold and pretty soon the skin is a weepy, smelly mess. Hot spots are extremely uncomfortable and your dog will want relief as soon as you can provide it.

Trim the hair from around the hot spot so you can get to it. Wash it well with an antibacterial soap or betadyne, sooth it with calendula tea, and then blot the area dry. Coat the spot with boric acid powder twice a day. Applying Australian tea tree oil *(Melaleuca)* can also be quite helpful in healing hot spots. If there is no improvement within twenty-four hours, take your dog to your veterinarian.

ITCHING—Itching can be caused by a number of different things, such as fleas, bites from other insects, or allergies, to name a few. You will need to do some detective work to find out what's causing the itching. Simply treating the symptoms isn't enough. Here again, the dog's diet plays an important role—make sure that he's eating nutritious food and get some fatty acids into him.

TEA TIME

You can soothe the skin with calendula tea. Put it on the itchy spots with a damp rag, letting it set there for a few minutes. Then let it dry without rinsing it off.

OILY COAT—When your dog's skin and coat are greasy, the hair sticks together and it smells bad. You'll know it when you see it. Dogs produce a natural oil in the skin called sebum. This keeps the skin flexible and the coat lubricated and shiny. Sometimes, however, dogs produce too much sebum and the coat gets saturated. Frequent shampooing with Joy, followed by a vinegar rinse, will clean that oil out of the coat. In addition, make sure the dog is eating a good diet with plenty of minerals.

MIRACULOUS MINERALS

Many dogs with an excessively oily coat are not getting adequate minerals from their diet. A powdered kelp supplement (from your local pet store or health food store) added to your dog's diet is an easy way to increase his mineral intake.

SHEDDING—Shedding is the dog's way of getting rid of the dead hair in his coat, making way for new hair. Some breeds—most notably Poodles and Bichon Frises—don't shed. Their hair grows constantly and is usually trimmed regularly. Other dogs shed twice a year, usually in the spring and fall. Female dogs usually shed just before or just after they have come into season and after having given birth to puppies. Some breeds—German Shepherds and Siberian Huskies, for example—shed heavily twice a year and a little bit all the time. Dogs will also shed while under stress, and some will show their stress by shedding immediately. It almost seems as though the skin loosens its grip on the hair and it begins to fall out. Not surprisingly, many dogs will shed after they have had surgery.

To evaluate shedding, you need to know what is normal for your dog and his breed. Excessive shedding with no obvious cause should be a concern as it might signal other health problems. If you can't pinpoint a reason for your dog to shed more than usual, call your veterinarian.

The best way to deal with shedding is to brush, brush, brush, and brush some more. The more dead hair you can brush out of your dog's coat, the less there will be deposited on your floor, furniture, and clothes.

AH, THE BENEFITS OF MASSAGE

Massage affects both the body and the mind. The practice of massage—particularly on people—has a very old and rich history. In many cultures, it is considered a spiritual as well as a physical practice.

Massage for animals has been performed for a long time, perhaps as long as we've had domesticated pets, but it's not a traditional practice that we can trace over time. As my grandfather once told me, "If your horse or goat or dog was hurt, you did what you knew to do. You didn't talk about it; you just did it."

A TRADITION OF HAND HEALING

Among the Tarahumara Indians of Mexico, sobadores, *which roughly translates as "hand healers," are held in high regard. Hand healers must be cleansed and initiated to remove evil spirits prior to learning their craft. Following ancient practices, a hand healer's massage focuses on the spirit of disease rather than the actual physical disease.*

Physically, massage loosens the muscles, aids in blood flow, and removes lactic acid from sore muscles. It will loosen scar tissue and tight tendons after injuries or surgery and will relax muscle spasms, strains, and sprains. Massage causes the release of endorphins (natural chemicals in the body) that relieve pain and promote feelings of well-being.

Emotionally, massage eases stress and allows your dog to relax. Aggression, over-protectiveness, anger, and other dark emotions can be diminished by such relaxation. Another benefit of massaging your dog is increased trust in your relationship—your dog must trust you to allow you to massage him. You reinforce that trust by making sure that your dog is relaxed and comfortable after the massage is over.

Spiritually, you will find the bond between you and your dog growing deeper as you spend this very personal time together.

Different Strokes

There is really no right or wrong way to massage your dog as long as you and your dog both enjoy the process. Some dogs prefer a lighter touch while others like to be manhandled roughly. How your dog needs to be touched on any given day may depend upon the dog's mood at the moment. Your dog may also like light touches around the head and paws but stronger touches on the neck or the hips. It will take practice to learn what type of massage will suit you both. In addition, the different types and strengths of massage have different purposes, so what you do will also depend on what you're trying to accomplish.

TTOUCH™

The concept of massage for pets really came into its own when Linda Tellington-Jones introduced Ttouch (pronounced "Tee-touch"). Ttouch is a circular motion massage, with the hands moving one and one-quarter circles. In other words, the hand makes a circle but doesn't stop until it's completed the circle plus one-quarter beyond the beginning of the circle. The Ttouch system applies many different types of strokes, and each stroke bears the name of an animal. For example, the Clouded Leopard stroke is made using the pads of the fingers while the hand is cupped or curved. In the Lying Leopard stroke, the fingers and palm are used. In the Raccoon stroke, only the very tips of the fingers are used, and the stroke is very light. Some of the other strokes are called Python Lift, Noah's Arc, Tiger Ttouch, and Bear. For more information about Ttouch books, videos, or seminars, see Appendix D: Resources.

As you practice, you will also find spots that your dog would rather you not touch. Respect your pet's preference, especially in the beginning. These spots may not feel good being kneaded, or your dog may just not like the idea of being massaged there. After all, it is your dog's body! It's also possible that that particular spot might be sore and so your dog doesn't want that area handled. If so, you might try again at another time with different types (and pressures) of massage strokes. As you become more experienced with the art of massage, your dog might accept a particular type or pressure on vulnerable spots.

You will also find spots where your dog really, really likes being massaged. The base of the tail is one that most dogs like. Another is the back of the neck. You should spend time massaging those spots, of course, but don't neglect the rest of your dog's body.

When you massage, actually move the skin. If your touch is so light that the skin doesn't move, you won't get the blood flowing or move toxins out of the muscles. Once you've got the skin moving under your fingers, you can vary the amount of pressure depending upon the type of stroke you're using and the purpose of your massage.

If your dog has a short coat, the coat won't interfere with the massage, but long-coated dogs present a bit of a challenge. While making strokes, work your fingers under the coat so that you can feel the dog's skin. It's much easier if your dog has been freshly brushed or combed and the hair is free of mats and tangles.

As you massage your dog, watch his face and the reactions of his body under your hands. His face will show you whether he's relaxed, apprehensive, or fearful. His body will move, twitch, or jump when you hit a sore spot. Keep in mind you want the massage to be both beneficial and pleasurable, so watch his reactions.

When you first begin to massage your dog, keep the massage sessions short and sweet. It's best to allow your dog to get comfortable sitting still and being massaged. Start with a two- or three-minute session and work your way up to longer time periods. If you try to start off with an extended massage, your dog may not enjoy the experience and fail to develop a positive association with it.

Some specific strokes include:

BASIC CIRCULAR STROKE—With this stroke, you simply move your hands in a circular motion. You can use one hand or two, depending upon how coordinated you are. This stroke is very relaxing and good to get the blood flowing under the skin.

EAR STROKE—This stroke almost seems directly connected to the brain. It calms a nervous dog, settles an aggressive dog, and allows the dog to think rather than react. This stroke was made famous in the movie *The Truth About Cats & Dogs,* in which a photographer used it to calm an aggressive dog. With the earflap between your thumb and fingers, rub gently around the base of the ear. Then stroke from the base to the tip of the ear. Repeat several times.

LONG STROKE—This stroke is quite relaxing and is quite similar to petting. Start at the base of the ears or neck and stroke slowly to the base of the tail. These strokes should be long and slow. The pressure can vary according to your dog's preference, but most experts recommend beginning with a lighter touch and gradually making it heavier.

KNEADING DOUGH—This stroke is actually more like kneading dough than stroking, but no matter what it's called, it's great for relieving muscle soreness. Once you have used the long stroke to relax your dog, begin this stroke on muscles that are sore. Isolate one at a time under your fingertips, and then gently knead that muscle as you would bread dough. If you've never made bread, think of a puppy nursing at his mother's breast. He kneads her to make the milk flow. This kneading motion makes the blood flow to the muscles and removes waste products.

Different Styles

If you've ever had a massage, you know that a systematic approach to the strokes feels best. This applies to your dog as well. Try some of the following massage techniques on your dog.

Invite your dog to lie down in front of you on the floor. Place both hands at the base of your dog's ears, on his neck, and begin making small circles with each hand. Don't use too much pressure to begin with; a heavy hand may scare your dog away. As you make circles, gradually move your hands around his neck to the front, and then back toward his spine. Gradually work down his neck toward his shoulders, then down the shoulders to each front leg, depending upon how he's lying. (You may have to do one side, and then roll him over and do the other.) Work down the rib cage, down his back, and down the hip. When you have completely massaged this side, roll him over and repeat the process.

As an alternative sit on the floor and invite your dog to lie down in front of you. Leaning forward toward him, rest your elbows on your knees (so that you aren't pulling on his ears), and with an ear in each hand, begin massaging the base of each ear. Gently rub with thumb and fingers. Place the earflaps between your thumb and fingers and gently stroke from the base to the tip of the ear. Return to the base and repeat the entire process. As you do this, watch your dog's face and eyes. He will gradually relax and may even fall into a trance.

Make sure that you give your dog a good grooming before this massage. Place both hands on your dog's shoulders at the base of his neck and stroke toward his tail with light, even pressure, finishing the stroke at the base of the tail. Go back to the shoulders and repeat it. With each pair of strokes, make the pressure slightly stronger. Watch your dog's body. He will twitch and move under your hands and will arch his back to feel the strokes even more. He may even push into your hands.

If your dog has some sore muscles, try the following technique. First, try to isolate the particular muscles that are sore. You can often do this simply by giving your dog a light massage with circular hand movements. A sore muscle will feel hard and tight under your hands, and your dog may twitch when you touch it. Using both hands, feel that muscle under the skin. Moving gently (remember it's sore), begin kneading that muscle, using fingers and thumbs. As you feel the muscle loosening and stretching, you may be able to use more pressure depending upon your dog's pain tolerance. Never make him uncomfortable.

THE POWER OF TOUCH

Touch is necessary for survival. Gentle massage can be invaluable to the well-being of your dog and is particularly helpful to orphaned puppies, newly adopted puppies, and newly adopted dogs. Older dogs who may be a little confused seem to be more grounded after a massage.

A Bounty of Benefits

In addition to the pleasure and bonding you and your dog experience when you massage him, there are some specific uses for massage.

If your dog is hurt, stressed, tense, or frightened, gently massage his ears. Start by rubbing the base of each ear, then moving up the earflap. Very gently press the earflap between your thumb and fingers and slide from the base to the tip of the earflap.

A massage of the pectineus muscle inside the thigh will loosen and relax it, giving dogs with hip dysplasia some relief from pain or stiffness. (This muscle is strong and usually feels like a tight band.) To be effective, a somewhat strong, kneading massage is required. Of course, you'll want to touch your dog carefully; an overly deep massage will hurt.

An all-body massage will relax a dog suffering from arthritis. Use strong circular motions over the entire body, emphasizing the muscles around and over the joints.

An all-body massage with slow, gentle circular motions will relax a dog with behavioral problems. Don't forget to stroke the earflaps.

An all-body massage using long, body-length straight strokes will wake up and stimulate an overweight, lazy dog or a dog that needs to get moving after an illness, injury, or surgery.

A TIP FOR CALMING YOUR CANINE

Is your young dog very excitable? Does he come into the house bouncing off the walls? Instead of yelling at him (which will make the problem worse), leash him as you bring him into the house. Have him lie down in front of you as you sit on the floor, and then begin giving him a massage. Start with an earflap rub, and then move to a standard circular massage. Use a firm, but not hard, touch. Massage his entire body. By the time you have massaged both sides, he will probably be quite relaxed. He will be able to control himself now, so tell him, "Stay," as you get up and hand him a chew toy.

HOT STONE MASSAGE

Hot stone massage is a popular technique that is exactly what it sounds like—a massage using hot stones. The warmth of the stones can stimulate blood flow so that toxins and wastes are flushed from sore muscles, and it can relieve soreness in arthritic joints. Heat can speed healing and improve the immune system. By using stones that will hold the heat, you can bring natural heat and a massage to your dog at the same time.

You will need to find five or six relatively flat stones that fit comfortably in the palm of your hand. Water-tumbled stones that are flat and smooth work very well, but if there is no river nearby, you might be able to find stones at your local garden center or craft store.

You'll also need to heat the stones. Some people like to light several candles—especially aromatic candles—and place the stones on a rack above the flames; however, you can heat the stones in the oven, too. You will use the stones when they are warm but not so hot that you cannot comfortably hold them in your hand.

Invite your dog to lie down in front of you and give him a basic massage to relax him. Then, with a stone in the palm of your hand, place the stone and your hand on his body, preferably over a sore muscle or joint. Do not press down; let the natural weight of the stone rest on him. Then gently begin moving the stone in a circular manner over that muscle or joint. If your dog is thin and the joints or bones are not well covered with flesh, be careful not to hurt your dog as you move the stones. Remember, move the stone but don't press down; the weight of the stone itself is enough.

When that spot feels warm to your other hand, move to another spot or joint. When the stone cools, put it back to reheat and bring out another stone.

Watch your dog's reactions. If he begins to pant, he's getting too warm, so stop and let him get a drink and cool off. If he's relaxed and accepting of the massage, however, you can continue for five to ten minutes or until the muscle or joint is relaxed and moving well.

YOUR SENIOR DOG

Older dogs will particularly enjoy a daily massage. A slow, gentle massage will ease his arthritis, loosen tight joints, and get the blood flowing again. In addition, your warm hands and caring touch will be emotionally and spiritually soothing. By massaging your elderly dog, you're showing him how much you treasure him.

COMBINE MASSAGE WITH GROOMING AND BODY CARE

I mentioned earlier that I groom my dogs before massaging them. I do this for several reasons. First, once the dog is groomed, my fingers will then slide through the dog's coat without getting stuck in mats and tangles. In addition, while grooming him, I can find foxtails, burrs, and fleas—nasty problems that should be addressed.

The massage, however, provides a much closer examination. While massaging my dog, my fingers are feeling every square inch of his body. I learn what he feels like when he is well. Then, should there be a problem, like a cut, a scrape, or a tick, my fingers will feel it.

Sometimes I begin massaging and find a tangle that I missed. I stop the massage, grab the comb again, and work out that tangle. Then I go back to massaging. That's okay. Massage, grooming, and body care should go hand in hand because they are all important for the care of your dog.

Chapter 6

YOU ARE WHAT YOU EAT APPLIES TO YOUR DOG, TOO

Sonny, a terrier mix, began scratching and chewing when he was about two years old. He scratched his ears so badly that they were bloody. He chewed at the base of his tail until he had hair caught between his front teeth, and the skin at the base of his tail was raw. He licked his paws, too, and did so until the hair was discolored from his saliva. During all this he showed a change in his personality.

Sonny's owner, Margie, was frantic. She didn't know what was happening to her dog. First aid remedies didn't seem to work, and her dog was becoming more and more unhappy.

Sonny's veterinarian explained to Margie that problems with these three areas—the ears, the base of the tail, and the paws—were fairly typical of food allergies. The vet explained that food allergies can be developed at any time, so Sonny could be allergic to the food that he'd eaten his whole adult life. Moreover, the food formula may have changed; the addition of even one ingredient is enough to cause an allergic reaction in some sensitive dogs.

When allergy tests were completed, they showed that Sonny had some very common food allergies. He reacted to beef, lamb, wheat, and corn. He was also allergic to some native grasses, trees, molds, and mildews. With allergy shots and a new food that was based on fish, Sonny stopped scratching, his skin healed, his coat grew back in, and his happy-go-lucky personality reappeared.

The food we feed our dogs is vitally important to their good health. Many dogs suffer from food allergies, and different types of foods will affect different dogs. One commercial food may nourish one dog quite well, but the same food may not be nutritious for another dog. The food a dog eats also affects his activity level, energy, immune system, growth, ability to heal, ability to reproduce, and many other aspects of his life.

We want our dogs to live long, healthy lives with us, and to do that, they must be well fed. It's up to us to become informed, knowledgeable consumers and dog owners.

NUTRITION

Good nutrition is the foundation for all life. What you choose to feed your dog is vitally important. Poor nutrition can result in a lack of energy and a great many health problems. Some behavior problems can also occur as a result of poor nutrition (and feeding your dog well is such an easy way to discourage them).

Your dog needs food made from good quality ingredients that satisfies his body's needs. Hopefully, it will also taste good to him and won't deplete your bank account at the same time.

ORGANIC EATING

The term organic food *is defined differently by different people. Some consider foods that are grown without pesticides, insecticides, herbicides, antibiotics, growth hormones, or any other chemicals with the exception of chemical fertilizers, to be organic. Other people state that truly organic foods should be grown with nothing but natural fertilizers. Many people prefer to eat only organic foods and would like to have their dogs eat only organic foods. Right now that's very difficult to do; some farmers produce plants organically, but very few meats are commercially produced in a truly organic manner.*

The Many Aspects of Nutrition

Every body needs good nutrition and what constitutes good nutrition depends upon the body being nourished. Obviously, an herbivorous animal (such as a horse or sheep) will not have the same nutritional needs as a carnivorous animal (like a lion or wolf). Dogs are scientifically considered carnivores, but all wild canine carnivores are known to eat other food in addition to meat. That's why your dog may eat a ripe strawberry or a grape.

Nutritional needs do not remain the same throughout an animal's lifetime. They will change as the body changes, for example, from puppyhood to adulthood to old age. Nutritional needs may differ depending on an animal's environment. Dogs living and working in colder climates will need more calories to keep the body warm than will dogs working in a warmer climate. Nutritional needs will change, too, with an animal's activity level—a hard-working dog will need more energy from food to perform his work than a couch potato.

Ideally, your dog's diet fulfills all of his nutritional needs. It should allow him to grow and remain healthy while having enough energy left for exercise and playtime. Just as with humans, good nutrition for dogs is composed of many elements. Vitamins, minerals, proteins, amino acids, enzymes, fats, and carbohydrates are all necessary for good nutrition.

When considering the vitamins and minerals your dog needs, it's important to remember that no one single vitamin or mineral is more important than another. Each has its own function and place in the system. Each is also dependent upon the others.

With that caveat, you should be familiar with the purpose and source of important vitamins and minerals.

Vitamins

Vitamins are organic compounds that are necessary for life. Without these compounds, there could be no metabolism of food, no growth, no reproduction, and there would be a total cessation of a thousand other bodily functions. Several vitamins, including A, D, E, and K are fat soluble, which means the body can store them in the body's fat. Other vitamins, including all of the B-complex vitamins and vitamin C, are water soluble. These are flushed out of the system daily in the urine and must be replenished through the foods consumed.

Vitamin A is a fat-soluble vitamin that has two forms: provitamin A and preformed vitamin A. Provitamin A is carotene, which must be converted into vitamin A before it can be used by the body. Preformed vitamin A is the result of that chemical conversion. As a fat-soluble vitamin, excess vitamin A is stored in the liver, fat tissues, lungs, kidneys, and the retinas of the eyes. This vitamin is an important antioxidant; it helps in growth, aids in digestion, builds resistance to disease, and helps repair tissues. A vitamin A deficiency will result in retarded growth, reproductive failure, skin disorders, and eye defects. On the other hand, too much vitamin A can be toxic. Vitamin A is found in leafy green vegetables, fish oils, and liver. The American Association of Feed Control Officials (AAFCO) recommends a minimum of 5,000 IUs of vitamin A per day per kilogram of dog food with no more than 50,000 IUs per day.

The B-complex vitamins are a group of water-soluble vitamins that the body uses in a variety of ways. Vitamin B1, thiamin, works with enzymes to convert glucose to energy. Also known as the "morale" vitamin, it affects the nervous system and is beneficial to a good mental attitude. Vitamin B2, riboflavin, works with enzymes to help cells utilize oxygen. It is needed for good vision and healthy skin, hair coat, and nails. Vitamin B3, niacin, works with enzymes to metabolize food. It also improves circulation and helps maintain a healthy nervous system. Vitamin B5, pantothenic acid, works with the adrenal glands, aids in digestion, and helps the body withstand stress. Pyroxidine, vitamin B6, aids in the production of red blood cells and is necessary for the absorption of vitamin B12. In conjunction with enzymes, vitamin B12, cyanocobalamin, assists in normal DNA synthesis. It also works with food metabolism and the nervous system. Vitamin B15, pangamic acid, ensures that the body, particularly the muscles, has enough oxygen. Other B vitamins, including biotin, folic acid, and choline, serve equally vital functions. The B-complex vitamins are found in brewer's yeast, liver, and whole-grain cereals.

Vitamin C is a vital part of the daily diet. Although dogs can produce vitamin C internally, most experts feel that they do not produce sufficient amounts to manage the stresses of modern life. A water-soluble vitamin, vitamin C is involved in many different functions, including maintaining a healthy immune system, growth, and aiding in the formation of red blood cells. Vitamin C also fights bacterial infections.

Exposure to the sun increases the body's use of vitamin D, and so it is called the sunshine vitamin. Vitamin D is needed for normal calcium-phosphorus absorption. It is also necessary for normal growth and healthy bones and teeth. Vitamin D is a fat-soluble vitamin, and excess quantities of it are stored in the liver, brain, and skin. Too much can lead to excess calcium and phosphorus in the system, causing calcification of the blood vessels. Fish oils and, as I mentioned before, exposure to the sun are good sources of vitamin D.

Vitamin E is a fat-soluble vitamin that works with the pituitary and adrenal glands, protecting them from oxidation. It also assists in the cellular respiration of muscle tissues, dilates blood vessels, and works to prevent blood clots. Vitamin E is found in vegetable oils, raw seeds, nuts, and soybeans.

Vitamin K is necessary for proper blood clotting and for normal liver function. It is useful for dogs with blood clotting disorders and is often given prior to surgery to help prevent excessive bleeding. Vitamin K is found in green leafy vegetables, yogurt, eggs, and fish.

Minerals

Minerals are inorganic compounds that, like vitamins, are necessary for life. Dogs need calcium, phosphorus, copper, iron, and potassium, as well as several other minerals. A delicate balance of mineral intake is required for good health—some minerals work only in the presence of others, and more is not necessarily better.

Calcium and phosphorus are two different minerals with closely related functions. Calcium is needed for normal growth, for strong bones, teeth, and claws, and for muscle contraction. Phosphorus is present in every cell and plays a part in every chemical reaction in the body. Working together, calcium and phosphorus keep the body healthy. A calcium deficiency will cause bone and skeletal disorders, muscle cramps, joint pain, and impaired growth. A ratio of 1.5 parts calcium to 1 part phosphorus is good for most dogs. Milk, milk products, and calcium carbonate are good sources of both minerals.

GNAWING ON NATURE

Dogs who eat dirt, chew on rocks, or chew on the stucco siding of the house are often craving minerals. If your dog has any of these tendencies, offer him a mineral supplement or feed a food with added minerals. Look for minerals listed on the label.

Iodine is a trace mineral that is vital to the proper functioning of the thyroid gland. It is found in fish, fish oils, and iodized table salt.

Iron works with protein to make hemoglobin, the part of red blood cells that transports oxygen throughout the body. Iron also works with enzymes to promote protein metabolism. For iron to be effective, the body must have adequate calcium. Iron is found in meats, fish, and liver.

Protein

Beef, chicken, lamb, fish, and other meats contain good quality protein. Protein is also found in other parts of an animal's body, including skin, nails, claws or hooves, and blood, but meat provides a better quality protein (nutritionally speaking). Proteins are in other sources, too, including eggs, dairy products, and some plants.

Complete proteins are those that contain all of the amino acids necessary for good health. Incomplete proteins are those that contain some (but not all) of the necessary amino acids. Good sources of complete proteins include: eggs, red meats, fish, milk, and dairy products. Incomplete proteins that are still good nutrition when combined with other proteins include: beans, peas, soybeans, peanuts, grains, and potatoes.

POWER SOURCES

Your get-up-and-go may be caffeine-driven, but your dog's energy comes from the healthful food he eats. To give you an idea: Each gram of protein provides four calories of energy, as does each gram of carbohydrates. Each gram of dietary fat provides nine calories of energy.

Amino Acids

Amino acids are necessary for many physical functions including growth and healing as well as the production of hormones, antibodies, and enzymes. Amino acids are created by the breakdown of proteins.

Enzymes

Enzymes are protein-based chemicals that cause biochemical reactions in the body and affect every stage of metabolism. Most people don't realize that every cell in the body contains enzymes. Some enzymes must work with a partner, such as a vitamin, to cause the needed reaction or metabolism.

Fats

In spite of all the bad press that fats have gotten lately, they are nonetheless a necessary part of good nutrition, especially for growing puppies and hard-working dogs. Fats are needed to metabolize the fat-soluble vitamins and to supply energy for activity.

Carbohydrates

Carbohydrates are sugars and starches and are used primarily for fuel for the body. Your dog's body runs on carbohydrates like your car runs on gasoline. Complex carbohydrates (such as potatoes, pasta, peas, grains, and rice) are intricate conglomerations of glucose (sugar) molecules.

THE BENEFIT OF BALANCE

Some young dogs and puppies who eat high-carbohydrate foods will show symptoms of hyperactivity and an inability to control their actions. These dogs simply cannot sit still. However, this overabundance of energy disappears when the dogs start eating a food with fewer carbohydrates and more meat protein.

COMMERCIAL DOG FOODS

When dogs were first domesticated, they probably ate the leftovers from kills that were butchered by the hunters. It's believed that pieces of muscle meat, scraps of organs, and the like were their standard fare. It's likely that the dogs also hunted for themselves. As people began buying commercially prepared food rather than producing their own, dogs relied increasingly on scraps from the table or foods (usually meats) bought specifically for the dog.

The first commercial dog foods originated in London and were prepared from the carcasses of workhorses that died on the streets. Butchers would sell the leftovers (entrails, brains, and scraps) as pet foods. In 1870, Spratt's Patent Meal Fibrine Dog Cakes were available, and although the British Royal Kennels fed them to their dogs, this food was too expensive for most dog owners.

In 1926, the Purina Company established the Pet Care Center for testing new animal foods, including dog foods. Purina's dog food, Checkers, a pelleted dry food, was introduced as a "nutritionally adequate ration for reproduction and growth." Other dog food companies soon entered the U.S. market, and in 1936 Carnation began selling their Friskies brand.

Today, commercial dog foods are designed to supply all of your dog's needs, including proteins, amino acids, enzymes, fats, carbohydrates, vitamins, and minerals. Many of the companies producing dog foods use feeding trials to test their foods and have fed, literally, generations upon generation of dogs. However, not all dog foods are created equal.

When it comes to commercial dog food, you usually do get what you pay for. The more expensive dog foods—as a general rule—are better quality foods. The less expensive foods—especially the generic or plain label foods—are lesser quality foods.

Testing is one of the many factors that play a role in determining the quality of a dog food. Feeding trials are performed by many pet food manufacturers but are not required by law. Companies may also test food in a laboratory to determine its nutritional value. Unfortunately, that testing doesn't measure the food as it is used or metabolized by the dog. Therefore a food could "test well" but still not adequately nourish your dog. Foods that are tested by actually being fed to dogs (feeding trials) will be labeled as such. If you're uncertain about how a food is tested, you can call the manufacturer; a phone number is usually provided on the label.

The quality of a dog food is also based on the quality of the ingredients. Grains grown in mineral-poor soils will have few minerals to pass on to the dog that consumes them. Poor quality meats will be less able to nourish the dog. Less expensive foods contain inexpensive and less nourishing grains and less of the more expensive meats. Again, the dog's nutrition can and often will suffer.

Many dog owners are concerned about the preservatives, artificial flavorings, and additives used in some commercial dog foods. The value of some of these additives to your dog's nutrition is questionable. If you have a question about a particular additive or ingredient, call your veterinarian and the manufacturer of the food. What do they each say about that ingredient?

LOOK FOR SIGNS OF POOR NUTRITION

Symptoms of inadequate nutrition may include some or all of the following: flaky skin, dull coat, brittle nails, less than normal energy for work or play, poor stamina, or insatiable appetite. In addition, the dog may eat strange things, including rocks, dirt, stucco off the side of the house, or wood.

Reading the Label

The label on each bag (or can) of dog food will tell you a lot about that particular food. One section of the label lists the percentages of nutrients. Most puppies and hard-working dogs will do well on a food that contains about 28 percent protein and 8 percent fat; while inactive dogs may do better with 24 percent protein and 6 percent fat.

The label will also tell you the ingredients of the food. When you're examining the label, remember that ingredients are listed in order of amounts contained. Therefore, if beef is listed first, followed by rice, corn, and wheat, you'll know that there is more beef in the food than there is rice, and there is more rice than corn. This listing can be deceptive, though. You might see wheat midlings, wheat germ, and wheat bran listed in a food, all listed after the meat ingredient. Because they're listed after the meat, does that mean there is more meat than wheat? Not necessarily. There might be more meat than wheat midlings or more meat than wheat germ, but if all the wheat is added together there might very well be more wheat than meat. You need to read the label carefully so you know exactly what you are feeding your dog.

THE MEANING OF *MEAT*

Pet food manufacturers can include in their products what are called "4-D" meats: the diseased, dying, disabled, and dead animals that arrive at the stockyard unfit for human consumption. The term meats *or* meat by-products *can also include feathers, beaks, hooves, hides, skins, horns, and other leftovers. Use the manufacturer's toll-free telephone number to ask a representative pointed questions about the quality of the ingredients in the food. If you aren't satisfied with the answers, don't buy the food.*

If you dog develops food allergies, the ingredients of his food become even more important. Many dogs are allergic to wheat, for example, and their owners must read the labels very carefully.

What Are the Chemicals Listed on the Label?

Most dog food labels list some ingredients you understand, such as beef, barley, rice, and so on, but many will also list ingredients such as sodium chloride, pangamic acid, and iron oxide. What are these things? Are they chemicals that could be dangerous to your dog? Let's take a look at some of the mystery ingredients seen most often.

- Ascorbic acid is a synthetic form of vitamin C.
- Biotin is a natural vitamin B.
- Calcium carbonate is a natural form of calcium often used as a calcium supplement.
- Calcium oxide is a natural form of calcium.
- Calcium pantothenate is a high-potency, synthetic form of vitamin B5.
- Calcium phosphate is a calcium salt found in or derived from bones or bone meal.
- Chloride or chlorine is an essential mineral, usually found in compound form with sodium or potassium.
- Choline is B vitamin found in eggs, liver, and soy.
- Choline chloride is a high-potency synthetic form of choline.
- Cobalt is a trace element, an essential mineral, and an integral part of vitamin B12.
- Copper is a trace element.
- Copper carbonate is a natural form of the mineral copper.
- Copper gluconate is a synthetic form of copper.

- Copper sulfate is a synthetic, high-potency source of copper.
- Ferrous sulfate is a synthetic, high-potency source of iron.
- Folic acid is a B vitamin found in yeast or liver.
- Inositol is a B-complex vitamin.
- Iron oxide is a natural source of iron.
- Magnesium oxide is a natural source of magnesium.
- Menadione sodium is a source for vitamin K activity.
- Pangamic acid is vitamin B15.
- Pantothenic acid is vitamin B5, a coenzyme.
- Potassium chloride is a high-potency, synthetic form of potassium.
- Potassium citrate is a natural form of potassium.
- Pyridoxine hydrochloride is a synthetic source of vitamin B6.
- Riboflavin is a synthetic source of vitamin B12.
- Selenium is an essential mineral.
- Sodium chloride is a synthetic form of salt; table salt.
- Sodium selenite is a synthetic form of the mineral selenium.
- Thiamine hydrochloride is a synthetic source of vitamin B1, thiamine.
- Thiamine mononitrate is a synthetic source of vitamin B1.
- Zinc carbonate is a source of the mineral zinc.
- Zinc oxide is a natural form of the mineral zinc.
- Zinc sulfate is a synthetic form of the mineral zinc.

Are Preservatives and Additives Safe?

Most commercial dog foods are preserved with something—chemical or natural—to preserve the food's shelf life. Unfortunately, some preservatives have been linked with health problems. The most controversial preservative currently used in dog foods is ethoxyquin, a chemical that prevents the fats in foods from becoming rancid and the vitamins from losing their potency. Ethoxyquin is approved by the Food and Drug Administration for use in human foods, but it has come under criticism from the general public. It has been alleged that ethoxyquin has caused cancer and kidney, liver, and thyroid problems, but none of these claims has yet been proven. Needless to say, many dog owners are avoiding the preservative anyway.

If you are concerned about ethoxyquin or any other chemical preservatives, look for a food preserved with tocopherols. These antioxidants are naturally occurring compounds of vitamins C and E. Just be aware that tocopherols have a very short shelf life.

Sodium nitrate and red dye number 40 are artificial colorings that give foods a fresh appearance. Both have been linked to cancer, epilepsy, and birth defects in laboratory animals. Although banned in Europe, both are widely used in the United States.

BHA, BHT, and MSG are all preservatives. Butylated hydroxysanisole (BHA) and butylated hydroxytoluene (BHT) are used to prevent fats from going rancid. They have been implicated in liver and kidney problems, birth defects, behavior problems, and many other maladies. They have even been called carcinogens. MSG is a flavor enhancer and preservative and has been known to give some people horrible headaches. It's not known if it has the same effect on dogs.

Many artificial flavorings have been linked to behavioral problems, such as nervousness, hyperactivity, hostility, and anxiety, in both children and pets.

Did you know that many dog foods contain sugar? Many semimoist foods contain as much as 15 percent sugar. Sugar aids in increasing palatability and prevents bacterial contamination, but your dog doesn't need this much sugar.

Salt is also added to many dog foods, again to affect the taste but also as a preservative. Your dog doesn't need a lot of salt and consuming too much will affect the calcium-potassium balance in his system.

Obviously, reading the label on your pet's food is very important. Know what each ingredient is and what it does. Again, if you don't understand an ingredient, call the manufacturer for more information.

Foods Causing Allergic Reactions

The ingredients in dog foods that most often cause allergic reactions include: beef and beef by-products; milk and milk products such as cheese; yeast and brewer's yeast; corn and corn by-products such as corn oil; pork; turkey; eggs; and wheat and wheat products. If you suspect your dog may be suffering from a food allergy, you can try to discover the cause yourself by restricting your dog's diet. To do so, you'll have to eliminate all but one food (ingredient) from your dog's diet, and then periodically add one ingredient at a time; while watching for reactions. It's much easier to ask your vet to run some allergy tests. The results will tell you exactly what your dog is allergic to and the extent of the allergy.

Different Forms of Food

Basically, there are three types of dog food. Dry, kibbled foods are small pieces that come in a bag, usually containing grains and meats. Dry foods have a good shelf life, and most dogs eat them quite readily. Generally, they are quite affordable.

Canned foods are mostly meats or meat recipes. These foods have a high moisture content. In the can they have a long shelf life, but once the can is opened they must be used right away. Canned foods are very palatable and are much more expensive than dry foods.

Semi-moist foods have a higher moisture content than dry, kibbled foods but not as high as canned. These foods contain a lot of sugar and salt as well as artificial colorings. Many dog treats fall into the category of semi-moist food.

However, these three basic types of foods are not all that is available. There are also frozen foods—usually meat-based with some grains or vegetables—and there are some dehydrated foods—again, mostly meat-based. Some dog owners like to feed food for humans to their dogs, cooking for them on a daily basis.

So what should you do? What kind of food should you feed? Most veterinarians recommend dry foods because they are easy to keep and reasonable in price. Vets also like the fact that chewing hard kibble helps keep a dog's teeth clean. Of course, the choice is ultimately yours, but in this situation, I think you might want to listen to the experts.

FOR MORE INFORMATION

Canine nutrition is a very complex subject. In fact, I wrote an entire book about reading labels and selecting the right food for your dog. It's called The Consumer's Guide to Dog Food. *You can order it from my Web site at www.lizpalika.com.*

HOMEMADE DOG FOOD

Commercial foods are formulated by experts. Formulating your own diet to feed your dog can pose risks to your dog's nutritional health, but many people have done so quite successfully.

The key to making a homemade diet work is using a variety of ingredients. Doing so will ensure that the dog is receiving all of the necessary amino acids and enzymes, as well as his required vitamins and minerals. Unless you are testing for food allergies under your veterinarian's supervision, never feed a diet based on only one or two ingredients. Such a diet will not supply everything your dog needs for good nutrition.

THE RAW FOOD DEBATE

Some owners are interested in feeding their dogs a raw food diet, with the belief that raw foods are the most natural. Raw plant foods are generally quite safe to feed although cooked grains are easier for the dog to digest than raw grains. On the other hand, raw meats can pose a significant danger to your dog. Cooking kills bacteria, viruses, and parasites that can threaten your dog's health. So yes, raw foods may have been the natural way for thousands of years, but dying young was natural, too. Moreover, the raw meats your dog would eat today are not the same as those found in the wild hundreds of years ago. Today, meat animals are housed in close quarters, exposed to horrible conditions, and fed a variety of chemicals. If you're not raising the meat animals yourself, for your dog's safety, cook that meat!

Basic Home-Cooked Diet

The home-cooked diet that follows is for dogs with no known food allergies. The amount fed each day will depend on your dog's weight (both actual and ideal), activity level, and energy needs.

1 pound cooked ground meat (chicken, turkey, or lamb)
  drained of most but not all of the fat
2 cups cooked whole grain brown rice
½ cup cooked, mashed barley
½ cup cooked oatmeal
½ cup raw, grated carrots
½ cup finely chopped or grated, raw green vegetables
  (no lettuce)
2 tablespoons olive oil
2 tablespoons minced or mashed garlic

Mix all ingredients together in a big bowl. Store in the refrigerator in a covered bowl, or divide into daily servings and store in the freezer. Thaw one day's serving at a time. When serving, mix the following into the portion:

Daily Supplements

1 tablespoon plain yogurt, with live active cultures
  Multivitamin/mineral supplement (in tablet or
  powder form)
  Pinch of kelp
  Dash of brewer's yeast

Deciding the quantity of a homemade diet to feed your dog is a trial and error process. If your dog has been eating a dry, kibbled food, he'll be so enthusiastic about this homemade diet that he'll really overeat if you let him. Offer one cup to one and a half cups of this recipe per thirty pounds of body weight to start. Then, watch your dog's weight closely. Adjust by adding more or cutting back depending upon your dog's weight gains or losses.

Working Dog Home-Cooked Diet

This home-cooked diet is for hard-working dogs, dogs under stress, or pregnant or lactating bitches.

1 pound ground lean meat, cooked, do not drain off the fat

4 large hard-boiled, shelled, crumbled eggs

2 cups cooked whole grain brown rice

1 cup cooked oatmeal

1 large cooked, mashed potato

¼ cup wheat germ (if dog is not allergic to wheat)

¼ cup grated, raw carrot

½ cup finely chopped or grated green vegetables

½ mashed avocado

2 tablespoons olive oil

1 tablespoon minced or mashed garlic

Mix together in a large bowl. Store in refrigerator in a covered bowl or divide into daily servings and freeze. Thaw one day's serving one day at a time. When serving, add the following:

1 tablespoon plain yogurt, with live active cultures

Dash of dry powdered milk

Dash of brewer's yeast

Pinch of kelp

Multivitamin/mineral supplement (in tablet or powder form)

As I mentioned in the previous recipe, dogs new to home-cooked meals tend to be very zealous eaters. Watch your dog's weight carefully when he's on this diet. It is meant for dogs who are very active or who need a strong boost in caloric intake. If your dog starts to get pudgy, you should probably switch him to less hearty fare.

Hypoallergenic Diet

This hypoallergenic diet is for dogs allergic to meats or grains.

5 large cooked, mashed potatoes

3 hard-boiled, shelled, crumbled eggs

1 cup finely chopped or grated green vegetables

1 cup cooked, finely chopped or mashed beans (not green beans)

½ cup grated carrot

2 tablespoons olive oil

1 tablespoon minced garlic

Mix together in a large bowl. Store in covered bowl in refrigerator or divide into daily servings and freeze. Add when serving:

1 tablespoon plain yogurt, with live active cultures

Multivitamin/mineral supplement (in tablet or powder form)

Pinch of kelp

For information about portion size, see Basic Home-Cooked Diet.

TIME FOR A TREAT

Healthy treats might be a piece of raw carrot, a chunk of squash or pumpkin, a piece of melon or avocado, or a piece of dried meat (jerky). Some dogs also like bananas.

Emergency Diet

This diet is for recuperating and ill dogs. It's also good for dogs suffering from extreme stress or shock. The goal of this diet is to get the dog to eat, to get some calories and good nutrition into him, and then get him back on a regular diet.

2 hard-boiled, shelled, mashed eggs

½ cup *very* finely ground cooked meat, most of the fat drained off

1 teaspoon kelp

1 tablespoon brewer's yeast

1 tablespoon molasses

1 teaspoon apple cider vinegar

¼ cup carrot juice

400 IUs vitamin E (open capsule and squeeze out the oil)

Enough water to make food very soft

Mix together in a medium bowl. Spoon-feed your dog, allow him to lap it up, or add more water and use a thick syringe to feed him. Feed small amounts often, even every hour for dogs in tentative health.

Adding Variety

For any of the preceding homemade diets, feel free to make substitutions, but substitute with a similar food. For example, for the meats, you can use beef, lamb, mutton, chicken, or turkey; assuming that your dog isn't allergic to any particular meat. You can even use tuna or other cooked fish. For the brown rice, you can use long grain white rice or wild rice (but don't use instant rice; it's been stripped of most of its nutritional value). For oatmeal, you can substitute any cooked grain, such as millet, amaranth, oat bran, or cornmeal. For the carrots and chopped greens, you can substitute any combination of grated or finely chopped vegetable. *Note:* Do not give your dog onions; they can be toxic to some dogs. Also avoid feeding your dog lettuce; it has virtually no nutritional value and will often cause diarrhea.

The basic premise of most homemade diets, including mine, is that a variety of good quality ingredients will supply your dog with all of the nutrients he needs for good health.

Today's dogs generally die at eight, nine, and ten years of age; often of cancer. While many of the preservatives and additives used in commercial dog foods cannot be tied directly to these deaths, it's interesting to note that years ago, before the use of these additives, dogs lived longer. Dr. Richard Pitcairn, author of *Dr. Pitcairn's Complete Guide to Natural Health for Dogs & Cats,* writes, "Since graduating from veterinary school in 1965, I have seen a gradual deterioration in pet health. I believe the chemical additives in pet food play a major part in that decline." So at a time when we are making remarkable advances in medicine and science, and we are living increasingly long lives, our pets are dying younger. There is something very wrong with that.

Many of today's informed dog owners now cook for their dogs, and many of these dogs are now living longer, healthier lives.

FROZEN BANANA SNACK

Mash one large, very ripe banana in a bowl. Add one and one half cups of plain yogurt. When thoroughly mixed, spoon into small (bathroom-sized) paper cups. Freeze. Let your dog lick the snack while still frozen from the paper cup or peel the cup off before serving.

CHOOSING THE RIGHT FOOD

Choosing the right commercial or homemade food for your dog can be difficult. Here are some questions to ask yourself when making a decision:

1. Does the food have a good variety of ingredients? Does it have complete and incomplete proteins? Does the food contain a selection of carbohydrates and fats? What about additives and preservatives? Do you understand what they are and why they are in the food? Are you comfortable with all of the ingredients?

2. What are the protein and fat percentages? Are you satisfied with those levels?

3. Will the food supply the needed calories for your dog without supplying too much?

If you have any questions about the food, talk to your veterinarian and call the food manufacturer.

After your dog has been eating the food for four to six weeks, evaluate the results. Ask yourself the following questions:

1. If your dog is a puppy, is he growing well?

2. How is your dog's weight? Is he too skinny? Is he too fat?

3. How is your dog's coat? It should be shiny and soft with no oily feel and no doggy odor.

4. How is your dog's energy? Does he have enough energy for work and play? Does he have too much energy? Does he act hyperactive? He should have plenty of energy for work and play without bouncing off the walls.

5. Does he act starved or always hungry? Often those dogs whose bodies are missing vital nutrients will chew on everything they can. They'll also act famished even though they are eating regularly.

6. How are your dog's stools? Healthy stools should be firm and compact. If the stools are very smelly, very soft, or very hard, there is a problem somewhere with the food.

Changing Diets

When changing from one diet to another, do so very slowly over a two- to three-week period. If you change foods too quickly, your dog may have a severe gastrointestinal upset. The need to make a slow transition is especially important when changing from a diet of commercial food to a home-cooked diet.

Cook up some of your new diet and begin adding it to his old food a tablespoon at a time, daily, for several days.

Then serve meals consisting of one-third the new diet and two-thirds the old food for a week. The following week, start serving one-third the old food and two-thirds the new food at each meal. If your dog is doing okay and his stools are fine (firm), then go ahead and switch him completely to the new diet.

THE UPSIDE OF DRY FOOD

Dry, kibbled foods help keep your dog's teeth clean by the scraping action that occurs when he's chewing. A home-cooked diet will not provide this benefit, so if you decide to become your dog's chef, you'll have to work harder and be more meticulous about keeping his teeth clean.

Should You Add Supplements?

If you're feeding your dog commercially prepared dog food, read the label. Most food labels will state that the food is complete and balanced nutrition. Many nutritionists agree that when you see that statement, you needn't supplement your dog's food.

On the other hand, some nutritionists (particularly those who are not hired by the manufacturers of commercial dog food) argue that what constitutes complete and balanced nutrition will differ from dog to dog. They believe that supplementation can make the difference between good nutrition and better nutrition.

MORE THAN A VITAMIN PILL

A supplement is anything that is added to the food or to the dog's regular diet. It may be a commercial vitamin, an herbal remedy, or additional foods.

Regardless of whom you choose to believe, you may simply feel better supplementing your dog's food. If you take vitamins yourself, you may also want to give your dog a vitamin, mineral, or supplement.

Some supplements that are high in nutritional value (but will not cause a nutritional imbalance) might include:

APPLE CIDER VINEGAR—This vinegar is full of minerals, trace elements, and vitamins. In addition, it is said to boost the immune system, help the body recover from illness and injury, and aid in digestion. Add a dash to the dog's food or add a tiny bit to drinking water. If your dog simply won't eat or drink it, you can try giving him the dehydrated form available in capsules.

BREWER'S YEAST—This is an excellent source of B vitamins and minerals, including the essential trace minerals chromium and selenium. In some dogs, depending upon the dog's own metabolism, a brewer's yeast supplement will help repel fleas. Sprinkle a pinch a day over the food, or serve according to manufacturer's directions.

EGGS—Give your dog cooked eggs only (raw eggs interfere with vitamin B absorption and have been associated with salmonella poisonings). Eggs are excellent sources of proteins, as well as a variety of vitamins, minerals, and amino acids. Serve one to three cooked eggs per week.

FISH OIL SUPPLEMENTS—Your local health food store will carry fish oil capsules. These concentrated supplements are a good source of omega-3 fatty acids. They are wonderful for the immune system, for healthy hair coat and skin, and are even good for alleviating heart disease and diabetes.

KELP—Kelp is a good source of iodine, calcium, potassium, and other minerals and essential trace elements. Use according to manufacturer's directions.

OATMEAL—Oatmeal is quite nutritious and will tempt many picky eaters. Use as a special treat or add a small amount to the daily diet.

YOGURT—Yogurt is a good nutritious food on its own, and is also a good source of protein, amino acids, and fat. Yogurt with live active cultures adds beneficial bacteria to the digestive tract. Add no more than one tablespoon per day for a medium-sized dog and less or more for smaller and larger dogs.

When adding supplements to your dog's food, make sure you add small amounts so that the total of supplements will not add up to more than 10 percent of the dog's daily diet. Oversupplementation could upset the nutritional balance of the commercial food.

DISCRETION ADVISED

Too much supplementation can upset the nutritional balance of an otherwise balanced diet. Supplement carefully and wisely. When in doubt, talk to your veterinarian, representatives of the dog food manufacturer, and the makers of the supplement. Then weigh their recommendations.

MEAL MANAGEMENT

In addition to what your dog eats, you'll also need to set a feeding schedule. Dogs appreciate regular meal times, so get in the habit of feeding him at the same time every day.

When Should Your Dog Eat?

Most young puppies need to eat two to three times per day. A big morning meal, a small lunch, and a big evening meal usually suit eight- to twelve-week-old puppies just fine. By twelve weeks of age, most puppies will be able to discontinue the midday meal and do quite well with just morning and evening meals. After about six months of age, most young dogs will eat one meal per day and usually indicate their preference for when they would like to eat. Some dogs will simply stop eating their morning meal and will eagerly consume the evening meal, while others will do just the opposite.

How Much Is Enough?

The label on your dog's commercial food will state feeding recommendations. If your dog eats the recommended amount of that food, he will be getting all of the needed nutrition available from it. Be aware, however, that those directions are just the beginning; every dog will have different dietary needs depending upon the individual dog's metabolism, activity level, and personality. A forty-pound dog that is more active and hard working will need more calories from his food than another forty-pound dog who is a little more laid back and relaxed.

Adjust your feeding amounts according to your dog's weight and activity level. If he is always hungry and is thin, give him more food. If some padding appears over his ribs and he is looking a little chubby, cut back on the food a little bit. Add more when your dog is working hard, and return to normal portions when he's not. If your dog is healthy and growing well, don't try to force him to eat more than he wants. The same recommendations apply to homemade diets.

No Free-Feeding

Don't leave food out for your dog to nibble on all day. This practice is known as free-feeding and is not recommended for several reasons.

First, if your dog does happen to get sick, one of the first questions the veterinarian will ask is, "How is your dog's appetite? How did he eat this morning?" If the dog eats sporadically throughout the day rather than at specific times, you won't be able to answer that question.

In addition, housetraining a puppy is much easier when the puppy eats at specific times. You know that he will need to go outside after every meal. If those meals are at set times, you know when to take him outside. If the puppy snacks all day, however, when should you take him out? It's much harder to tell.

Food left out all day can spoil. Homemade diets, in particular, should not be left out. Bacteria develop quickly in cooked foods allowed to set out for hours. Moreover, food that is set out for free-feeding is easily invaded by pests. Ants, flies, and other insects can soil it; it may also attract rodents.

Finally, regular meals also help develop a firm relationship between you and your dog. As the giver of the food at each mealtime, you assume a very important position in your dog's life. Why not reinforce your special bond?

Chapter 7

A RETURN TO ANCIENT MEDICINES

My grandmother was quite the character, or at least that's what everyone used to say. Personally, I didn't care whether she was a character or not when I was a child; she was my hero. She never went anywhere without a dog by her side, she loved her family, she was very creative, and she always let the world know how she felt about something. Of course, she had her flaws, too. She was very outspoken, sometimes embarrassingly so. Her dogs were always spoiled rotten, and sometimes they weren't very nice to us grandkids. And she drove really, really fast, which I thought (as a kid) was neat but my folks thought was dangerous. I can remember more than one conversation about Grandma's driving.

Grandma had something else that always fascinated me; she had a memory the proverbial mile long of old remedies for all kinds of illnesses and ailments. Grandma grew up on a farm and her parents did, too. Their parents immigrated to this country from Ireland where they had been farmers. All of these ancestors had their own remedies that had been passed down to each successive generation, and Grandma knew them all.

Unfortunately, most of her descendants were too infatuated by modern medicine to pay any attention to her old-fashioned cures. But I was interested and was able to record many of her remedies before she passed away.

Today many people—including scientists, researchers, doctors, and patients—are re-examining these old remedies. We're finding that many of them were based on real results and that many are medically sound and quite effective.

EARLY MIND-BODY PRACTICES

In many societies, ancient healers combined their healing practices with ceremonies. Physical health was connected to spiritual health, and dancing, chanting, songs, plays, and other rituals played a role in ancient medicines.

ANCIENT ARTS

In most ancient cultures, the healer was greatly respected. The healer or medicine woman or man may have also served as a religious leader or shaman. Regardless, he or she was always an important person. After all, the healer could save your life someday.

Generally, the healer didn't have to perform normal, manual labor such as hunting, picking food, or farming; instead, other members of the group would donate food and other supplies to the healer. Some cultures, including many Native American tribes, required that the medicine man or woman be given the best pieces of meat, the best hides, and the most attractive furs.

The healer's job was to maintain his or her medicinal staples—the healing herbs that members of the group might need in the future. If the group was large, two or three children might be assigned to the healer to help harvest medicinal plants and perhaps, if they worked hard enough, to train to serve as the medicine man when the time came.

Today, the herbal arts performed by these medicine men and women are coming back into favor. Folk medicine, as it is sometimes called, or medical botanics, has even been discussed in some medical schools. Japanese, Chinese, Indian, and some African doctors are returning to the use of their ancient healing arts—not just the herbal medicine but also acupuncture and acupressure—and are combining them with modern medicine. Although those who study and employ these ancient arts may chuckle to see that the things they have long believed in are now reaching mainstream medicine, they probably aren't too surprised, either.

ANCIENT PRACTICES REVIVED

Acupuncture is a practice in which fine, strategically placed needles are used to stimulate healing.

Acupressure uses the same principles as acupuncture, including the same placement on particular energy points, or lines, but acupressure uses touch, massage, or pressure rather than needles.

HERBAL MEDICINE

Most of my Grandma's remedies were based either on foods, such as those mentioned in the last chapter, or herbal remedies. Herbal remedies are derived from plants and may involve the use of the fresh plant but usually are in the form of teas, dried plant materials, juices, or extracts.

Although many modern medicines were originally made from plants, the herbal medicines are more natural and haven't been refined. They're also often safer than traditional medicines. Willow bark, for example, contains a chemical very similar to aspirin. However, willow bark may be the preferred treatment because it also contains chemicals that protect against gastric ulcers, a common side effect of long-term aspirin usage.

Herbs (and other plants) contain a variety of substances in their roots, stems, bark, leaves, flowers, or seeds. Because of the different chemical composition of each part of the plants, the various parts may have different medicinal usages. In addition, the efficacy of any plant- or herb-based treatment may vary depending on how the plant is harvested, processed, and used.

AYURVEDIC MEDICINE

In India and areas of the Middle East, Ayurvedic medicine has been practiced for thousands of years. This type of healing focuses on the metabolic body type of an individual, as well as the strengths and weaknesses of each individual. A combination of herbs, diet, meditation, and other practices are employed to bring the individual's mind, body, and spirit back into balance.

Animals have instinctively used plants as medicines for as long as they both have shared the planet. Some plants will purge an animal of intestinal worms while others will stimulate the immune system. Some will help an animal who is getting ready for hibernation to put on fat. Instinct and a natural knowledge taught animals how to use the world around them to enhance their well-being.

Herbal medicine uses plants to aid in maintaining health as well as assisting the body to heal itself. Whereas modern medicine generally treats symptoms and tries to kill or stop diseases, herbal medicine works with the body. The body has a miraculous ability to care for itself, as seen by the workings of the immune system and in its ability to heal. Sometimes the body just needs a little help, and that's where herbal medicine can step in.

If you decide to use herbs as medicine for your dog, keep in mind that herbs may not be as concentrated in certain elements as modern medicines. This is particularly important to note if you're using herbs in place of traditional medicines. Herbs usually act more gently on the system and work more slowly than manufactured drugs. Some people get frustrated when using herbal remedies because there is often no immediate reaction, alleviation of symptoms, or healing. If you are patient and wait a day or two or three, however, there should be signs that the herbs are working, granted, of course, that you are using the correct herb for that problem.

An Herbal Cornucopia

Although there are thousands of herbs commonly used for domestic animals, not all have been established as safe and effective for dogs. The safe use of the herbs in the following list has been well documented.

ALFALFA—Alfalfa is widely grown as livestock feed for good reason. It is very nutritious, contains plant protein (up to 50 percent by weight), and vitamins A, B-complex, C, D, E, and K. It is also high in chlorophyll. Alfalfa has many medicinal uses and is well known for easing the inflammation of arthritis. It also has anticancer properties. The leaves and flowers buds are used medicinally as food, in capsules, or in a tea. A member of the pea family, alfalfa is easily grown in gardens or planters. It blooms first in the spring but will continue growing and blooming after several harvests.

The considerable vitamin K content of alfalfa has made it especially useful for dogs with bleeding disorders. It is known to help with fat-soluble vitamin absorption, and it may help stimulate natural growth hormones. Alfalfa also has an alkalinizing effect in the bladder, easing overly acidic urine.

Alfalfa can be given as a food supplement (fresh or dried) every day with no long-term toxic or detrimental effects.

ARNICA—Arnica is a daisylike plant with bright yellow flowers. The entire plant is used medicinally as an aid to heal wounds, including fractures, sprains, and bruises. The plant matter can be used fresh or dried and is used as a fresh poultice, an oil infusion, or water infusion. Arnica is primarily a mountain plant but will grow in gardens when the soil is very rich in organic matter.

Topically, preparations of arnica open blood vessels to increase circulation to speed healing. The open blood vessels also help move out fluids found in the injured area. The preparation should be applied two to three times daily as long as needed until healing is complete.

Warning: Do not let your dog lick arnica off his skin; many dogs are sensitive to it. Instead, after applying the arnica, completely cover the skin with a bandage. Secure the bandage so that it's not uncomfortable, but be sure that the dog cannot remove it.

BLACK WALNUT—The black walnut is a large tree that grows to one hundred feet in height, sometimes taller. The green, unripened fruit hulls are used medicinally as extracts. Fruit bearing usually begins in early summer. Black walnut trees are common throughout eastern North America but are often found as transplants in other parts of the continent.

Warning: Black walnut extracts are one of the best and safest worming extracts known, but they must be used with care. If administered improperly, they can be toxic to your dog. Before using a black walnut worming extract, consult with an herbal medicine practitioner for guidance.

BURDOCK—Burdock is a Eurasian import that has spread throughout North America. It prefers rich, deep, moist soil and so is found often at the edges of farmer's fields and along roadside ditches. This herb produces light lavender to purple thistlelike flowers that produce seed-bearing burrs. The root is used medicinally as an alcohol or glycerin extract or tincture, or fresh or dried decocted, which is then poured over the dog's food.

Burdock is used medicinally as an aid to good nutrition; it's a healthy food containing many minerals and trace elements including calcium, phosphorus, iron, thiamin, and riboflavin. In addition, it is beneficial to the liver as a tonic and blood cleanser. It is good for dogs with oily skin or inflammatory skin disorders. Burdock has been shown to be particularly effective in helping the body eliminate environmental toxicities by flushing them from the bloodstream before they cause a problem.

Burdock is one of the safest plants that can be given to your dog; it's right up there with alfalfa.

CALENDULA—Calendula is a popular garden flower with yellow and gold daisylike blossoms. It is usually available at garden centers in the spring, and can be found in all types of climates. The plant grows well in gardens or planters. The flowers are used medicinally as a water or oil infusion, tincture, poultice, salve, or ointment.

Calendula has excellent anti-inflammatory properties. When used as a first aid ointment, a calendula salve or ointment can be applied to the wound and will bring quick relief from pain and swelling. It will also aid in healing and helps to prevent infection. Washes will bring relief to skin irritations, including those from flea bites, sunburn, and poison ivy.

A tincture of calendula can be used internally to treat digestive problems, where it will also reduce inflammation. It has also been shown to be effective in the treatment of colitis.

CAYENNE—Although we usually think of cayenne as a flavoring agent for food, the capsicum in cayenne and other peppers is actually good medicine. Originally grown in the tropics, peppers are now grown everywhere, in gardens, in planters, or even as houseplants. Only the fruits of the pepper plants are used medicinally, not the stems, leaves, or roots.

Internally, capsicum dilates blood vessels, thereby increasing blood circulation. By increasing blood flow, it also strengthens tissues. Externally, it also has anti-inflammatory and analgesic properties.

The fruits are usually dried and then can be used in oil infusions. The oil can be used internally or can be made into a salve or ointment for external use.

CHAMOMILE—German chamomile was one of my grandmother's favorite herbs and it's one of mine too. This lovely plant with daisy-like flowers—with white petals and a raised yellow center—is gentle and soothing with many uses. Originating in Europe, chamomile is now grown all over the world. It makes a wonderful addition to the garden because it will often bloom throughout the spring, summer, and fall, stopping only when it freezes.

Chamomile is wonderful for the digestive system. It expels gas, soothes an irritated intestinal tract, stops intestinal tract spasms, stimulates digestion, and expels worms. Chamomile also works as a sedative and is wonderful for dogs who are too nervous or stressed to sleep.

The flowers of the chamomile are used medicinally and can be used as a water or oil infusion. Most dogs will accept glycerin extracts of chamomile. Dried chamomile makes a good tea.

CLOVER, RED—Red clover was at one time found only in Europe, but it has spread throughout North America and is often found growing wild near human habitation. It can also be grown domestically but be careful; this is one invasive plant. This handsome clover has red, round flowers and, unlike other clovers, somewhat pointed leaves.

Red clover is a good diuretic. It also helps cleanse the body as an expectorant and a tonic. Red clover increases estrogen production in the body and is also nutritionally very good. It is high in plant proteins, vitamins B-complex and C, and in the minerals calcium, potassium, and magnesium.

The flowers of red clover are used medicinally. They are usually used as a food with two or three fresh flowers per day (per medium-sized dog) sufficient as a diuretic and tonic. This plant can also be used as a dried herb in a tea.

TRY THIS

Soothe the discomfort of teething by rubbing chamomile extracts directly on the gums where the new teeth are coming in. Repeat as often as needed.

COMFREY—Comfrey is found in Europe, western Asia, and throughout North America. It is hardy and grows well as a garden herb. Comfrey has pink, purple, or yellow flowers on sturdy stems with long, narrow leaves. Leaves, stems, and flowers are used medicinally.

Comfrey is best known for its ability to help heal wounds. Fresh or dried herbs can be mashed with water and made into a poultice that can be placed on or bandaged directly over the wound. It also has anti-inflammatory properties. Comfrey can be used on cuts, scratches, flea and other insect bites and stings, or any other skin problem.

Comfrey has also been used internally for hundreds if not thousands of years. It is thought to have anticancer properties and is supposed to be good for stomach ulcers as well as other digestive ailments. Comfrey, however, can also be quite toxic. The FDA discourages the internal use of comfrey. If you feel that the internal use of comfrey might be beneficial for your dog, consult with a knowledgeable herbalist first.

DANDELION—This weed is every gardener's nightmare but every herbalist's dream. Believe it or not, dandelions didn't originate in North America. Originally from Europe and Asia, they are now found virtually everywhere plants grow. With their jagged leaves and bright yellow flowers, dandelions are quite distinctive and well known.

All parts of the plant are used medicinally. A good food, dandelions are rich in vitamins A, B-complex, C, D, and K. They are also good sources of iron, phosphorus, and other trace minerals, including potassium. A handful of fresh dandelion leaves and flowers can be chopped up and mixed with your dog's food to enhance its nutritional content.

A dandelion tea is a good diuretic. It also stimulates digestion and serves as an anti-inflammatory agent in the intestinal tract. A larger dose of dried dandelion will serve as a laxative.

DILL—Dill is a tall plant with feathery leaves and bright, yellow flowers. Dill grows all over the world and is often considered a weed, spreading quite well on its own. Of course, it's also grown in herb gardens.

Dill's leaves, flowers, and seeds all have medicinal uses. A tea made from dried dill leaves and flowers is soothing to the digestive tract, easing nausea and expelling flatulence. This tea will also have a diuretic effect. For a bad stomachache, make a stronger tea from crushed dill seeds. The oil in the seeds is much more potent than that in the leaves and flowers.

Dill contains volatile oils known to stimulate the production of anticancer enzymes. Dill is also said to increase milk production in lactating mothers.

ECHINACEA—Echinacea is a North American native. Also known as coneflower, it has purple, pink, or white daisylike flowers whose petals arch downward rather than up toward the center of the flower. Although this flower used to grow wild throughout North America, harvesting has reduced most wild populations. Today, it is being cultivated domestically.

The root of echinacea is the strongest part of the plant medicinally, although the leaves and flowers are sometimes used for weak teas.

Echinacea's claim to fame is its ability to stimulate the body's immune system. When given prior to or shortly after exposure to viruses, colds, or bacterial infections, it can help the body fight off disease. The body will stop responding to echinacea if it is given continuously, so it's best to use echinacea only when needed.

A decoction of dried root is quite effective, as is a tincture made from dried root. For a less potent dosage, echinacea's leaves and flowers can be made into a tea or sprinkled over food.

AN OLD REMEDY FOR THE NEW WORLD

My grandmother was a fan of echinacea long before it became popular in mainstream America. I can remember her urging my mother to put my brother and me on echinacea a week before school started each fall. She knew that if our immune systems were "kick-started" prior to being exposed to our schoolmates, we would be less likely to get sick.

FENNEL—Fennel is another Eurasian native that was transplanted to our west coast by settlers to the area. It quickly naturalized and is now found throughout southern California. Fennel closely resembles dill with its feathery leaves and yellow flowers. You can identify it by the odor. Dill smells like dill while fennel smells more like licorice.

The roots, leaves, and seeds of fennel all have medicinal properties. The fresh and dried leaves are used as a tea to dissipate intestinal gas, soothe the digestive tract, and stimulate digestion. An extract made from dried, ground roots is a nutritious food high in vitamins A and C as well as calcium, iron, and potassium.

FEVERFEW—Feverfew was imported to North America from Europe as a medicinal herb. It has now naturalized in a few areas but is primarily grown in herb gardens. It has serrated leaves and tiny, white, daisylike flowers.

Feverfew is a strong anti-inflammatory herb that reduces the pain of arthritis quite effectively. It also dilates blood vessels, which can aid in flushing toxins from the system. Moreover, unimpeded blood flow can be of great assistance in the general healing process. It also has insecticidal properties.

Feverfew is usually used in a dried form (leaves and flowers) steeped in a tea. The tea can be taken internally for arthritis relief. Another great use for the tea is as a healant for the skin. Use as an external rinse for all types of irritations and fleabites.

FLAXSEED—Flax is a Native American plant and is found throughout the prairies and meadows of mid-America. Flax has tiny leaves and lovely purplish-blue, five-petaled flowers.

Flaxseeds contain linoleic acid, linolenic acid, and omega-3 fatty acids, all of which are necessary for the development and maintenance of a healthy brain and immune system.

Flaxseeds are good nutrition but cannot be fed as seeds as they will cause gastric distress. Instead, drop a handful of roughly cracked and ground seeds into a Mason jar. Pour olive oil over the seeds, filling the jar. Let this set for two to three weeks, then strain the seeds from the oil. Throw away the seeds and use the oil as a nutritional supplement to your dog's food.

GARLIC—I can't imagine anyone—anywhere in the world—who doesn't know what garlic is. This root is what makes food taste so great! It has been used in food and medicine for so many thousands of years scientists don't even know where garlic originated. Today, it grows all over the world, primarily as a domesticated plant, but it also grows wild in North America. Garlic grows extremely well in gardens or planters.

Garlic is a known antibacterial medicine. It also stimulates the immune system and works as an anticancer agent and an antioxidant. It has antiviral and antifungal properties, and is known to help lower blood pressure. It is also nutritious (full of plant protein, trace minerals, vitamin A and B-complex) and works as a decent tonic. What can't garlic do? Not much.

Use only the bulb of garlic, not the stems or flowers. The fresh or dried cloves of the bulb can be used in cooking your dog's homemade diet, or they can be chopped up raw and sprinkled over his food. Keep in mind that excess heat from cooking will destroy some of garlic's beneficial properties. If you want to use it medicinally, it should be used raw.

Garlic also makes a good oil infusion that can keep in the refrigerator for as long as a year, although if you use it regularly, a full Mason jar won't last but a month.

GINKGO—Ginkgo is a tree that can grow to more than 100 feet in height. It has unique, fan-shaped leaves. Originally from China, ginkgo trees have been introduced to North America and Europe. It is handsome and will make a great addition to your yard if you have room for such a large tree.

The nuts from the ginkgo tree were used for thousands of year—both medicinally and for food—but today, the leaves are of more importance. Gingko dilates the blood vessels, increasing circulation, and works as an anticoagulant, preventing the formation of blood clots. It is also an antioxidant and a tonic.

The dried leaves of the ginkgo tree are used to make a tea. It is often sold as a dried herb in capsule form.

GOLDENSEAL—Goldenseal's deeply lobed leaves are large (up to six inches wide). It can be grown in gardens or in planters.

Originally from North America, goldenseal has been used as a natural remedy for the respiratory and digestive systems for hundreds of years. Its dried, ground root can be used in a glycerin tincture or extract, or in a tea where it works to relieve inflammation in the respiratory tract as well as the digestive tract. It also acts as an intestinal antiparasitic.

Goldenseal is also very effective as an eyewash for dogs with conjunctivitis. Make a tea from the roots of the plants (dried or fresh), and then add a dozen drops of the tea to one ounce of sterile saline solution (which you'll be familiar with if you wear contact lenses). A few drops in each eye three to four times a day will quickly clear up the problem.

HAWTHORN—The hawthorn is a small tree with large, sharp, deadly thorns and small, purple berries. A North American native, it is found wherever there is enough moisture; it likes moist marsh meadows. Some subspecies are available for growing in the garden; however, most hawthorn trees grow wild.

Fresh or dried berries are used in a tincture, tea, or decoction and are known primarily for their ability to strengthen the cardiovascular system. They steady and strengthen a weak or uneven heartbeat. They increase the blood flow from the heart and at the same time dilate the blood vessels so that this increased blood flow can move through the body. In turn, the body obtains greater access to oxygen and nutrients carried by the blood.

For an old dog or a dog with heart disease, a few fresh berries per day (for a medium-sized dog) will work well as a tonic. When the fresh berries are available, use some to make a tincture that can be stored for use through the rest of the year.

LICORICE—This North American native is a tall member of the pea family. Licorice has long, narrow leaves and small, hooked spines on its seedpods. The native licorice plant is found all over the continent in moist areas, particularly ditches. It can be raised in the garden but needs deep, rich soil with lots of organic compost and lots of water.

Licorice root—fresh or dried, in a tea or tincture—has many medicinal uses. It acts as an expectorant, while at the same time, it soothes and protects mucus membranes. It has anti-inflammatory and antiviral properties and helps stimulate the immune system.

When taken internally as a tea or tincture, licorice root's anti-inflammatory properties make it very useful for dogs with arthritis. Externally, a tea or salve can be used to relieve skin irritations.

MARSHMALLOW—Marshmallow is a handsome plant with two-inch, pink flowers that grow on spires. The plant's stems and leaves are covered with fine hairs.

Marshmallow roots, used as teas from fresh or dried root, make a soothing wash for irritated skin, including fleabites, other insect bites, abscesses, and wounds. Taken internally, teas are soothing for an upset digestive system, will reduce inflammation of the urinary tract, and will help boost the immune system.

NETTLE—This North American native gets its name "stinging nettle" from the fine, stinging hairs on its stems. It's not-so-amusing defensive abilities aside, nettle is still good medicine.

When dried, the leaves can be fed directly to your dog, or they can be made into a tea. Internally, nettle can work as an antihistamine when taken on a regular basis throughout the allergy season. Nettle is also very nutritious, providing plant proteins, vitamins A, B-complex, C, and D, and many trace minerals including calcium, iron, magnesium, potassium, and phosphorus.

Externally, a tea makes a very soothing rinse after a bath, easing the irritation of insect bites and moisturizing dry skin.

THINK TWICE BEFORE GROWING NETTLES

If you decide to grow nettles in your garden, do so with care. Wear gloves and a long-sleeved shirt when anywhere near nettles; their fine, stinging hairs work their way into the skin and cause great discomfort. In addition, nettles spread by putting out horizontal roots and will invade your yard very quickly. You might be better off growing them in a planter or pot.

OATS—Oats are a staple food for many people and are grown commercially throughout the world. The ripe seeds of the oat plants are the part used as food, and they contain plant proteins, vitamins, minerals, and many necessary trace elements. Medicinally, the green seeds are used before they are fully ripe. These green seeds can be used fresh or dry, crushed, and made into a tincture.

Oats have anti-inflammatory properties, particularly for the nervous system. Old dogs, or dogs with nervous tendencies, will relax when given oat tincture or oat tea.

Dogs suffering from depression will feel better when given oat tea or tincture for a period of time.

A poultice made from crushed seeds and water makes a very soothing skin remedy.

OREGON GRAPE—When most people think of grapes, Oregon grape is not what comes to mind. Although Oregon grape does produce purple fruits, they are quite sour and are different from table or wine grapes. The leaves of the Oregon grape are spiked at the edges, much like holly. A North American native, Oregon grape is found from New Mexico and California north into Canada. It can be cultivated in gardens.

The roots of the grape plant have the medicinal uses and are primarily made into tinctures, oil infusions, and decoctions. It is a good anti-inflammatory and antimicrobial, especially in the digestive system and respiratory system. In the digestive system, it is known to be effective against many staff bacteria and *E. coli*. It stimulates bile production and as such is good for the liver. Oregon grape is also an effective antiparasitic.

A few drops of the oil infusion can be used to clean your dog's ears if you suspect ear mites.

PARSLEY—Parsley is more than a pretty plant; it also has some good medicinal properties. A native of Eurasia, it is cultivated worldwide and can easily be grown in gardens, planters, and even in the house on a sunny windowsill.

The roots, leaves, and even seeds of the parsley are used in tinctures, teas, or as fresh or dried herbs. Parsley helps the digestive system in several ways, first as an antimicrobial, then as an antiparasitic, and finally, it helps to expel gas. Parsley is also known to work as a diuretic. For old dogs, the anti-inflammatory properties will aid in reducing the pain of arthritis.

PEPPERMINT—One of my grandmother's favorites, peppermint is always available in my house, too. Peppermint is very soothing to the digestive tract; it will stop nausea and vomiting, calm an irritable bowel, and expel gas. It is also wonderful for motion sickness.

Peppermint can be used as a tea from fresh or dried herbs. Oil tinctures are also effective. As a last resort, if nothing else is at hand, dissolve a peppermint candy in hot water. The peppermint oils are there although your dog really doesn't need that sugar.

Peppermint grows easily in the garden (sometimes too easily). It spreads quickly so you might want to grow it in a planter or pot.

PLANTAIN—Plantain is widespread throughout most of North America and is often found along roadsides, sidewalks, and vacant lots. Most people, seeing this low-growing plant with small flowers on spires, would consider it a weed rather than a medicinal herb. However, the leaves of the plantain are very soothing to the digestive system.

Plantain leaves, when used in a tincture or tea, will help relieve diarrhea, reduce inflammation of the intestinal tract and bowel, and relieve the symptoms of irritable bowel disease. When a dog eats something that he shouldn't, give several doses of plantain after the episode.

Plantain teas are also very good for the urinary tract and will reduce the bleeding and irritation associated with a bladder or urinary tract bacterial infection.

RASPBERRY—Raspberry vines are native to western North America and are found near pastures, along roads, and in the mountains. These thorny vines are easily cultivated in the garden, but be careful, they spread easily and will take over.

The leaves of the raspberry, when dried and used in tinctures and infusions, have several medicinal properties, as do the fresh berries. Internally, raspberry tea is soothing to the digestive tract, including an irritable bowel. It also has calming properties and is good for nervous dogs, newly adopted dogs who may be anxious, or dogs startled by thunder.

Female dogs in season, or coming into season, who may be upset, nervous, or having cramps will benefit from a raspberry tincture. Add one teaspoon of dried leaves to eight ounces of hot water to make a strong tea that your dog can drink or that you can pour over her food. Offer it three to four times a day.

SAGE—Wild sage grows all over the world, although the common sage is a native of the Middle East. The southern California area has several native species, as do Washington and Oregon. Sage can be grown in a garden but it needs full sun.

Used externally, a sage poultice has astringent and antiseptic properties and is excellent for skin irritations and wounds. A poultice can be used for fungal infections of the skin, too, including ringworm.

A sage tea used as a mouthwash is good treatment for gum disease, mouth ulcers, or wounds. It will speed healing and help prevent infection after dental surgery. A tea can also be used as a gargle to help treat infections and inflammations of the throat.

Taken internally as a tea, sage is soothing to the digestive tract and is known to kill harmful bacteria, including *E. coli* and candida.

SENNA—Senna, a bush with large, oblong leaves, is a powerful natural laxative. Usually used as a dried herb (made from the leaves), you may be able to find senna in capsule form. Senna stimulates the bowels, but because it is quite strong, be sure to use it cautiously. If diarrhea results (rather than simply a bowel movement), your dog could suffer potassium loss.

SLIPPERY ELM—Slippery elms are large trees that grow to eighty feet in height. They're commonly found throughout the eastern part of North America. The inner bark is used medicinally.

The inner bark, used in tinctures or teas, is very soothing to the digestive tract and internal mucus membranes. It is good for colitis, diarrhea, and irritations of the stomach and digestive tract. Without causing spasms of the colon, it will help eliminate wastes and so is very useful for incidences of constipation.

ST. JOHN'S WORT—St. John's Wort has lovely yellow, five-petaled flowers on long stems, with long, numerous stamens. This is another European immigrant that has made itself at home in North America. It can be grown in gardens, but because it spreads easily, you would be better off planting it in a planter.

The top third of the plant—the new leaves and flowers—are used medicinally. Older leaves generally are not as potent. The dried herbs can be used in tinctures, oil infusions, glycerin infusions, or teas.

In recent years, this herb gained worldwide recognition as the "herbal Prozac" and became an instant bestseller; however, herbalists have known of St. John's Wort for hundreds of years—it isn't new— and have used it for a number of different things.

This herb's most popular use is as an antidepressant and it works very well that way. Dogs suffering from anxiety, stress, nervousness, or depression will react more positively after a few weeks on this herb. Give ten to twelve drops of oil or glycerin infusion (less for smaller dogs and more for larger dogs) at least twice per day. Don't expect immediate results; it will take two to three weeks for any noticeable change.

This herb also has very strong antiviral properties and is thought to be effective in helping the immune system manage exposure to a virus.

VALERIAN—Valerian has long, narrow leaves that progressively become smaller toward the top of the plant. Its flowers bloom in small clusters on very long stems. The roots are very smelly, like dirty gym socks. Valerian can be cultivated in a garden but likes lots of water; keep it moist and plant it in compost-rich soil.

Even though the roots smell so bad, they have the stronger medicinal properties. When dried and used in tinctures or teas, valerian root has strong sedative properties. It calms the nerves, relaxes the body, and allows even the most anxious dog to fall asleep. It will help dogs afraid of loud noises, especially thunderstorms, and eases pain after surgery or injury.

Valerian is also an antispasmodic and works much like phenobarbital but with fewer side effects. By inhibiting the increased neural activity that precedes a seizure, it prevents seizures from occurring.

WORMWOOD—Wormwood is an attractive plant with small, yellow, ball-like blossoms. A native of Europe, wormwood has been introduced to North America and has flourished.

Wormwood has been used as an antiseptic and antifungal for skin problems, and as its name suggests, as a natural wormer for the intestinal tract. It is particularly effective against roundworms.

Make an alcohol tincture with wormwood for use on the skin. For use against worms, capsules of the dried herb are used. Be aware that wormwood is quite strong and should be used cautiously. Only administer wormwood to treat roundworms if the worms are present in the dog's feces.

YARROW—A member of the sunflower family, this Asian native has feathery, fernlike leaves and lovely, small, white and yellow flowers born in clusters. When used as a dried herb in teas, tinctures, poultices, or oil infusions, it has many medicinal uses.

As a poultice on wounds, yarrow stops bleeding, while at the same time it works as an analgesic and antiseptic. Internally, it dilates blood vessels, increasing and strengthening the circulatory system, and it lowers blood pressure.

In the digestive tract, it works as an antiparasitic, expelling worms. It will also soothe the intestinal tract, expelling gas and easing inflammation.

Warning: Yarrow is quite strong, and some dogs may show allergic sensitivities to it. Watch your dog carefully the first few times you use it and stop using it should your dog show any allergic symptoms. Look for panting, vomiting, diarrhea, swelling, or redness of the skin. However, because allergic symptoms can show in almost a countless number of ways, discontinue if you see anything out of the ordinary.

YUCCA—Yucca grows domestically but it grows very slowly. In addition, its stiff leaves with pointed tips can be quite dangerous. Grow it at your own risk.

The roots of the yucca, when dried and used in a tincture, are very soothing to the digestive tract, actually increasing food metabolism. It also decreases the odor of the dog's urine and feces. Yucca works to decrease the pain and inflammation of arthritis, and it aids in healing.

Yucca is good food. It is rich in vitamin B-complex, C, and the minerals calcium, iron, phosphorus, potassium, and magnesium.

A WORD OF CAUTION

Most herbs are quite safe, but be aware that some dogs may have sensitivities to specific herbs. Signs of sensitivities include vomiting, diarrhea, and itching. If you feel that your dog is having an untoward response to an herb, immediately stop giving that herb.

Forms of Herbs Used as Medicine

Herbs are used in many different forms. Why a particular herb is used in any given form is based in large measure upon its chemical makeup. Depending upon the individual plant, the plant may be used fresh, dried, as a tea, or in some other way. You can buy herbs in these various forms, or if you grow the herbs, you can process them yourself.

Fresh herbs, straight from the garden, are rich in nutrients. Alfalfa, garlic, parsley, and a variety of other herbs can be consumed in their fresh state, and they can be eaten as food or sprinkled on food.

Dried herbs are usually created in a dry place away from the sun. To dry herbs, pull them up from the garden, shake the dirt off the roots, and then hang them in bunches to dry. If the roots are the potent part of the plant, hang the herbs top side up. If the stems, leaves, and flowers are the most potent, hang them upside down with the roots up. This way, as the plant begins to dry, the fluids remain in the part of the plant to be used. Once dried, the herbs should be stored in airtight containers away from sunlight. Dried herbs usually retain their potency for about a year. After that, they tend to oxidize and lose their medicinal value. Dried herbs can be sprinkled on food or used as a tea.

Tinctures or extracts are made by soaking herbs in a solution of alcohol and water or in a solution of glycerin and water. The alcohol or the glycerin breaks down the plant material releasing the active ingredients. There are many ways to make tinctures, but an easy way consists of putting the plant material in a jar and pouring a 50/50 alcohol and water mixture over the plants. (I recommend using unflavored vodka; it doesn't have much taste.) Put on an airtight lid and let it set for two weeks. Then strain the alcohol mixture off. Discard the remaining plant material. The alcohol solution can be stored in small airtight bottles and will remain fresh and potent for a long time.

Alcohol tinctures are very common, popular, and effective, but most dogs absolutely hate the taste, and many will disappear when they see the bottle come out of the cupboard. If your dog thinks alcohol tinctures are the worst thing that could happen to him, you have an alternative. You can also make glycerin and water tinctures. Although they are not normally as potent as alcohol tinctures, they are sweeter in taste and most dogs accept them.

To make a glycerin tincture, buy some vegetable-based glycerin, which you will probably find at your local health food store. Chop the plant material and place it in a jar. Pour a mixture of 50/50 glycerin and water over the plant. Cover it with an airtight lid and let it set for two to three weeks in the refrigerator. Drain the glycerin mixture off the plant material. Throw away the plant material. Store the glycerin tincture in airtight bottles in the refrigerator. If kept refrigerated, it will remain potent for at least a year.

Oil infusions are also accepted by most dogs. To make an oil infusion, place the plant material in a jar and pour olive oil (undiluted) over the plants. Let it steep in a warm place (your kitchen counter is good) for a month. You can then put the entire mixture into the refrigerator, or you can pour off the oil, save it in the refrigerator, and discard the plant material.

Teas are made by pouring hot water over some dried herbs just as you would with some Earl Gray tea. Teas are a weaker solution than most other forms of prepared herbs. Obviously, this can be beneficial if you want a weak solution, such as when giving your dog some peppermint tea when he has an upset tummy. Teas (also called water infusions) are very effective as rinses to soothe skin irritations.

Decoctions are made much like teas (with water poured over dried herbs) except that decoctions are simmered over very low heat for a few minutes. Decoctions are usually used with plant roots that need the heat to break down the plant material. Never let the water come to a boil, however, as excess heat will destroy many of the plant's beneficial properties.

Poultices are made by mixing dried or fresh herbs with water, and then mashing them to break down the plant's cellular structures. The paste is then applied directly to the skin or wrapped in cheesecloth and applied to the skin. Your dog may accept the poultice better if it's warm rather than cold.

Create a salve or ointment by first making an oil infusion. Add to the infusion a thickening agent such as beeswax. One ounce of beeswax to six to eight ounces of oil usually works well.

Capsules are made from dried herbs. Although you can buy empty capsules and stuff dried herbs into them yourself, it's much easier to simply sprinkle the dried herbs over your pet's food.

COMMERCIAL HERBAL PRODUCTS

If you buy premade capsules containing herbs, or tablets made from herbs, buy from a reputable manufacturer and read the label. Many commercial preparations contain a number of ingredients other than simply the herb you want. If you have any questions, call the manufacturer (a toll-free telephone number is found on most labels). If you aren't comfortable with the answers, don't buy the product.

Using Herbal Remedies

As you can see from the herbs I described earlier, there are a variety of plants with similar functions. How do you know what to use? Sometimes you'll just have to experiment. Give each herb a few weeks to work (of course, if your dog seems to be allergic to an herb, discontinue it at once), and then look at the results. Does your dog appear to be benefiting from the herb? Is it accomplishing what you had hoped? If it isn't, try a different herb and give it the same amount of time to work. Each dog's body is different and will react in slightly different ways to each herb.

If you would like to know more about using herbs, see Appendix D: Resources, for more information. In addition, consider consulting an herbalist. He or she can help guide you in choosing specific herbs for your dog.

GROW YOUR OWN

For many years, people have gathered wild herbs for personal use. Today, this gathering—in addition to commercial gathering—is severely depleting the number of many wild plants. In some areas where certain herbs were found in abundance, they can no longer be found at all. Therefore, it is wise to grow your own herbs. You can plant the herbs you want and need and assure yourself of their quality; in turn, you are saving those plants remaining in the wild.

TAKING A LOOK AT ACUPUNCTURE

Acupuncture is a very old healing art with its roots in ancient China. In fact, acupuncture needles have been found that date back at least 7,000 years. It was used on both people and animals, although the animals were not pets, but rather domestic animals who worked for a living.

For many years, the Western medical community looked upon acupuncture with disdain, considering it "folk medicine" or simply mumbo jumbo. More recently our medical experts have rethought acupuncture and realized that it can be very effective. Although the spiritual aspects of acupuncture tend to be dismissed in the West, the sound science behind it cannot be ignored.

Acupuncture is conducted by the placement of very fine needles in specific spots on the body. These spots, called acupuncture points, are located along energy lines or meridians. Physically, acupuncture works because these spots contain small blood vessels and nerve endings. The insertion of the needles causes the body to release endorphins, hormones, and other healing and pain-relieving mechanisms, thereby triggering the healing process.

Spiritually, acupuncture also strives to balance the opposing forces—the yin and the yang—in the body. The body's yin and yang can be considered opposites of just about anything: balanced and unbalanced, happy and sad, and so forth. If you think of the process of acupuncture as restoring the proper balance, that is reasonable.

Acupuncture is not something you can practice at home. It is a very complicated science. Knowing exactly where the energy lines or meridians are located, where to place the needles, and how many needles to use, takes considerable study. With the increasing acceptance of acupuncture, however, an increasing number of veterinary acupuncturists are practicing it. See Appendix D: Resources, for more information on how to find one in your area.

ACUPRESSURE BASICS

Acupressure is based upon the science of acupuncture, but pressure is used (as with massage) rather than needles. Because there is no penetration of the animal's body, this is something you can learn to do at home.

The points where pressure should be used can be felt as slight depressions or dimples under your dog's skin. You can find them by gently massaging your dog, but obviously, his coat can make this somewhat challenging. These points are associated with a specific part of the body, although they are not necessarily the part closest to that point. For example, massaging just under your dog's dew claw on his front leg affects the lungs.

If the dog is having a problem with the part of his body associated with a particular point, there will be a clogged or heavy feeling at that point when you massage it. A few seconds of gentle massage will release the pressure. Your dog may wince slightly as you massage that specific point, but he'll stop when the massage takes effect.

Examples of some remedies and the acupressure points associated with them are:

- To aid in treating shock—Massage just to the side of the nose on the muzzle.
- For upper respiratory problems—Massage the tip of the nose.
- For conjunctivitis and enlarged third eyelid—Massage just above the eye.
- Gastritis and upset stomach—Massage the mid-back, just past the shoulders toward the tail, to either side of the spine.
- Respiratory problems—Massage just under the shoulder blade, on the dog's side, on the second rib, mid-way.

There are many, many more points for specific problems, and I could probably write an entire book about acupressure points. I'm sure it would be very difficult for every dog owner to master them all. There are, nonetheless, five points you should learn in case of emergency. Those emergency points are:

- In case of injury to the head or illness centered in the head— Massage in the indentation on the inside of the front leg between the dew claw and the paw itself.

- In case of a threat to the immune system, including allergies—
  Massage in the depression at the inside of the elbow on the
  front leg.
- In case of cardiac arrest—Massage just above your dog's nose
  (toward his eyes), slightly to the side of his muzzle (either
  side).
- In case of emergency or serious respiratory problems—Massage
  just above the wrist joint of the front leg, to the inside.
- In case of severe gastrointestinal upset—Massage on the hind leg,
  just below the hock (or knee joint) on the outside of the leg.

As you can see, the practice of acupressure takes some expertise,
but why not try it when you massage your dog? This is one of those
practices that can, literally, do no harm and possibly a great deal of
good. For more information, see Appendix B: Remedies for Your
Dog, in which specific acupressure points are listed along with other
possible remedies for your dog.

Chapter 8

NEW AGE MEDICINE

Ginger, a Chow Chow, was very concerned about her owner, Claudia. Like many Chows, she was primarily a one-person dog. Although she liked several of Claudia's friends, she could take them or leave them. She was so dedicated to her owner that she developed separation anxiety. Whenever Claudia left her, she would pace, whine, and drool, and wouldn't stop until she came home. Both Ginger, and Claudia's apartment, were a wreck.

Claudia clearly had a dilemma: "I have to go to work," she said. "I can't stay home and baby-sit my dog all day. My job pays the rent and buys dog food."

A visit to an animal communicator failed to provide any concrete reason for Ginger's anxiety, nor did it lessen it. The communicator asked Claudia if she had ever tried any Bach flower remedies with Ginger, specifically Rescue Remedy™.

Dr. Edward Bach was a bacteriologist and homeopath practicing in England in the 1930s. He believed that the emotional, intellectual, and physical aspects of each individual were one, and needed to be treated that way. He developed thirty-eight homeopathic remedies using flowers (usually the petals) for various illnesses of the mind and body. In one mixture, he combined five different flowers. This mixture, called Rescue Remedy, is used to treat extreme fear, shock, or trauma.

Within several days of beginning the Rescue Remedy, Ginger began to calm down. Although still anxious when Claudia left, she was obviously relaxing once her owner was gone. "When I come home now," Claudia said, "Ginger's ruff and chest aren't soaked with drool like they used to be."

ALTERNATIVE VERSUS TRADITIONAL APPROACHES TO HEALTH

Alternative medicine—which includes a wide variety of techniques not generally recognized by the modern medical (including veterinary) community—has been rapidly gaining popularity. In 1990, Americans made more than 425 million visits to alternative health practitioners, and that's more visits than were made to primary care physicians. Although statistics of the same kind are not available regarding our pets, an increasing number of veterinarians are finding that their patients are asking about alternative veterinary treatments.

Alternative therapies are usually safer and just as effective as many modern medicines and medical techniques. As a society, we're becoming more proactive concerning our health care, and we're examining the benefits and side effects of traditional medicine more closely than we used to. This same behavior extends to our pets. A look at alternative veterinary medicine is a natural second step.

Some differences between traditional medicine (including veterinary medicine) and alternative medicine include:

- Traditional medicine emphasizes diagnosis and treatment, while alternative medicine emphasizes disease prevention.
- Traditional medicine views disease as warfare and is always looking for better "weapons" to "combat" illness, while alternative medicine views treatment as a means of restoring balance to the mind, body, and spirit.
- Traditional medicine encourages patients to be passive and accept treatment, while alternative medicine encourages the active participation of the patient.
- Traditional medicine views the mind and body as two separate entities, while alternative medicine views the mind, body, and spirit as one interrelated being.
- Traditional medicine views the body as something that is "broken" when disease or injury occurs, while alternative medicine views the body as unbalanced or "out of sync" when disease strikes.

AN OVERVIEW OF ALTERNATIVE MEDICINE

When thinking of alternative medicine, the terms *holistic* and *homeopathic* generally come to mind. These terms are used in many different contexts. Some people consider them synonymous, and although they are related, they are not the same thing.

There are several definitions in use for things or subjects classified as holistic, but for the purposes of this book, I'll define *holistic* as meaning *whole*. Holistic methods are those in which the entire dog is treated: the mind, spirit, and body. Whereas traditional or modern medicine treats the injury (such as the broken leg), holistic medicine encompasses the whole dog. For example, a holistic approach to a broken leg is to respond to the break but also to the fact that the dog is in shock, is emotionally frightened, and will need his immune system to be kick-started so that he can heal well.

Holistic medicine may incorporate many different techniques into any given treatment. Herbs, massage, Ttouch, flower essences, aromatherapy, psychic communication, and the power of stones may all be called into play. Generally, in the case of an ill or injured pet, the body is treated first and stabilized. A good diet supplemented with vitamins, minerals, and food supplements appropriate to the individual case is always part of the treatment. Herbal remedies are also used when appropriate. First aid (including traditional medicine) is used when needed.

Depending upon the problem to be treated, homeopathic remedies, such as the Bach flower essences I mentioned before, may also be used. I'll discuss homeopathic remedies in more detail later in this chapter.

Another ancillary line of treatment may involve psychic communication. Diane Stein, author of *The Natural Remedy Book for Dogs and Cats,* writes: "Healing the three bodies—the emotional, mental and spiritual—becomes holistic healing." She encourages us to "Ask your pet what's wrong!" And be prepared to listen to the answer. Psychic communication can also reassure the dog that he is being cared for and that he can relax and allow the treatments to work.

If your dog will tell you what is wrong emotionally, you can move on to other healing techniques. Massage and Ttouch both speed healing by stimulating the circulatory system and the blood flow. In addition, because of the value of touch, they can also heal emotional or spiritual problems.

By treating all aspects of the illness or injury—physical, mental, and spiritual—holistic medicine incorporates the entirety of your dog's well-being into the healing process, leaving nothing to chance.

PSYCHIC HEALING

Whether it is called psychic healing or the laying on of hands, or by some other name, this type of healing has been in use for as long as we've kept records, told stories, or made art.

This healing method consists of transferring vital energy from one person to another. Healers can often identify what ails a person simply by looking at him or touching him. Often they can't explain how they know what the problem is. Some healers can soothe, calm, or even heal those they touch. Very often people attracted to the healing professions (doctors and nurses) have an exceptional healing ability but are not consciously aware of it.

HOMEOPATHIC MEDICINE

Homeopathy is the practice of treating disease with very small doses of a remedy that would produce symptoms of the disease in healthy people. As counterintuitive as it may be, homeopathy works.

A History of Homeopathy

Dr. Samuel Hahnemann studied medicine in Germany in the late 1700s. He was unhappy with the medical techniques of the time, which included laxatives and enemas, emetics, and blood letting. He felt that medicine should cure disease rather than just treat the symptoms. He sought to develop a technique of medicine that was safe, gentle to the patient, and yet effective.

Using a very scientific method, which was almost unheard of in that era, Hahnemann studied the effects of many herbs and other plants on the human system. He kept detailed notes, maintained strict controls, supervised the people being used as test subjects, and finally published his work, *Organon of Medicine,* in 1810. His theories were based on the principle that "like treats like." A substance that produced the same symptoms in a healthy person as the disease does can cure a person with that disease.

Hahnemann found, during his experiments, that when he diluted his plant-based remedies, they became more effective. Ten parts plant matter to millions of parts water is not an unusual combination in homeopathic medicines. During each stage of dilution, the mixture is shaken, and the potency of the mixture refers to the number of times it is diluted and shaken. A label that reads 3C, 6X, or 12X indicates relatively few dilution stages (X equals dilutions of ten and C equals dilutions of 100). A label reading 200C is obviously very dilute and well shaken.

Although one might think that this dilution would weaken the mixture, and logically that would be correct, it isn't necessarily so. Scientific study has revealed that a substance leaves behind a "footprint" even after it has been diluted. Quantum physics tells us that physical substances can leave behind energy fields, and this is what makes these diluted mixtures so potent.

Hahnemann spoke out against the medical practices of his era. Not only was he cast out of the conventional medical community, but he was reviled and his theories dismissed as "outlandish."

Modern Homeopathy

Today, there are many homeopathic remedies available commercially; some of Dr. Hahnemann's are still in use and others have been discovered. Remedies based on plants, minerals, and other natural substances stimulate the body's natural defenses and help the body heal itself.

As a rule, a particular homeopathic remedy is suitable for specific illnesses, injuries, or situations. To treat common ailments, you may want to keep a homeopathic first aid kit. Some basic remedies follow:

- Aconite, made from the monkshood plant, is a good remedy for the early stages of a fever. Your dog may appear to be restless, fearful, or uncomfortable without showing any other symptoms of illness.
- Arnica, made from leopard's bane, relieves the discomfort of bruises and muscle soreness.
- Gelsemium, made from yellow jasmine, eases the discomfort of upper respiratory distress.
- Ipecacuanha, made from ipec root, relieves nausea.
- Ruta, or rue, helps heal sprains, strains, and sore muscles and will also relieve the pain of a broken bone.

Use these basic guidelines to treat your dog with homeopathic remedies:

- Give the remedy to your dog at least thirty minutes before or after eating. Depending on your dog's diet, the remedy may be less effective when given with food.
- Don't touch the remedy with your hands, as homeopathic remedies can become easily contaminated. If giving a liquid, do not touch the stem of the dropper or the liquid with your fingers.

If giving pills, shake them from the bottle into the cap or onto
a paper towel in your hand.

- Drop the medication into your dog's mouth and let it dissolve
there where it will be absorbed through the mucous membranes. Don't make him swallow.
- Be patient. Give the remedy time to work.

Homeopathic medicine is quite a complex science. If you would
like more information about using homeopathic remedies for your
dog, see Appendix D: Resources, for information on how to find a
homeopathic veterinarian and for references that can help you learn
more about this fascinating subject.

FLOWER REMEDIES

As I mentioned in the introduction to this chapter, Dr. Edward Bach,
a bacteriologist and homeopath, originated what are now known as
the Bach flower remedies in the 1930s. Although people all over the
world were using flowers (as well as other parts of the plants) as herbal
remedies for thousands of years, Dr. Bach created the formulas for his
specific homeopathic flower remedies.

Dr. Bach was a firm believer in holistic ideology. He believed that
one's state of mind very much influenced one's physical state of health
and vice versa. Therefore, his flower essences were made to help balance both the mind and the body.

Dr. Bach's flower remedies are still very much in use today and can
be found in any health food store. Although originally made for people, they are also very safe for dogs and are used frequently for them
and for other pets.

Flower essences are sold in rather small quantities, and when you first see the little bottles on the store's shelf, you may feel as though you're about to be ripped off. Remember, however, that these flower essences should be diluted and not given to your dog straight. Put five drops of a flower essence in a clean, one-ounce bottle, fill three-quarters of the bottle with distilled water, and then fill one-quarter of the bottle with brandy (or, if your dog hates alcohol, glycerin). You can combine up to five different flower essences in one bottle. This remedy can then be dispensed by eyedropper on or under your dog's tongue.

Some of the best flower essences for dogs include:

AGRIMONY—Agrimony is used most often for dogs with skin conditions, including flea and other insect bites, and mange. A common sign of a skin problem is restlessness: pacing back and forth or refusing to lay down and get comfortable.

ASPEN—Aspen is useful to dogs who are anticipating danger. A few drops of aspen prior to a visit to the veterinarian's office will help calm fears. This is also good for dogs who are afraid of thunderstorms.

CENTAURY—Centaury is good for dogs who are fearful and submissive, especially those who urinate in submission. It enhances the will to live so it's also recommended for dogs undergoing surgery or those recuperating from a serious injury.

CERATO—Cerato helps an unfocused dog concentrate and learn more easily. It is excellent for dogs going through training, either basic obedience or advanced training.

CHESTNUT—Chestnut is very good to use with dogs undergoing training to break bad habits, such as destructive chewing, digging, and other annoying behaviors. It enhances memory and makes training more effective.

CHICORY—Chicory is useful for treating dogs with separation anxiety. It also helps ease the dog-owner bond of dogs who are overly dependent upon their owners or who are jealous.

CRAB APPLE—Crab apple is particularly good for dogs competing in dog sports, as it boosts self-esteem.

ELM—Elm helps take the edge off dogs undergoing a stressful or overwhelming event. A few drops prior to a trip to the grooming salon, nail trimming, a dog show, or even training class will ease the stress.

GORSE—Gorse helps ease grief. If a dog has lost a companion, or if a dog is terminally ill, gorse will ease the depth of the grief without interfering with its natural course.

HOLLY—This remedy is for dogs with short tempers. Those dogs who easily become aggressive, or who always accept the challenge, will benefit from holly. It makes dogs just a little more accepting of the world around them.

HONEYSUCKLE—This sweet flower is for dogs who have overexerted themselves. It is good for working dogs, service dogs, and performance dogs who try too hard. It is also good for mother dogs who are overwhelmed by the nursing and care of their puppies.

MUSTARD—Mustard is used for dogs with hormonal imbalances, bitches in season, or older dogs who are achy and grumpy. It helps mitigate mood swings.

OAK—Oak is a good remedy for working dogs, specifically those under stress. It builds perseverance and stamina. It is also good for dogs suffering from a long-term illness for the same reason; it gives the dog the will to carry on.

OLIVE—Olive is particularly helpful to elderly dogs who are easily tired and overwhelmed. It stimulates the adrenal glands and maintains energy levels.

PINE—Use pine to help alleviate the pain of rejection or abandonment. Dogs who have been given up by their owners, left at shelters, or in a rescue program are candidates for this remedy.

ROCKROSE—Rockrose is an excellent treatment for dogs who exhibit strong fears, even terror. This is for those dogs who would jump through windows during a thunderstorm. By instilling courage and trust, it helps dogs see through their fear.

STAR-OF-BETHLEHEM—Like pine, star-of-Bethlehem is very good for dogs who have been given up by their owners or are newly adopted. It helps alleviate past fears or a sense of abandonment. It is also good for dogs who must spend time in the veterinary hospital.

VERVAIN—For dogs with high-energy behavior problems, vervain is an excellent remedy. Those dogs who chase cars, run back and forth along the fence, bark incessantly, or chase other animals will find some calm in vervain.

VINE—Vine is the remedy for overly dominant dogs who feel they must boss all the other pets in the household or neighborhood. It is particularly good for dominant dogs with aggressive tendencies.

WALNUT—I recommend walnut to help dogs adapt to changes in their environment. If you are planning to move to a new home, or remodel your current one, or if a child is leaving for college, walnut can help the dog cope.

WILD OAT—Dogs who are bored, or who get into trouble because they don't feel needed, will benefit from wild oat.

The remedies listed here are only a few of those available. For more information about flower essences and the Bach flower remedies in particular, see Appendix D: Resources.

RESCUE REMEDY

Rescue Remedy is always in my home and in my first aid kit. A combination of five different flower essences, I use it (for people and dogs) in any emergency—major or minor—it's the first remedy I try. Rescue Remedy contains cherry plum, clematis, impatiens, rockrose, and star-of-Bethlehem. It is useful for distress of any kind, anxiety, fear, sudden accident or injury, and even the onset of severe illness.

AROMATHERAPY

Do certain smells evoke memories for you? Do the smells of Christmas pine, gingerbread, and fruit pies make you think of Christmas? If so, then you understand aromatherapy. Aromatic oils and scents (especially those of plants) have been used for thousands of years to relieve pain, alleviate tension and fatigue, and invigorate the entire body.

Researchers believe that aromatherapy as we know it was established in ancient Egypt. Ancient Egyptians used aromatic oils for massage, bathing, and medicine. The dead were even embalmed in cedar oil. The Europeans used fragrant oils, too, and during the Black Plague, oils were used to ward off disease.

Rene-Maurice Gattefosse was a French chemist who first used the phrase *aromatherapy* in the 1930s. Remarkably, an accident in his laboratory led Gattefosse to become a proponent of healing with essential oils. During an experiment, an explosion occurred and his arm was burnt. In pain, he plunged his arm into the nearest container of water, one which contained lavender oil. Not only did the lavender oil help suppress the pain of his burn, but over the next few days, he watched his arm heal with little pain and even less scarring. He then devoted the rest of his life to the study of fragrances and their effect on mood as well as healing.

Although aromatherapy is still new to many people, the technique is not new at all. Many large corporations, including those that produce cosmetics, air fresheners, and cleansers, use fragrances in their products. Those fragrances are carefully selected. For example, why do so many cleaners use a lemon scent? Citrus scents create a positive mood and are very uplifting. So after you clean with a lemon-scented cleanser, not only is your kitchen counter clean, but you feel good about it. Hmmm. Interesting, isn't it?

People who enjoyed the effect that scents had on them went on to share the techniques with their pets. It only makes sense that aromatherapy would be effective with dogs; after all, the dog's sense of smell is very highly developed. (The dog's ability to detect a scent is really quite amazing. In fact, no manmade machine has proven to be as accurate.) Why not give both of you a special sensory treat now and then?

Some common essential oils for aromatherapy include:

CITRUS OILS—Citrus oils create an uplifting mood and a sense of well-being.

LAVENDER—Lavender should be in every homeopathic first aid kit. It is soothing for injuries and eases stress.

PEPPERMINT—Try peppermint as a stimulant; it "picks up" a dog who is tired, bored, or upset.

PENNYROYAL—Pennyroyal is an excellent flea and insect repellant. Put a few drops on your dog's bed.

Scented candles are great for use with dogs (make sure the dog can't touch the candle or knock it over). As an alternative, drop some oil onto a cotton ball so that the dog can sniff it. A few drops can also be placed in his bed where he can smell it all night.

Aromatherapy oils are very concentrated; a little goes a long way. Keep in mind when using aromatherapy that your dog has a much more sensitive nose than you do. For your dog, less is much better than more.

DON'T DOUSE THE DOG

Although some aromatherapy oil may be used on the skin (with people), do not do the same with your dog. Your dog often licks his coat and skin, and should one of those oils be too concentrated or toxic, he could poison himself.

HOT AND COLD THERAPIES

Heat and cold therapies have been around for a long time. Before people were able to create different states of temperature, they undoubtedly relied on the elements to provide hot and cold therapies. Nonetheless, there is still considerable debate as to when to use heat and when to use cold. Some people say to put heat on a sprained wrist, while others say to put cold on it. For the sake of your canine's well-being, let's clear up the mystery.

Heat, as in a wet, hot towel, a hot stone (for use in hot stone massage), or a monitored (watch it closely) heat pad, can be used to ease the following:

ARTHRITIS—Heat helps loosen the joints, making movement less painful.

MUSCLE SORENESS—Heat eases the stiffness and opens blood vessels, allowing better circulation for better healing.

RESTLESSNESS—Heat helps relax and calm the nervous dog, allowing rest and sleep.

Cold therapy, usually in the form of ice packs, is good for:

FEVER—A cold pack can provide relief while other therapies work internally.

INJURIES—A cold pack placed over a muscle or joint injury immediately following the injury will reduce pain somewhat, but more importantly, it will reduce swelling.

WHEEZING—Dogs with exercise-induced asthma will find relief from a cold pack over the shoulders or chest.

So what's the answer—should you use heat packs or cold packs on sprains, strains, and muscle soreness? You should use both. Use cold immediately after the injury to reduce swelling. Then, after twenty-four hours, use heat to increase blood circulation and speed healing.

LIGHT THERAPY

When my husband and I were transferred from our native southern California to a military base in the northeast, I looked upon it as a challenge. I enjoyed seeing new places and meeting new people. It would be fun. What I didn't expect was the winter depression. As the nights grew longer and the days shorter (and grayer), I found myself getting mentally and physically depressed. I didn't understand it. A wise physician friend recommended basking a few minutes each day (or a couple of times each day) under the UV fluorescent lights that we used to simulate sunlight for our reptiles. Sure enough, after just a few days of light, I was feeling better.

CONTROL THE TEMPERATURE

Be very careful when using both heat packs and cold packs on your dog. Heat packs, especially heating pads, can cause burns. Cold packs should chill the affected spot but should not cause your dog to shiver. Leave each pack on no longer than fifteen minutes at a time. Then remove it, let the spot come back to body temperature, and reapply the pack again if needed.

This syndrome, which is called "seasonal affective disorder" or SAD, is not uncommon. In fact, many people speculate it is one of the reasons why so many northerners retire to Florida. Sure the weather is great but so, too, is the sunshine.

SAD can affect your dog as well as you. When days get shorter, you may both take fewer walks, you may both go to bed earlier, and you both will have less exposure to sunshine. If you find your dog behaving in a manner that suggests depression, some exposure to bright lights could help. I used the fluorescent lights used to create the effect of sunshine over reptiles because I had them available. These lights were not designed for use as light therapy, however, so if you use them for your dog for an extended period of time, be sure to cover his eyes with a towel for protection. See Appendix D: Resources, for resources for lights made specifically for SAD.

In addition to combating SAD, light has other therapeutic uses. Researchers know that when light enters the eye, it signals the pineal gland, which then produces melatonin. Melatonin, which has attracted a lot of attention recently as a means of fighting jet lag, regulates sleep.

Different types of lights have other effects on the body. UVA fluorescent lights, used as greenhouse "grow" lights, are known to cause aggressive behavior in some reptiles exposed to them. However, when exposed to UVB fluorescent lights, the reptiles' behavior didn't change. These lights, moreover, allowed them to metabolize calcium better, hence leading to better captive health. In another experiment that resulted in widespread use, farmers used blue lights to calm their animals and make them easier to handle.

Exposure to natural sunlight is vitally important to good health, and if your climate cooperates, a few hours each day is fine. As far as artificial light is concerned, there is still much we don't know.

COLOR THERAPY

Color therapy is closely related to light therapy. Colors are energy, and I'll elaborate on their use in chapter 9 in the discussion of gemstones and their colors. Color can be used for your dog as colored lights, as a colored towel or blanket, a special collar and leash, or with colored gemstones.

Colors and their effect on your dog include:

RED—A strong, potent color, red conveys power. In healing, red stimulates the sensory nervous system.

YELLOW—Yellow is bright and lifts the spirits. It alleviates depression. In healing, it stimulates the lymph system.

ORANGE—Use orange to stimulate the respiratory system and relieve cramps and spasms. A warm color, orange is very attractive to many dogs, especially as a blanket for their bed.

GREEN—Green works to bring the body into balance. It aids in healing and strengthens the immune system.

BLUE—Blue is a cool color and works as a coolant for the skin, relieving itching and inflammation. It is also a mild sedative.

PURPLE—Purple is relaxing and aids in sleep. It lowers blood pressure and body temperature, reduces the heart rate, and calms emotions.

Color is often used with other therapies and is an effective adjunct to herbal and homeopathic remedies. For more on color therapy, including its ties with other New Age techniques, see Appendix C: The Significance of Color.

EXERCISE

Exercise as a New Age medicine? Well, if a goal of alternative medicine is to stay healthy, exercise certainly fits the bill of preventive medicine.

Our dogs were made to be active. Their ancestors hunted and traveled great distances to do so. As they became domesticated, dogs were bred to work—to hunt, retrieve, herd, or protect the family. They had to be athletic and physically fit to do their job.

Today, our pet dogs rarely get the exercise they need, and it shows in both their mental and physical health. Dogs who get inadequate exercise often (not just sometimes but often) develop behavior problems. Digging, destructive chewing, barking, fence-running, self-mutilation, and a host of other problems can be associated with a lack of exercise.

When a genetic heritage to work and inadequate (or no) exercise are combined, it leads to problems. Although all dogs need to get regular workouts, herding, working, and sporting dogs particularly need good aerobic exercise each and every day.

Lack of exercise leads to physical unfitness, such as poor cardiovascular recovery after playtimes, muscle weakness, and a lack of stamina, but it can also lead to obesity, a widespread problem in dogs today. Some veterinarians say that more than 50 percent of the dogs walking into their clinics are not just overweight but obese. This has detrimental effects on our dogs' health and leads to countless maladies, including heart problems and back and hip problems. The impact of obesity on the overall health of dogs is not unlike its impact on the health of people.

A walk is good exercise for a baby puppy or an elderly dog, but a healthy adult dog needs to run, jump, climb, and use all of his muscles. A good jog followed by a game of catch the tennis ball or Frisbee™ would be excellent exercise.

As with any exercise program, start slowly. Let the dog's muscles gain strength and his pads toughen. Sore muscles are no fun for anyone, human or canine.

VACCINATIONS AND NOSODES

The value of vaccinations has been in dispute for some time. In fact, Dr. Samuel Hahnemann, the father of modern homeopathy, discovered that after people and animals received vaccinations, they often became ill. He called this illness vaccinosis. Another homeopath, C. Compton Burnett, author of *Vaccinosis and Its Cure by Thuja* (no longer in print) used the herb thuja (or thuya) to treat those people suffering from vaccinosis.

Although people and their pets are still being vaccinated, an increasing number of people are questioning the wisdom of traditional medicine's vaccination protocol. You may have noticed, as I have, that after a vaccination, my dogs are listless, don't have their normal appetite, and generally just seem out of kilter. The response is more pronounced in puppies and older dogs.

A vaccination is made up of bacteria or a virus of a specific disease. This bacteria or virus has been weakened or killed so it is no longer active or alive (hence the name "killed vaccine"). This weakened or killed vaccine is given to your dog (or to people) with the expectation that the body's immune system will be triggered and will develop antibodies against that specific disease.

OBSERVE YOUR DOG AFTER HE'S BEEN IMMUNIZED

If your dog receives a vaccination, watch for a reaction. Serious reactions usually occur fairly quickly, often before your dog even leaves the vet's office. Wait about thirty minutes after the vaccination before heading home; if your dog has a serious reaction, you want to be at the vet's. Minor reactions may be subtle—a little fatigue, some muscle soreness, or a loss of appetite. You can treat them yourself with the homeopathic remedy thuja, but do so only under the supervision of a homeopathic or holistic veterinarian. Thuja is quite potent and must be used with care.

Many experts believe that repeated vaccinations (especially annual vaccinations such as those dogs and cats receive) may be causing an increase in the development of autoimmune diseases in dogs and people. Such diseases include asthma, allergies, warts, tumors, and irritable bowel disease. No vaccine, moreover, is 100 percent effective. Variables that affect the build-up of antibodies include the quality of the vaccine and how the vaccine was handled during manufacture, shipping, and storage, as well as how it was administered to your dog. In addition, your dog's state of health and immune system are variables; how does your dog's body react to a particular vaccination?

So what should you do? What can you do if you live in a state where vaccinations are required? Richard Pitcairn, DVM, a holistic veterinarian and the author of several books on natural pet care, suggests that dog owners vaccinate their pets only for diseases prevalent where they live. He recommends the administration of killed or modified live vaccines, rather than live virus ones. In addition, he advises pet owners to repeat the vaccinations less frequently than recommended by the manufacturer.

Some experts, including Dr. Pitcairn, support the practice of giving only one vaccination at a time, rather than the combined shots. Combined shots may include distemper, hepatitis, parvovirus, and a variety of other diseases all in one injection. Combination shots can completely overwhelm a dog's immune system, causing him to become sick or to develop inadequate antibodies to the different diseases.

Nosodes are homeopathic vaccinations that serve as an alternative to the traditional product. Active parts of the disease are prepared in a diluted solution much like a homeopathic plant or flower remedy. There are nosodes available for distemper, leptospirosis, hepatitis, parvovirus, kennel cough, and many other diseases that could threaten your dog's health.

Because they are taken orally, nosodes cause no pain or shock. They are generally less expensive than vaccines and do not cause the allergic or sick reactions sometimes attributed to vaccinations. Nosodes have been proven effective by holistic veterinarians, dog breeders, exhibitors, and pet owners.

If vaccinations are required by law in your state, your options are more limited. One approach is to discuss a combination technique with your veterinarian, whereby your dog receives those vaccinations that are legally required and nosodes for those that are not.

Deciding not to vaccinate your dog is a serious matter. Although vaccinations do carry with them some risk, so too do the diseases they are designed to prevent. Distemper and parvovirus, just to name two, have killed thousands of dogs and have the potential to kill thousands more. Think this decision over thoroughly. If you decide to discontinue your dog's vaccinations—any vaccinations—make sure you do so with the guidance of a holistic veterinarian and follow through with the correct nosodes. It is an irresponsible dog owner who simply chooses to do nothing. Do *not* leave your dog unprotected!

AN OUNCE OF PREVENTION

To lessen the number and severity of possible reactions to a vaccination, take time to prepare your dog. First of all, make sure he is healthy. Don't vaccinate a sick or injured dog, or even one who is "just a little under the weather." Start giving your dog an extra dose of vitamin C, beginning a few days before the vaccine and continuing a few days after. Begin giving echinacea a few days prior, also, and continue for at least a week after the vaccination.

NEW AGE MEDICINE TODAY

More and more mainstream veterinarians are advocating (and using) holistic and homeopathic remedies. They may not be able to understand the treatments, but they've seen them work—and you can't argue with success.

Quite a few veterinarians use a combination of techniques in their practice. For example, Mary L. Brennan, DVM, author of *The Natural Dog: A Complete Guide for Caring Owners*, uses homeopathic remedies as well as modern medicines. She writes, "Sometimes I am able to integrate homeopathy with other types of treatment. For instance, certain cardiology (heart) cases can be assisted by the use of homeopathics. I have been able to take dogs off the toxic forms of medication and use homeopathics instead."

Other traditional medical and veterinary practitioners, however, are much less accepting of holistic methods of medicine. The Food and Drug Administration (FDA) has taken a cautious approach. The agency has been monitoring food supplements, herbal remedies, holistic techniques, and homeopathic medicine for quite a while, but only recently has it allowed the manufacturers of holistic remedies to indicate the product's purpose on the label.

Most natural remedies—herbs, food supplements, vitamins, minerals, flower essences, and homeopathic remedies—are safe and effective. Some, especially herbs, have been used for thousands of years, and their benefits are well known. Nonetheless, the FDA has begun examining the sale and usage of many different herbs and other remedies, and some, even with long histories of effective usage, have been banned.

It is hopeful, with the increased demonstration of the utility of natural remedies, that these products gain an ever-wider acceptance among all members of our society.

TAKING YOUR DOG WITH YOU AS YOU EXPLORE

In part 3 of this book, I'll take you down some unconventional paths. This may be new, uncharted territory for some dog owners; make sure your bring your dog with you!

Chapter 9 will focus on powers from the earth, specifically the powers of gemstones, crystals, and stones. I'll explore their powers and how you can use them. I'll also look at the powers of magnets and how they can be used to alleviate pain.

In chapter 10 I'll move from the earth to the stars. Astrology, Chinese astrology, and numerology are the focus of this chapter. I'll also show you how to see your dog's aura. Finally, I'll help you learn to discern and interpret your dog's dreams.

In chapter 11 I'll explore the issues that we often find hard to discuss. What happens when your dog grows old? Is death the end? Do dogs go to heaven? Will you meet again?

CRYSTALS, STONES, METALS, AND MAGNETS

It had been a bad day. Clients were fussy, demanding, and short-tempered, and I could feel myself moving in the same direction. To try and short-circuit the coming bad mood, I called to my dogs and we went out for a walk. Walking the dogs always calms me down and centers me.

As we walked, I consciously took in deep breaths of fresh air, clearing and cleaning my lungs. I made it a point, too, to look around me; to appreciate the new green leaves on the trees and the sounds of the songbirds as they stopped to eat on their northward migrations. I also watched my dogs. I take pleasure from their enjoyment of the world, and they make me see things I might not have otherwise seen—like the raccoon tracks in the sand and the deer hiding in the bushes.

When we reached the riverbed, a favorite place of ours, I took the leashes off the dogs. They ran, played, and sniffed as we walked alongside the river. I could feel myself starting to relax, but my mind kept going back to those conversations earlier in the day that had made me angry and tense. The point was to let go of them, but the more I tried to *not* think about them, the more I *did* think about them. It was a vicious circle with no end in sight.

As I tried to clear my mind, I noticed that Riker appeared to be searching for something. He was sniffing near the river, too close for my comfort, so I called him back. He turned away from the river, looked at me (even making eye contact), and then went back to sniffing. I'm not used to being ignored—especially by Riker—so I went over to find out what he was so intent upon. As I walked toward him, he found it. I could see him pick up something. He mouthed it a few times, rolling it around in his mouth, and as he did, he closed his eyes as if he really needed to concentrate on this thing. Apparently it was good, because he then dashed toward me, bouncing over big rocks and through the bushes, with the thing still in his mouth. Curious, I held out my hand. He dropped a rock in my hand. A rock?! Why a rock? Riker doesn't play with rocks.

Then I looked at it. Granted it was covered in dog drool, but it was a lovely piece of rose quartz. It had been in the water for quite some time; all the edges were as smooth as if it had been in a rock tumbler. About the size of a cherry tomato, the rose quartz was a clear, deep pink; the pink of a sunset just before it turns orange.

It took me a moment to realize what Riker had given me, and then I had to sit down on the ground to hug my dog. Happy that he got such a positive response from me, he proceeded to lick my face and crawl into my lap.

Rose quartz is a powerful stone. Even small pieces are good for healing, but most importantly, rose quartz can calm and ease aggressive mental turmoil. Had Riker felt my distress and approaching bad mood and searched out this stone to help me release it? When he rolled the stone around in his mouth, was he testing it to see if it had power? I can't say for sure. Riker is still very much a puppy, and although we have a wonderful relationship, our mutual psychic connection isn't particularly strong. Nonetheless, I like to think he sensed the perfection of that rose quartz for me.

OUR RELATIONSHIP WITH STONES

From earliest times, mankind has believed that the earth itself was powerful. Many cultures, including those of Native Americans, believed that the sky was our father and the earth our mother. In their "Song of the Loom," the Tewa people recited, "O our mother the earth, O our father the sky, Your children are we, and with tired backs we bring you gifts." A Winnebago saying provided, "Holy mother earth, the trees and all nature are witnesses of your thoughts and deeds." Cherokee legends say that the earth herself comes from the sky and that the Mother Earth is the outer body of the Great Spirit. Within that legend, when we walk upon pebbles, rocks, and minerals of the earth, we are walking on stardust. The belief that the earth is mysteriously powerful, however, is much older than even the oldest Native American cultures.

Thousands of years ago, early mankind experimented with the first tools. A woman used a strong, heavy stick to pry up some tubers to eat and a man used a long, pointed stick to hunt game. As the shortfalls of their wooden tools became apparent, they began looking at other materials. They discovered that some stones, flint in particular, could be shaped, and began to make spear points, arrow points, knives, and awls.

SOLID LIGHT

The ancient Australian aborigines believed that crystals were sacred. Clear quartz crystals were said to be solidified light that fell from the sky like rain. To become a healer or shaman, the young person had pieces of crystal inserted into his body (including under the skin or in the tongue). This process filled him with the light from the sky and gave him the power a healer needed.

As early man became more skillful at shaping different types of stones, and as he began to appreciate the beauty of the stones and crystals around him, art was developed. Stones were shaped into figures, both real and imaginary. Jade figures were highly valued in China as well as South America. Obsidian and amber were both treasured stones and were used for early art and jewelry pieces, but perhaps the most important stone was red ocher. Red ocher was sacred to many people, including those in Australia, North America, Africa, and Europe. Associated with life energy and power, red ocher has a special relationship with mankind dating back more than one hundred thousand years.

The oldest known use of stones or crystals for healing occurred in India. Many ancient texts recorded the various uses of different stones and the sources of those stones. Some stones were said to be created from the light from planets, while others were from a supernatural being. The stones and crystals were made into sacred images, religious statues, prayer beads, and amulets because they had greater powers than other materials, thus offering greater benefits.

In North America, the Apaches considered turquoise to be a vital part of the medicine man's tools. In addition, warriors would put on turquoise stones or jewelry to protect themselves and to ensure success when they went on a hunt. Seen as a link between heaven and earth, turquoise was also important to the Central American people (including the Aztecs, Mixtecs, and Mayans), who used it to decorate the images of their gods.

The Bible also mentions the use of stones, crystals, and metals. In most instances, the references are for the purpose of describing color and clarity, using the crystal as a guide. However, they were also used to emphasize richness. In Revelation, Ezekiel has a vision of heavenly beings, "And I looked, and behold, a whirlwind came out of the north, . . . and a fire infolding itself, as of the color of amber. And above the firmament that was over their heads was the likeness of a throne, as the appearance of a sapphire stone."

Even today we see crystals and stones being used in modern religion. Many prayer beads and rosaries are made from precious stones or crystals. People may simply think the beads are pretty, but there is a long-standing reason why these stones and crystals are used—they have power.

Metals, too, have played an important role in our lives. After the Stone Age, when mankind learned to use flint and other stone tools, came the ages of metal. During the Iron Age and Bronze Age, mankind learned to mine and work metals, to form new shapes and develop new tools. These two stages of development quickly led mankind to the Industrial Age—for better or for worse.

More recently, we have seen the effects of a desire for certain metals. The gold rushes in California and Alaska in the 1800s changed the face of North America forever. Even though gold is found naturally and in some places is quite common, it is still a metal that people place great monetary value on.

EARTHLY ENERGY

As you know, stones, crystals, and metals come from the earth. And the earth, if you like, can be thought of as one gigantic battery. The earth has its own energy and is taking it in from the sun and elsewhere. Stones, crystals, and metals absorb, retain, and emit that energy. When Riker picked up the rose quartz and rolled it around in his mouth, he was probably feeling the stone's energy. If its energy were depleted, it wouldn't have done me any good. Riker would have discarded it and continued his search for one that was fully charged.

Lauren Chattigre, D.V.M., a holistic veterinarian in Boring, Oregon, believes that crystals work like little generators. They store and focus energy from nature and pass it along. According to Chattigre, "You will actually feel a little zing from the resonance when you hold the right stone."

This energy, because it was not well understood, was often called magic. Magic and stones, crystals, and metals have had a long relationship. The stones used in amulets, those carved into figurines, and those used in religious services were all of value due to their energy. This energy, this magic, could cause an occurrence or prevent one. Metals given a useful shape—even something like armor or a sword—were sometimes believed to have special powers of protection or courage.

People who can channel and use the energy found in stones, crystals, and metals have been called gods, deities, or magicians (depending upon the culture). You don't have to be a god, deity, or magician to take advantage of this energy, however; you just have to know it's there and believe in it. When there is a need for a stone—such as Riker felt within me that day—knowledge as to how to use the stone, and belief in the stone's ability, then the stone can do its work (or magic).

As we discovered the powers of crystals and stones, and used them on ourselves, we shared them, too, with our canine companions. A crystal in a wire cage hung from the dog's collar can help protect him from harm while a different stone tucked under his sleeping blanket can help relieve the pains of arthritis. A stone in his drinking water, one held in your hand during a massage, or another placed on an energy point during a healing ritual can all help your dog.

The energies that make the powers of the earth so effective for us work just as well on our canine companions. In return, sometimes our canine companions turn the tables on us as Riker did for me. The next time your dog brings you a stone from outside, look at it carefully. It may be just a rock, or it may be a special treasure that your dog knew was absolutely meant for you.

CRYSTALS, STONES, AND METALS—A TO Z

Before you learn how to use crystals, stones, and metals for your dog, you need to be familiar with their powers. In the following, I'll describe the most commonly used stones and their effects. Keep in mind, though, that a stone's abilities are not set in stone, as it were. Lots of different factors play a role in a stone's powers, including you, your dog, and, of course, the stone itself.

AGATE (also called red agate or blood agate)—Agate produces strength, courage, longevity, and healing. It is of special benefit to dogs on farms. An agate hung from the dog's collar can help protect the dog from snakebite and insect bites and stings. An agate amulet will remove negative emotions, especially spite and jealousy.

AMBER—Amber is probably the oldest substance used as jewelry. Beads and pendants have been found that date back to 8000 B.C. It produces luck, healing, strength, beauty, and love. Amber protects the wearer against jealousy, and a piece of amber in an amulet will help maintain good health. Amber can be quite stimulating and may be too much so for some dogs.

AMETHYST—Amethyst, a purple- to violet-colored crystal, is the stone of peace; it has no negative associations. Amethyst raises the spirits, elevates moods, and promotes happiness. It has also been known to enhance psychic awareness. A working or performance dog with a bit of amethyst on his collar will make the right decisions.

AQUAMARINE—A pale, blue-green stone, aquamarine is associated with the sea. When hung from the collar of water rescue dogs such as Newfoundlands and Portuguese Water Dogs, it provides protection from the ocean's dangers. This stone elevates psychic awareness, promotes peacefulness, and emphasizes courage in dogs who wear it.

AVENTURINE—This green stone is a good luck stone. When tucked under the dog's bedding, aventurine enhances intelligence, strengthens eyesight, and guards against bad luck.

AZURITE—Azurite is a lovely, deep blue stone used for healing and to increase psychic abilities. It is best used tucked into the dog's bedding.

BLOODSTONE—This green chalcedony has red spots (hence the name) and has been used for thousands of years as an aid to warriors. A working guard dog with a bloodstone amulet will be brave, courageous, and calm.

CARNELIAN—This red form of chalcedony, when worn in an amulet, bolsters the courage of the shy or fearful. Carnelian promotes self-confidence and counteracts doubt and negative thoughts. It is a good, all-purpose healing stone.

CHRYSOCOLLA—Chrysocolla is a green stone known to increase wisdom, dispatch fear, and attract love.

CITRINE—Citrine will soothe the restless sleeper when tucked under his sleeping blanket. In an amulet, it will also increase psychic awareness. This stone works to integrate intuition with reasoning as well as spiritual energies.

COPPER—Copper reduces inflammation and eases arthritis. It releases tension, strengthens the body, and aids in the flow of internal energy. It works best when actually touching the body.

EMERALD—You undoubtedly know that emerald is a brilliant green stone. If you don't wear an emerald, you may have forgotten that it's wonderful for strengthening the memory. In fact, emeralds are said to help the living remember past lives. A dog having trouble learning will do much better with a bit of emerald tucked into an amulet. Try the same technique with an older dog who seems confused. Emeralds will calm a troubled mind and create harmony.

GARNET—This fiery red stone strengthens the body and promotes courage. Working dogs wearing a garnet will be brave, protective, and strong. This is a very strong stone; an aggressive dog should not wear this stone unless that strength and aggressiveness is needed.

GOLD—This precious metal balances the nervous system, brain, and bioelectric functions of the body. Gold reduces stress.

HEMATITE (or volcano spit)—Hematite is a heavy, silver-black stone primarily used for healing. It focuses attention on the physical body and away from the psychic or spiritual. Hematite supports the circulatory system and aids in detoxification.

JADE—This green stone has been sacred to the Chinese for thousands of years. Jade is associated with longevity, wisdom, and healing. It is also protective, guarding against accidents.

JASPER, BROWN—Brown jasper will center and ground one who carries it. It will help a working dog concentrate or a daydreamer finds his way.

JASPER, GREEN—This is a healing stone. Green jasper is used in healing rituals or carried in amulets.

JASPER, RED—Red jasper is very protective and defensive. It sends negativity back to its originator.

MICA—Mica is an all-purpose protective stone. It can be placed under your dog's bedding or hung above his feeding place. Try placing a piece in an amulet for your dog.

OBSIDIAN—This black stone is a centering, grounding stone. Obsidian will help the dog in training to return his focus and the distracted dog find his work.

ONYX—Onyx protects against conflict and negative energy.

QUARTZ, CLEAR CRYSTAL—Crystal quartz has been used in many different ways over thousands of years. It is one of the strongest and most versatile stones. When tucked under the dog's bedding or carried in an amulet, this stone promotes psychic abilities. When held in your hand during a massage or when placed on one of your dog's energy centers, it promotes healing. Quartz also amplifies the powers of other stones held near it and strengthens the dog's aura.

QUARTZ, ROSE—This is a powerful healing stone, for both the body and the mind. It will calm the mind, deflect aggression and negativity, and return that negativity back to the sender. Normally a gentle stone, rose quartz responds to its environment.

RUBY—This red stone is powerful and protects its wearer against all foes. A ruby on a protective dog will guard the dog and all the property and people that the dog is to protect as well. Rubies are also very strong healing stones and work particularly well with the heart and circulatory systems.

SAPPHIRE—The blue sapphire has been used defensively for thousands of years. It was known to scare away evil and send negativity back to the sender. As defensive magic, sapphires also keep the body healthy. These stones are also known to increase communication on many levels, including the spiritual and psychic.

SERPENTINE—Serpentine guards against snakebites, bee stings, and spider bites as well as other threatening creatures.

TIGER'S EYE—Tiger's eye, a gold and brown stone, builds courage and energy, attracts good luck, and protects the wearer. The tiger's eye has strong vibrations and feels warm to the holder. The wearer of tiger's eye can remember incidences from past lives.

TOPAZ—Topaz relieves depression, worry, and other emotional strains. Under bedding, it relieves sleeplessness and nightmares. It will also alleviate the pain of arthritis.

TURQUOISE—This has long been considered a healing stone and was always present in the medicine man or shaman's bag. Turquoise is an all-purpose healing stone that strengthens all of the body's organs. Native American warriors wore this stone to protect them in battle and to ensure a good hunt. A piece was placed on their horse to protect it from danger or a misstep. Turquoise is a power stone and draws power to its wearer.

The Magic of Shape

Naturally created stones and metals are found in an endless number of shapes—from simple masses to elegant crystals. The shapes are formed by the actions of the earth such as water and wind or from breaking from a larger stone. Some stones appear to be in magical shapes; they might be stars, crescents, or diamonds.

Stones that are formed naturally into recognizable shapes are much more powerful than stones shaped by people. Such stones are said to have deep magical significance. Native Americans treasured stones found in animal shapes; these were used in important rituals. Other cultures, both ancient and contemporary, value stones in certain shapes.

Some of the interpretations for these shapes include:

ANIMAL SHAPES—Stones shaped like a particular animal will bring you the protection of the animal they represent. Interpreting animal-shaped stones is an entire science all unto itself.

HEART-SHAPED—These stones are used, as you might expect, to attract love.

LONG AND THIN—Long thin stones serve as phallic symbols and represent the male aspect of reproduction or power.

PERFECTLY ROUND—Round stones are associated with women and child bearing, or fertility.

TRIANGULAR—Triangular stones protect the people who carry them close.

If you find a stone shaped by nature, treasure it. These stones are truly magical and are always bearers of good luck.

SPECIAL STONES

A stone with a hole that goes through it, worn by water, winter, or other natural forces, is very special and very strong magic. In some cultures, members believe that a holed stone represents the first woman, or Eve, or the mother of all creation.

The Meaning of Color

Color is very important to us, and it's just as important to our dogs. For many years researchers believed dogs saw only in black and white, but for many of us that didn't make any sense. In the wild, a predator needed good vision, and one that saw only in black and white would be severely handicapped. Recently, however, researchers have finally agreed that wild and domestic canines do see color—not as we do, but they do see color.

In the last chapter, I discussed color therapy, and the same things apply to colored stones. Not only can stones of a particular color be used in color therapy as are lights, blankets, and other objects, but stones of the same color often share similar qualities or powers. For example, throughout ancient times, red stones were used to banish negativity and promote healing, just as rubies do today.

Many people (and dogs) are attracted by certain colors more so than others. I, personally, love the color red. Even though red is often regarded as the color of war, of violence, of blood and of birth and death, it is still a very attractive color to me. Rubies are definitely one of my favorite stones. Rubies protect their wearer against all foes (emotional, spiritual, and psychic) and are strong healing stones. Because I like to consider myself a teacher and healer, perhaps I can say that I have chosen wisely.

When I allowed my dogs access to all my stones and asked them to choose the color they liked the most, I found that Kes always chose a red stone, too. But Kes, like myself, is also a teacher. Red stones are strong and powerful, and teachers need to convey that they're leaders.

Riker is very much the lover, not the fighter, and is a peaceful dog. He chose a pink stone—the rose quartz—just as he did for me that day by the riverbed. Rose quartz and other pink stones repel negative thoughts and promote peace, goodwill, happiness, and joy. And that is Riker.

Dax, on the other hand, is fiery, protective, and willful. She invariably chooses stones with more than one color. Multi-colored stones are complex, just as Dax is, and their powers will vary depending upon the situation.

When choosing stones for your collection, I'd recommend looking for a variety of colors. You'll want to be able to access the power of as many different colored stones as possible.

USING CRYSTALS, STONES, AND METALS

The key to using stones, crystals, and metals is that your (and your dog's) feelings, intuitions, and needs tell you what stone you should use. Give yourself permission to make the right choice, and then abide by it.

Charging the Stones

Before using any stone, crystal, or metal, it must be charged (or more correctly, recharged), especially if the stone has been in your possession for a while. When laying on the earth, either in the sunlight or buried in the earth, the stone was constantly being recharged with energy from the earth, the sun, or the moon. The stone's energies are depleted when they are used, however, and are not recharged when away from the elements and natural light.

There are several ways to recharge a stone. One way is to set the stone in a safe place outside in the sun. Let it set there for several hours. Some stones that do best when recharged in the sun include amber, calcite, carnelian, tiger's eye, and topaz. Most metals recharge best when in the sun and in contact with the earth.

Some stones are more receptive to energy from the moon. These stones, which include aquamarine, beryl, moonstone, sapphire, and selenite, can be set outside in a safe place under the light of a full moon. In several hours, they will be vibrating with energy.

If you are full of energy and feeling powerful but need a charged stone to help your dog, you can also use your energy to charge the stone. Hold the stone tightly in your hand and visualize in your mind your need for the stone's energy. Picture what you will be doing with the stone, how you will do it, and the end result. For example, if your old dog's arthritis is acting up, you may wish to place a charged piece of topaz under your dog's bedding to help ease the pain in his joints. As you envision this process, visualize the energy moving from your center down your arm to your hand and into the stone. When the stone is warm and vibrating with your energy, place it under your dog's bedding.

A stone should be recharged before each use. If it's difficult for you to remember to do this, you may want to find a safe place where your stones—when not in use—can remain outside in view of the sun and moon and in contact with the earth. When you need them, they'll be fully charged and ready to work for you.

Using Stones Indirectly

The easiest way to use a stone's power is indirectly. The previous example of placing a charged piece of topaz under your dog's bedding to alleviate the pain of arthritis is an indirect use of the stone's energy. The stone is being used, but it is not directly touching the dog. In many situations, indirect use is all that is needed, especially for long-term effects.

Stones can be used indirectly in several others ways. A bit of mica, tucked into an amulet, can be hung above the dog's feeding place as a general-purpose protector. Several small chips of emerald and aventurine can be mounted in a decorative pattern on your dog's training leash to aid his learning. Indirect contact allows the stones to do their work quietly and without a lot of energy or force.

VISUALIZATION

As I discussed extensively in chapter 3, visualization is "seeing" without using your physical eyes. Instead, you are using your mind to "see" or picture an event. This is a powerful mental tool but is really quite simple to do.

For example, close your eyes and "see" your dog's face. Picture him sad and lonely. When you see him clearly, change his expression to one of happiness. When you have changed his expression and it is remaining happy (not reverting back to sad), open your eyes and look at your dog.

He'll probably be looking at you, either with that same happy face or, if he's not accustomed to being the subject of your visualizations, he may look questioningly or slightly confused.

Direct Contact

Direct contact refers to when the stone is actually touching your dog, and there are numerous methods to apply.

One of the most commonly used means of direct contact is the practice of hanging a stone from the dog's collar. The stone can either be mounted as jewelry, in a metal mounting, or it can be carried in an amulet. If the stone is to be hung from your dog's collar, make sure it is a small piece of stone. Stone is heavy, and your dog may protest carrying a heavy stone from his neck.

If your dog decides to chew the stone off his collar, listen to him. The stone may be too heavy, physically, or your dog may disagree with your choice of stones. If your dog doesn't want the energy from a ruby, for example, don't force him to wear it. It may be too strong for him at this time. You might want to choose another stone that has the same powers but is less forceful.

ONE AT A TIME

Please, please, please, use small stones and don't use more than one stone at a time on your dog's collar. Although your dog may seem quite strong, a stone is heavy. After a while all the energy in the world isn't going to cure the neck ache from dragging around that stone. Besides, a large stone could get quite annoying beating against the dog's chest as he moves.

A fully charged stone, moreover, produces a lot of energy. If several stones are hanging off your dog's collar, his senses will be overloaded. Let him deal with one stone at a time.

Another common method of direct contact is by using a stone while massaging your dog. As I discussed in chapter 5, a massage can relax your dog, releasing tension and stress. Massages also have tremendous healing potential, from the massage itself and from the tools you use when you massage your dog. By having a rose quartz, clear quartz, sapphire, or other healing stone in your hand or resting on your dog while you massage him, you can harness the power of that stone at the same time the massage does it's own magic. Double the effectiveness of the massage!

Your Dog's Energy Centers

Your dog's energy centers (or chakras) are located along the centerline of his body. These energy centers are some of the same spots you focus on for massage or acupressure. Each of these points is a gathering spot for a multitude of influences on your dog's mental, emotional, spiritual, and physical health. Each spot has a different effect on your dog, and because each stone, crystal, or metal also has a different effect or purpose, a variety of things might be accomplished by placing stones on these particular spots.

When you want to use stones on your dog's energy centers, sit on the floor with your dog and invite him to lie down. When he's lying down with you, give him a full body massage to relax him, and as you do, tell him what you are going to do, visualizing it as you speak. Once your dog is relaxed and accepting of your planned use of the stone, you can proceed to employ the stone's powers. Do not attempt to hold the dog still if he doesn't want to; that is counterproductive.

EXPERIMENT FREELY

You can combine many different techniques during the same session. You can massage your dog, use acupressure, do a hot stone massage, and use a crystal on several energy points. None of these techniques conflict with each other and, in fact, are often quite complementary.

Make sure each stone is fully charged before you begin. Hold each stone in your hand for a moment before placing it. As you hold it, visualize what you want the stone to do. For example, if your dog has been feeling overwhelmed by training and appears to dislike his

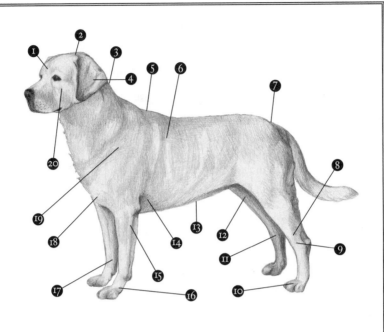

CHAKRA AND MASSAGE POINTS

1. *3rd eye/middle of forehead*

2. *flat of skull between ears*

3. *base of skull where it meets the neck*

4. *ear flaps*

5. *where neck meets shoulders*

6. *midback, on side of spine*

7. *base or root of tail*

8. *outside of rear leg above hock*

9. *outside of rear leg below hock*

10. *outside toe of rear foot*

11. *inside rear leg at hock*

12. *inside rear leg, up close to body*

13. *navel*

14. *left side over the heart*

15. *outside of elbow on front leg*

16. *hollow above and behind front paw*

17. *inside front leg, above wrist joint*

18. *crease where front leg meets body*

19. *below shoulder blades*

20. *outside corner of eye*

training sessions, use a piece of amber, warm it in your hand, and as you place it, visualize the negative emotions flowing away from him, leaving him happy and carefree, even during training sessions. You might visualize the negative emotions as dark vapors leaving your dog. You can then envision your dog, during a training session with you, bouncing around with his tail wagging.

Each of your dog's energy centers affects him in a different way.

HEAD—This spot is located on the flat part of the skull between your dog's ears. Stones affecting the mental processes may be used here. A topaz can ease depression, a sapphire can increase communication, or a rose quartz can calm mental anguish. Copper and gold also work well here.

THIRD EYE—Your dog's "third eye" is in the middle of his forehead. This energy point relates to psychic communications and abilities, including memories of past lives. Sapphires, hematites, and emeralds work well on this energy point.

HEART—The heart chakra is the center of both the physical and psychic. Physical problems with the body manifest themselves here, as do widely swinging emotions and desires. Rose quartz is a wonderful healing stone and works well here, as do rubies, green jasper, and copper.

NAVEL—This energy point usually absorbs the stresses of daily life, both physical and emotional. When this energy point is working well, your dog will be full of life, with bright eyes eager to do anything. When your dog appears overwhelmed or overstimulated, this energy point needs recharging. Agate is good for use on this spot as it removes negative emotions. Amber also removes negative emotions and jealousy but can be quite stimulating for some dogs, so use it carefully.

ROOT OR BASE POINT—The root point is located at the base of the spine, where the dog's tail attaches to the spine and hips. Use this spot to help your dog ground himself to find himself emotionally and physically. Obsidian, brown jasper, and carnelian all work well here.

As you work with these energy points or centers, keep in mind that there are no "right" or "wrong" choices to be made. If your dog really dislikes having stones placed on the third eye location, don't fight him about it. Try a different spot instead; his protest of that spot may be his only way of telling you that spot (or stone) is wrong for him.

There is also no "right" or "wrong" crystal, stone, or metal to use. Your decision will depend upon you, your dog, and the specific stone. Amber might work well for your best friend's dog, but that doesn't mean it will be a good stone for yours. The best thing to do is to try a few different stones; see what feels right to you and what seems to have the best effect on your dog.

Most people accumulate a variety of stones. A friend of mine keeps her special stones, crystals, and bits of metal in a nice felt-lined wooden box. When a stone is needed, she opens the box but doesn't search for a stone; instead, without looking, she reaches in and takes the stone that her hand reaches for. She says that invariably, that is the one that was needed.

TALISMANS

Talismans are small objects, sometimes stones, crystals, or metals, usually in a special shape, that have significant meaning. A small cross representing a religion is a talisman, a piece of clear quartz on a chain around your neck is a talisman, and a piece of pewter shaped into a bear's paw print is a talisman. What makes a talisman special is not what it is but what you believe it means.

I have Riker's piece of rose quartz hung on a chain and keep it as a special talisman. In my van, I have several special talismans, all of them protective, because I believe that driving on today's freeways can be risky business!

There are no talismans that are right or wrong, none that are more important than others. If something calls to you, has significant meaning, or just seems "right," then it probably is. Keep it close because you were meant to have it.

THE POWER OF MAGNETS

Magnets are manmade and so might seem out of place here; however, their power originates from the earth as does the power of crystals and stones. Magnets have been used in Eastern medicine for hundreds of years, primarily for treating pain.

When placed on the skin near a painful or injured spot, magnets use the earth's energy (and the magnetic pull on iron and ions in the bloodstream) to increase blood flow to that spot. The increased blood flow, which is fully oxygenated blood, aids in healing and reducing pain. Magnetic energy also quiets the nerves that may be stimulated after an injury. By decreasing the electrical energy sent to the brain, the pain signal channels to the brain are closed.

The most effective magnets are made of neodymium, as they're strong enough to penetrate your dog's tissues and energize and oxygenate the blood.

There are three types of magnets: north, south, and bipolar. The north pole magnets are cooling and sedating. These are most effective against inflammation, acute pain, infections, and the nervousness that accompanies these conditions. South pole magnets are stimulating and accumulating. They are used to strengthen the body, especially during healing. They will also work to help stimulate the immune system.

Bipolar magnets have the characteristics of both the north and the south poles, and should be used when a dog is severely debilitated.

Magnet therapy is a very safe, noninvasive, and economical method of treating your dog, especially for minor injuries such as a pulled muscle or strain. It can be easily combined with other holistic techniques, including herbal and homeopathic remedies and massage.

Many pet supply stores and Internet shopping sites now offer magnet therapy alternatives for dogs. Collars are available with magnets inside for dogs with neck or shoulder pain. There are magnetic rollers available for massaging your dog and sleeping pads with magnets inside. See Appendix D: Resources, for more information.

Chapter 10

ASTROLOGY, NUMEROLOGY, AND YOUR DOG'S DREAMS

It had been a wonderful day. We were up in the coastal redwoods, camping at a favorite spot, and the weather was cooperating wonderfully. We had walked through the forest, enjoying the majesty of the huge, old trees, and the dogs romped, played, and sniffed for chipmunks and squirrels. As the sun went down, we lit a campfire and relaxed while the dogs fell asleep.

Shortly, though, we heard whining from Kes. Turning to look, we saw her legs thrashing, muscles twitching, and lips blowing in and out. She was obviously dreaming but what was she dreaming about? Was she chasing the squirrels that chittered at her earlier today? Or was she trying to catch that fish in the river that got away from her? Within a few seconds, her dream was over and she fell back into a sound sleep.

Have you ever awakened from a dream and wondered what it meant? Or wondered if it actually had any meaning at all? Many people believe that dreams have connections to our lives and that if we want to we can learn from them. Our dogs' dreams can teach us too, so in this chapter I'll take a look at what dogs dream about.

I'll also discuss the fascinating subjects of astrology, Chinese astrology, and numerology as they pertain to your dog. Each of these sciences can be applied for a better understanding of your relationship. Then I'll tell you about your dog's aura. So let's continue our explorations.

IT SAYS SO IN THE STARS!

Astrology is a science that dates back thousands of years, but it is also a science that is constantly evolving. As long ago as 3000 B.C., mankind built observatories to watch the stars and planets in the skies.

Sun sign astrology, the type from which our daily newspaper horoscope is derived, is a very simplified form of a very complicated science. Astrology studies how the date and time of someone's birth (you, your spouse, significant other, or even your dog) affects his or her life. It can help you use your strengths to your advantage or to aid you in overcoming weaknesses. Most people think of astrology as a means of learning more about themselves or those who are close to them.

Sun sign astrology today is based on the relationship between the twelve zodiac or sun signs, the planets, the sun, the moon, and the twelve aspects of life, called houses. This is a very, very complex science and students of astrology must devote long hours to mastering its intricacies and nuances. That said, the following overview will give you a basic understanding of the twelve sun signs and how they apply to you and your dog.

The Astrological Sun Signs

When were you and your dog born? Which sign applies to each of you?

Aries	March 21 to April 20
Taurus	April 21 to May 20
Gemini	May 21 to June 20
Cancer	June 21 to July 21
Leo	July 22 to August 21
Virgo	August 22 to September 21
Libra	September 22 to October 22
Scorpio	October 23 to November 21
Sagittarius	November 22 to December 20
Capricorn	December 21 to January 19
Aquarius	January 20 to February 18
Pisces	February 19 to March 20

As examples, I was born under the sign of Aries, as was my youngest dog, Riker.

IF YOUR DOG'S DATE OF BIRTH IS UNKNOWN

If you obtained your dog from a shelter, you might not be sure when he was born and be uncertain of his sign, but you can make a guess. You were probably told your dog's age when you got him, and you can calculate back from that time. If his age was related more vaguely, for example, fourteen to sixteen months, determine the two or three signs that he might be. Read the character traits found in those of each pertinent sign. Chances are, you'll be able to pick which sign applies to your dog.

More About the Sun Signs

ARIES—Aries is the ram and is the first sun sign. People who study astrology joke that if Aries hadn't been first it would have rearranged the zodiac so that it was. As an Aries, I can testify to that personality quirk. Rams are known for their strong will, pushiness, and tendency to be a little egocentric. Aries is a fire sign, loves the color red, and is known to rush in where angels fear to tread.

TAURUS—Taurus is the bull, known for having its feet firmly planted on the ground. A bull will get things done, but only when he's good and ready. Bulls are reliable, steadfast, and calm, but they can also be resistant to change and sometimes can be a "stick in the mud." Taurus loves the color emerald green.

GEMINI—Gemini, the twins, loves the color yellow, and is the sign signifying change. The twins are always in motion, see everything, and love to take advantage of opportunities. Geminis are quick, witty, and flexible, but they can also be emotional.

CANCER—Cancer, the fourth sign, is the sign of the crab. Crabs relate to the color silver, and as a water gem, the pearl. Crabs are quite emotional and can be hurt badly by the people they love. Crabs are dependable, loving, and self-sacrificing, but they can also be overly emotional and sensitive.

LEO—Leo, the lion, is self-confident and a born leader. Leos are generous, ambitious, and proud. As good leaders, Leos are loyal and expect loyalty in return. They'll be hurt if they find that they've misplaced their trust. Leos enjoy the color gold.

VIRGO—Virgo is the sign of the virgin representing purity, practicality, and perfection. Of course, not all Virgos are perfect, but most will strive for perfection in some aspect of their lives. Not surprisingly, Virgos have a tendency to be worriers even when there isn't an obvious problem. Virgos are often healers and like the color sky blue.

LIBRA—Libras strive for balance and harmony. They are charming, active, and social. Librans have a tendency to worry about what others think of them, and this can make a Libran seem insincere. They're at their best with other people, however, rather than alone. The Libra's color is blue.

SCORPIO—Scorpio, the scorpion, is intense. Powerful, decisive, and mysterious, Scorpios are often warriors who look life and death in the face. Scorpios are sometimes humorless; as such, you can understand why the favorite color of Scorpio is black.

SAGITTARIUS—Sagittarius loves freedom and is hesitant to be tied down by responsibilities. Optimistic, generous, and adventurous, Sagittarius can also be easily led astray. The favorite color is purple.

CAPRICORN—The goat is intense and goal-oriented as well as very practical. Goats have good self-control, both of body and emotion. Goats can also be very kind, surprisingly so in face of the intensity of their ambition. Earth tone colors of brown flatter the Capricorn.

AQUARIUS—Aquarians are very much individuals and eccentrics. Those born under this sign follow their own path and don't really care what other people think. Aquarians are idealistic, independent, and imaginative. The best color for Aquarius is violet.

PISCES—The fish is highly intuitive, very compassionate, and easily the most giving of the twelve signs. They are known to be shy and passive, but also somewhat talkative. A Pisces couldn't keep a secret if his life depended on it. Obviously the best color for Pisces is sea green.

Although these descriptions may seem quite straightforward, there are innumerable variations. Astrologers look at much more than just your sun signs, they also look at the positions of the sun, moon, and planets. The positions of these heavenly bodies also have a bearing on your horoscope. For more information, see Appendix D: Resources, for references.

Applying Astrology to You and Your Dog

So does the sign your dog is born under make any difference to your relationship? Sure it can. You may find that you and your dog are always fussing at each other; or you may find that you are perfectly compatible. Looking at your sun signs, either one of those traits or tendencies may show up.

If you are looking for a new dog or puppy, you can also use your sun sign to find a compatible canine companion and to avoid one that might be a poor match. Let's take a look.

ARIES—Rams need an exciting relationship and do well with other Aries, Leos, or Sagittarians. Aries should avoid Libras, Capricorns, and Scorpios.

TAURUS—The bull enjoys a dog born under the signs of Cancer, Pisces, or even their opposite, Scorpio; however, bulls should avoid Aries, Geminis, or Sagittarians.

GEMINI—The twins form strong relationships with other Geminis, a Libra, or a Scorpio. Avoid Taurus and Pisces.

CANCER—If you are a Cancer, your dog should be another Cancer, Taurus, Scorpio, or Pisces. Relationships with a Gemini, Virgo, or Leo probably won't work out as well.

LEO—If you are a Leo, the best relationship will be forged with a dog who is another Leo, a Sagittarius, or an Aries. Avoid Cancer, Scorpios, Taurus, and Aquarius.

VIRGO—If you are a Virgo, the dog best suited for you would be either another Virgo, Taurus, or Capricorn. Don't look for a dog born under the sign of Cancer; that would be a mismatch.

LIBRA—If you are a Libra, the best dog for you would be born under the sign of Gemini or Aquarius. Although another Libran would be fine, two personalities so alike could be trouble. Try to avoid a dog who is a Capricorn.

SCORPIO—Scorpios need a dog who can handle their intense personality and stern outlook. A Virgo, Cancer, or Capricorn is a good dog for a Scorpio, while a Taurus, Scorpio's opposite, can give the Scorpio balance. A Scorpio should avoid Aries; they are too much alike.

SAGITTARIUS—If you are a Sagittarius, look for a dog born under the sign of Aries. An Aries dog can keep up with a Sagittarius and can keep him safe. Gemini, Libra, and Aquarius might also be compatible.

CAPRICORN—If you are a Capricorn, the best canine companion should be born under the sign of Cancer. Scorpio, Taurus, and Pisces are also good choices, but Aries, Libra, and Aquarius are not.

AQUARIUS—Aquarians bond well with Libras, so a dog born under that sign would be fine. A Sagittarius would also do well. Avoid a Capricorn.

PISCES—A Pisces needs a dog who can keep him focused, channeled, and moving in one direction. A dog born under the sign of Capricorn would be very good for a Pisces, as would a dog born under Scorpio. Pisces should avoid Aries and Sagittarius.

TRY THIS

What is your sun sign? _____

What characteristics do you have of that sun sign? _____

_____

What is your dog's sun sign? _____

What characteristics does he have? _____

In what ways are your sun signs compatible? _____

In what ways does your relationship with your dog demonstrate your astrological compatiblity? _____

CHINESE ASTROLOGY

According to Buddhist legend, when the Buddha invited all of the animals of the world to meet with him and help him celebrate his enlightenment, only twelve showed up. The rat, ox, tiger, hare, dragon, snake, horse, goat, monkey, rooster, dog, and pig all came to the celebration. He honored each of those animals by giving them each a year to rule, and those twelve became the twelve animals of Chinese astrology.

The twelve animals of Chinese astrology were in use in other astrological systems long before the Buddha, however, so the legend is probably just a legend. Many Asian countries have their own type and style of astrology, most based on the twelve animals.

The animals each have certain characteristics that are bestowed upon the people or pets born under their protection. This doesn't mean there are only twelve types of personalities; instead, other factors come into play. Each personality is influenced by three animals: one for the year of birth, one for the month of birth, and one for the time of birth. Those who study Chinese astrology also examine other factors as well. It takes years of study to be truly adept at working with this astrological system. I'll stick to the basics here.

Traits Symbolized by the Animals

Westerners have developed broad assumptions about certain animals. For example, most of us think of rats as vermin, dirty, and carriers of disease. However, that is not how Chinese astrology views the rat. So don't make any assumptions—good or bad—until you find out more.

The chief characteristics of the twelve animals are as follows:

RAT—The rat is resourceful and ambitious, hard-working, determined, and intelligent. Rats are busy souls; if they're not actively doing something, they're planning it. Rats like fine dining and usually eat heartily (if the food is good). Their favorite colors are light blue and white.

Male rats are quick thinkers and always charming, but they can also be short-tempered. Female rats are hoarders and will hide toys, treats, or even bits of food. Female rats love their family above all else and will sacrifice all for them.

OX—The ox is patient, shrewd, conventional, reliable, and courageous. The dog who is an ox may appear to be slow in mind and body, but he's not. The ox just likes to take his time and think things through. An ox craves peace and quiet, especially at home.

He'll gravitate toward items that are violet or pale pink.

The male ox is strong and sometimes standoffish, but when he gives away his heart it is forever. His love, loyalty, and affection are steadfast. The female ox is strong-minded and somewhat stubborn.

TIGER—The tiger is passionate, entertaining, daring, dangerous, fast, and even a bit exhausting. The tiger often acts before he thinks, reacting to stimuli without thinking through the consequences. However, the tiger is notoriously lucky and things usually turn out fine. He likes reds and oranges—bright colors that reflect the sun.

Male tigers are enthusiastic and energetic. They are the instigators, sometimes pushing others beyond their limits. They can also be too bouncy and are sometimes quite annoying. It's hard for a male tiger to learn self-control. Female tigers are very similar, but tend to behave in a subtler manner. The female tiger may hide her claws, but the claws are still there.

HARE—The hare is sensitive and generous, but egotistical. The hare is also tactile and intuitive. He is quick-thinking, clever, and shrewd and occasionally intimidates other animal signs who have a slower pace. Hares like pale green, pale pink, white, and gray.

The male hare is physically active, athletic, and strong. He likes to test his physical limits and sometimes hurts himself doing so. The female hare is very intuitive, tends to have psychic abilities, and quite often is even prophetic. The female hare is also a listener, and people like to confide in her.

DRAGON—As a steadfast, loyal, hard-working horse, I often dream of being a dragon. The dragon is daring, independent, enthusiastic, and inspiring—mysterious, things that the horse is not. The dragon is larger than life, exciting, and magnificent—just like he's portrayed in fairy tales. The dragon's colors are dramatic—gold, black, and forest green.

Male dragons are attractive (physically and intellectually) and are admired by the other animal signs. Male dragons like to be right, and when they aren't, they won't admit it. Their stubborn streak can get them into trouble. Female dragons tend to be the center of attention even when they don't try to be.

SNAKE—In many cultures, the snake is looked upon as the lowest of the low, the betrayer. In others, the snake is viewed as the sacred symbol of knowledge and wisdom. Chinese astrology sees the snake as intelligent, intuitive, organized, and brave. The colors of the snake are yellow and green, especially the paler shades. Many snakes also like black, a deep, dark clear black—not gray.

Male snakes are romantic charmers and very attractive to the opposite sex. They're also hard workers. Like the males, female snakes are regarded as sexy but are not particularly interested in conquest. They prefer to focus on their family. Female snakes are regarded as witty, entertaining, and wise.

HORSE—The horse is loyal and hard-working, friendly, sociable, and well liked. The horse is a known motivator, an inspiration to those bogged down in everyday life. Horses don't understand the meaning of the word *can't*. A horse's favorite colors tend to be earth tones— browns, golds, and natural shades.

The male horse is very social, enjoys being surrounded by friends, and is quite the communicator. The female horse is a little more reserved than the male horse but that isn't saying much; she is also quite gregarious. Family and friends are very important to the female horse.

GOAT—The goat is peaceful, sincere, honest, and adaptable. He is also creative, passionate, and a bit crazy. Goats may give the appearance of respectability, but then, at any given time, they may go off the deep end. Goats like the colors mauve, pink, and violet.

Male goats are often rebels; they don't follow the pack but instead make their own path. If everyone else follows, fine, but they don't worry about being alone, either. Female goats can be quite unconventional, too, but are less likely to strike out on their own than the males.

MONKEY—The monkey is quick-witted, lively and entertaining, bold and independent. Monkeys are optimistic. Intelligent, cunning, and manipulative, they can take advantage of many of the other animal signs. Only dragons can see through the monkey's shenanigans. The monkey's colors are yellows, golds, and browns.

The male monkey is cheerful and enjoys socializing. He will take risks and is sometimes deceitful. Female monkeys are coy and flirty, sometimes too much so. Both male and female monkeys dislike rigid rules.

ROOSTER—Roosters are protective, courageous, communicative, and honest—they're loyal friends. He also tends to be old-fashioned and slightly pompous. The rooster may not agree with you—and will tell you so to your face—but when you are a friend, you're a friend for life. Roosters love the color red as well as various shades of orange.

The male rooster is determined, capable, and goal-oriented. The male rooster is also a flirt, but he is not promiscuous. The female rooster is well balanced, patient, and capable. She too may like to flirt, but she's just being playful. Family is very important to her.

DOG—The dog is loyal, responsible, trustworthy, sensitive, and moral. He is everything we think a dog should be and more. Dogs are forgiving, tolerant, and caring. The dog sometimes takes on more than he can handle, but it always seems to work out. Dogs like earth tones, including browns, golds, beiges, and other sand colors.

The male dog feels things deeply. He is much more emotional than the males of the other animal signs. He can be prone to depression when things don't go his way or when he feels betrayed; however, he also takes great joy in his relationships. Female dogs are also quite emotional, although they seem to more comfortable with their feelings than the males. Female dogs are good listeners, and their friends are treasured.

PIG—The pig is cheerful, tolerant, eager, generous, and lucky. Of all the animal signs, the pig is the most fun. They're warm, friendly, and forgiving and really enjoy time with others. Unfortunately, pigs can also be lazy and self-indulgent. The pig's favorite colors are blues, especially a deep navy blue.

The male pig is a good listener and is often considered a good friend, but he will rarely make an effort to maintain a friendship; that's up to the other person to do. Luckily for him, he's appealing enough to keep people around him. The female pig can seem somewhat self-centered. Be patient with her, as she is sincerely interested in her friends and family.

Finding Your Dog's Animal Signs

To assess the signs that govern your dog, you'll need to know his year, month, and time of birth. Dogs born in the years listed below were born in the year of:

YEAR

Horse	1990 (Jan. 27, 1990 through Feb. 14, 1991)
Goat	1991 (Feb. 15, 1991 through Feb. 3, 1992)
Monkey	1992 (Feb. 4, 1992 through Jan. 22, 1993)
Rooster	1993 (Jan. 23, 1993 through Feb. 9, 1994)
Dog	1994 (Feb. 10, 1994 through Jan. 30, 1995)
Pig	1995 (Jan. 31, 1995 through Feb. 18, 1996)
Rat	1996 (Feb. 19, 1996 through Feb. 7, 1997)
Ox	1997 (Feb. 8, 1997 through Jan. 27, 1998)
Tiger	1998 (Jan. 28, 1998 through Feb. 15, 1999)
Hare	1999 (Feb. 16, 1999 through Feb. 4, 2000)
Dragon	2000 (Feb. 5, 2000 through Jan. 23, 2001)
Snake	2001 (Jan. 24, 2001 through Feb. 11, 2002)
Horse	2002 (Feb. 12, 2002 through Jan. 31, 2003)
Goat	2003 (Feb. 1, 2003 through Jan 21, 2004)
Monkey	2004 (Jan. 22, 2004 through Feb. 8, 2005)
Rooster	2005 (Feb. 9, 2005 through Jan. 28, 2006)

Finally, you need to know the animal that applies to the month and time of your dog's birth.

MONTH		TIME	
Ox	January	*Ox*	1 A.M. to 3 A.M.
Tiger	February	*Tiger*	3 A.M. to 5 A.M.
Hare	March	*Hare*	5 A.M. to 7 A.M.
Dragon	April	*Dragon*	7 A.M. to 9 A.M.
Snake	May	*Snake*	9 A.M. to 11 A.M.
Horse	June	*Horse*	11 A.M. to 1 A.M.
Goat	July	*Goat*	1 P.M. to 3 P.M.
Monkey	August	*Monkey*	3 P.M. to 5 P.M.
Rooster	September	*Rooster*	5 P.M. to 7 P.M.
Dog	October	*Dog*	7 P.M. to 9 P.M.
Pig	November	*Pig*	9 P.M. to 11 P.M.
Rat	December	*Rat*	11 P.M. to 1 A.M.

Putting It All Together

I'll use one of my dogs as an example as to how you can apply this information. (Of course, you can apply the same type of analysis to yourself.) My youngest dog, Riker, was born on April 20, 1999. I called his breeder, and she thought that he was born between 7 P.M. and 9 P.M. that night.

Riker was born in the year of the hare, and that is the part of him that he shows to the world, his outward, visible personality. According to the chart, he is sensitive and generous, but egotistical. The hare is also tactile and intuitive. Riker fits all of those descriptions. (I don't normally find him egotistical even though he does think he's pretty handsome.)

The month in which Riker was born tells us how he conducts himself in his relationships with others, or in this case, with me. April is the month of the dragon. The dragon is daring, independent, enthusiastic, and inspiring. I can agree with those descriptions.

The time that Riker was born describes the real Riker, the inner dog. The time of 7 P.M. to 9 P.M. is attributed to the dog. The dog is loyal, responsible, trustworthy, sensitive, and moral. Is Riker trustworthy and sensitive? Absolutely.

Applying Chinese Astrology to You and Your Dog

Can you use Chinese astrology to evaluate your relationship with your dog? Sure. You may learn why you and your dog seem to mesh well, or perhaps you will learn why you keep butting heads.

Find your year of birth on the following chart:

Tiger	1950, 1962, 1974, 1986
Hare	1951, 1963, 1975, 1987
Dragon	1952, 1964, 1976, 1988
Snake	1953, 1965, 1977, 1989
Horse	1954, 1966, 1978, 1990
Goat	1955, 1967, 1979, 1991
Monkey	1956, 1968, 1980, 1992
Rooster	1957, 1969, 1981, 1993
Dog	1958, 1970, 1982, 1994
Pig	1959, 1971, 1983, 1995
Rat	1960, 1972, 1984, 1996
Ox	1961, 1973, 1985, 1997

This is a simple example: I was born in the year of the horse. According to Chinese astrology, the "me" that I show to the world is loyal and hard-working, friendly, sociable, and well liked. The horse (me) and the hare (Riker) should get along quite well. The horse can be emotional (true), but the hare balances it in his desire for stability (also true).

Take a look at the compatibility of you and your dog.

RAT—Rats don't always get along well with other rats; in fact, squabbles between them are likely. A rat and an ox can be good companions as long as the ox will allow the rat to be the boss. The hare will make the rat relax a little, often a very good thing. The rat and dragon will get along fine, as will the rat and snake. Don't try to match a rat with a goat; it rarely works.

OX—An ox and a rat will get along fine, but a tiger and an ox is cause for trouble. The ox and snake, ox and horse, and ox and rooster can all be good friends and companions. Relationships between an ox and dog, an ox and dragon, or an ox and another ox should be avoided.

TIGER—A tiger and a horse can create an interesting friendship; the tiger is daring and quick but the horse is strong, steadfast, and loyal. A tiger and goat will create a wonderful relationship. A tiger should not be paired with a pig, another tiger, or a dragon; these signs just don't work out.

HARE—A hare and a rat usually get along quite well—although a rat will occasionally try to take advantage of a hare, he rarely succeeds. The hare is a good companion for many of the other animal signs, including the horse, ox, snake, and pig. A hare also gets along famously with other hares. The hare should not attempt a relationship with a monkey; these two are sure to conflict.

DRAGON—Dragons and rats have personality traits that complement one another and are known to develop exceptional friendships. Dragons also get along with pigs and monkeys; however, a dragon should not be paired with a dog or a horse; he is too flamboyant for these two animals.

SNAKE—It's said that opposites attract, which explains why a snake and a hare make such a good team. Other fine matches for a snake are an ox, a dragon, or another snake. A snake should never attempt a relationship with a tiger, a monkey, or a pig; those are doomed to failure.

HORSE—A horse will have a solid friendship with another horse, a tiger, and a goat. The horse and the dog are two of a kind and can form a strong relationship. On the other hand, a horse will not tolerate the ego of a dragon nor does a horse care for a monkey.

GOAT—A goat gets along very well with a tiger; after all, they are quite a bit alike. Goats and hares, snakes, horses, and pigs will also become fast friends; however, a goat and a rooster, a monkey, a dragon, or an ox will not work and should be avoided.

MONKEY—The best match for a monkey is with a dragon; both are colorful and social. A monkey can also have a good relationship with a rat or with a rooster. Relationships with hares, snakes, and goats are not desirable for a monkey; each party will exasperate the other.

ROOSTER—A rooster is best paired with a tiger. These two complement each other very well. A rooster also fares well with an ox, a horse, and a dog. A rooster and a goat will clash frequently. A rooster should never try to develop a relationship with another rooster; that is a disaster waiting to happen.

DOG—A dog gets along well with a horse as they share many personality traits. A dog and a monkey also make good friends because their differing personalities seem to balance each other out. However, a dog should not be paired with a dragon; a dragon is too showy for the serious dog.

PIG—A pig and a rat are compatible, although a rat may take advantage of a gullible pig. A pig and a goat can share many interests, but the best companion for a pig is probably a rooster. Two pigs should never try to establish a relationship; it won't work.

Only the Beginning

I have touched on the very basics of Chinese astrology; there is much more to learn and master. If you're interested in more detail about this science, see the resources in Appendix D: Resources.

NUMEROLOGY

My birth name is Elizabeth Anne, and as a child I was called Betty. For as long as I can remember, I didn't like the name Betty. I don't know why, but I always felt it didn't suit me. Finally, when I started high school, I informed everyone I knew that my name was Liz and it has remained that way. Liz suits me, fits me, and is comfortable. Why the problem with a name? Our name, and our dog's name, is who we are. I have nothing against the name Betty; it just wasn't me.

More than 2,500 years ago, in Greece, Pythagoras and his followers believed that the essence of everything, from a tree to a concept (such as justice) was a number, and that everything could be expressed through numbers. Numerology is a science that converts everything about you to simple numbers.

Today, several different systems of numerology are in use. One is based upon Pythagoras's system. It analyzes the person's given birth name, in my case Elizabeth Anne or in my dog Kes's case, Watachie's Empathic Kes, her AKC registered name. The Chaldean method uses the name a person is best known by; in my case now, Liz, or in Kes's case, simply Kes. There are other differences in each system, of course, and the practice of each can be quite sophisticated. I'll explain a simplified version of numerology that you can use without a calculator.

Meanings of the Numbers

Numbers say a lot about us. Read on.

NUMBER 1—One is the center and leader of the cosmos. It signifies leadership, originality, and independence. One's colors are yellow, gold, and orange, and one's gemstones are topaz and amber.

NUMBER 2—Two tends to see both sides of each issue and tries to have things both ways. A two is very social and versatile; he tries to make peace wherever he goes. Two's colors are green and cream, and his gemstones are jade and pearl.

NUMBER 3—Three is versatile and busy; he's got a finger in a lot of pies. A three is creative, imaginative, artistic, and good-natured. A three likes purples, lilacs, and mauves. Three's gemstone, of course, is amethyst.

NUMBER 4—Four tends to be a worrier, and he prefers to live life in the slow lane. A four is practical, stable, and dependable. The colors of a four are blue and gray, and the gemstone is a sapphire.

NUMBER 5—Five hates to waste time; he also craves stimulation and dislikes boredom. A five is energetic, resourceful, and productive. Five's colors are gray and white, and his gemstone is diamond.

NUMBER 6—Six is a romantic. Six loves love itself and loves to be loved. He is family-oriented, compassionate, and considerate. Six's colors are blue-greens, and the gemstone is emerald.

NUMBER 7—Seven likes to stimulate his mind; inner searching is his quest. He's intellectual, imaginative, and psychically oriented. A seven's color is green, and the gemstone is moonstone.

NUMBER 8—Eight will experience the highs and lows of life; extremes are the norm. Materialistic, an eight can be strong-willed and strong-minded. His colors are black and black-purple and his gemstones are ruby and amethyst.

NUMBER 9—Nine is a caring soul. Nines are humanitarians who desire to save everyone and everything. In keeping with his preference for red, a nine's gemstone is bloodstone.

Your Destiny Numbers

Your destiny number and your dog's destiny number reflect the life lessons you will each experience during your lifetimes. Obviously, your destiny number is very important.

To calculate the numbers, write down the date of your birthday. For example, I was born on the 11th day of April (the 4th month) 1954, so I will write each number down and add all the single digits together:

$$1 + 1 + 4 + 1 + 9 + 5 + 4 = 25$$

I will then add the numbers that appear in the previous total (25), to arrive at a single digit.

$$2 + 5 = 7$$

My destiny number is then number 7.

I can do the same thing for my dog Riker. He was born on the 20th of April 1999.

$$2 + 0 + 4 + 1 + 9 + 9 + 9 = 34$$

I will then add the numbers in the result.

$$3 + 4 = 7$$

Riker and I share the destiny number 7. That doesn't surprise me at all, and it shouldn't you, after reading about him in this book. He is a wise soul and quite mystical.

Your Zodiac Numbers

Each of the twelve sun signs of the zodiac is associated with a number. Find your zodiac number and your dog's, and then jot them down. I'll return to them in a minute. The zodiac numbers are:

Aries:	9	*Libra:*	6
Taurus:	6	*Scorpio:*	9
Gemini:	5	*Sagittarius:*	3
Cancer:	2	*Capricorn:*	8
Leo:	1	*Aquarius:*	4
Virgo:	5	*Pisces:*	7

Often, your zodiac number is the same as, or is complementary to, your destiny number. (You may find, however, that this number is opposite your destiny number. Such opposition can cause discord and upheaval throughout your lifetime.)

What Is the Number of a Name?

Your name is who you are. I often wonder if I didn't want the name Betty because Betty is a number 9 and in numerological terms (as I'll show you in a moment), number 9 doesn't work well for me with my other numbers. Liz, however, is a 2, which is much more compatible with my destiny number of 7.

To obtain the number of your name, you'll need to use the conversion table of letters to numbers that follows.

CONVERSION TABLE

1	2	3	4	5	6	7	8	9
A	B	C	D	E	F	G	H	I
J	K	L	M	N	O	P	Q	R
S	T	U	V	W	X	Y	Z	

To convert names into numbers, write down the number above each letter. For example, Betty converts to 2 + 5 + 2 + 2 + 7 = 18. Any two-digit number is then reduced to a single digit, so 18 becomes 1 + 8 = 9.

Liz converts to 3 + 9 + 8 = 20, which reduces to 2 + 0 = 2.

Riker converts to 9 + 9 + 2 + 5 + 9 = 34, which reduces to 7.

Combine Your Numbers

By combining your destiny number, zodiac number, and name number, you can come up with one number. This one number represents you best.

If I add my destiny number of 7, my zodiac number of 9, and my name number of 2, I get the following result:

$$7 + 9 + 2 = 18$$

The two-digit number needs to be reduced.

$$1 + 8 = 9$$

So the number that best represents me is number 9.

To discover Riker's numbers, I'll add his destiny number of 7, his zodiac number of 9, and his name number of 7.

$$7 + 9 + 7 = 23$$

I will reduce the result to a one-digit number.

$$2 + 3 = 5$$

The number that best represents Riker is 5.

There's no doubt in my mind that our numbers suit us. Look back at the meanings of the numbers for a moment. What do you think?

CHOOSING A NAME THAT YOUR DOG CAN LIVE WITH

When a new puppy or dog joins your household, get to know him before you name him. Ask yourself if any names you have in mind seem to fit his personality. Then, calculate each name's number and analyze how the name combines with his destiny number and zodiac number. Does the final number suit the essence of this dog? If not, don't use that name. Try a different name.

Going Further with Numerology

I've presented a very simple explanation of numerology. If you find the field of numerology as fascinating as I do, you'll want to learn more about making calculations and analyzing numbers. For more information, see Appendix D: Resources.

YOUR DOG'S AURA

An aura is an electromagnetic energy field that surrounds all living things. In chapter 8 I mentioned that homeopathic medicine works because even when a substance is greatly diluted, it still leaves behind an energy "footprint," and it's this footprint that makes the diluted medicine so effective. This is very similar to the energy field, or aura, that surrounds living things. Many people can actually see this energy field, whereas we cannot see the energy "footprint" except with specialized tools.

The aura that surrounds living things is much like a cloud that extends away from the body. It is usually in layers of colors, and the size and denseness of the cloud varies from individual to individual. In addition, the clarity with which you'll see an aura depends largely upon your devotion to practicing.

Most people see an aura as a light, a colored light, that encompasses each living thing. The colors are representative of each individual's behavior, personality, and being. A healthy individual usually has a stronger, denser aura than someone who is less healthy, emotionally, physically, or spiritually.

Understanding Aura Color

Each color of an aura has significance, just as color does to light therapy and color therapy, which I discussed in the previous chapter.

BLUE—Blues are nurturers and caretakers. People with a blue aura are often found in the health care fields, and dogs with a blue aura make excellent therapy dogs. Blues are sensitive, intuitive, and emotional.

EARTH TONES AND BROWNS—Those who give off an earth tone aura are grounded, practical, and logical. Earth tones are often very physical and have a tendency to be nonverbal. Earth tone dogs will move heaven and earth for their owner but will not be communicative about it.

GREEN—Greens are intellectuals and do not act on impulse. One with a green aura will think something through thoroughly. Greens dislike exertion, and green dogs should never be asked to participate in physically demanding sports.

ORANGE—Those who give off an orange aura are those who like to push themselves physically. They're athletes and explorers. Orange dogs benefit greatly from participating in dog sports and activities.

PURPLE—Those with a purple aura are psychic, spiritual, and intelligent. Purples want to make a difference in the world, and they want their time in this life to mean something. Dogs that have purple auras strive to be the best at whatever task is laid before them.

RED—Red, as always, is a strong color. It is very physical, and those who give off red auras enjoy physical activities. Reds are confident, strong, and are often leaders and teachers. Red dogs are leaders of the pack.

YELLOW—Those with a yellow aura are joyful; they love life and live to experience it. Yellows can be impatient, though, and are sometimes a little pushy. Yellow dogs have fun with life; their owners had better like to play!

Seeing Your Dog's Aura

Learning to see your dog's aura takes some practice, but most people are able to learn to do it. Invite your dog to join you in your quiet place. Turn on a light so that the room is well lit but not overly bright. Ask your dog to lie down on the floor about five to ten feet away from you. A white background—a white wall or white sheet—behind your dog will help you in the beginning.

Sit down on the floor facing your dog and relax. Your dog can go to sleep if he likes. As you relax, breathe deeply but normally. Don't stare at your dog, and don't try to "see" the aura. Instead, relax, blur your eyesight slightly, and look at the white background behind your dog.

You will begin to see slight colors—not like a crayon—but instead, subtle colors like very diluted watercolor paints. When you begin to see the colors, don't get excited and try to stare at them; they'll disappear. Remember, the colors are given off by electromagnetic energy, and you really can't see that with your naked eyes. That's why you're looking at the white background.

When you see the colors, make a mental note of what they are. Your dog may have more than one color in his aura. It may be yellow all around him with some blue around his head; or it may be blue all around him with a brown ring outside of that. Just remember the colors. A dog who is healthy mentally, emotionally, spiritually, and physically will give off a clear, wide aura. A dog with problems in any of those areas will have a weaker aura; it will lay close to him, and the colors may appear dull or muddy.

DREAMING ABOUT DREAMS

In this section, I'll be discussing the dreaming that occurs during sleep, not daydreaming. Daydreaming is affected too much by your conscious mind whereas dreaming during sleep reflects everything going on in your life.

Dreams have long been given importance, especially in decision making. Shamans, medicine men, religious leaders, and the leaders of armies often used dreams to give them guidance. Many shamans and medicine men would induce dreams by entering a trance, or a dream state, or by ingesting or smoking hallucinogenic substances to bring on dreams.

The fact that people dream during the REM (rapid eye movement) stage of sleep is not controversial; however, the interpretation of dreams as messages from our subconscious (or beyond) has been debated long and hard. Some argue that these messages are real and should be listened to carefully. Others contend that our dreams are simply subconscious thoughts that are affected by our day, our activities, or even what we've eaten before going to bed.

To find out what you've been dreaming, put a pad of paper and a pen next to your bed within easy reach. If you wake up during the night, relax for a moment and think about your dreams. Did you dream at all? What do you remember? Do the same thing when you wake up in the morning. Do you remember anything? If so, write it down immediately. In your notes, answer the following questions:

1. When did you dream? Day and time.
2. Was it pleasurable or a nightmare?
3. Did the dream focus on any particular time period?
4. What was the dream about?

Don't try to remember what you dreamed later in the day. Dreams don't remain in our awareness for long, and attenuated recollections are generally distorted by our conscious thoughts. You'll have the most accurate memory of a dream right after you wake up.

Many of the things we dream about have been accorded special meaning. Sometimes, of course, when we dream about something, it is actually about that particular thing. For example, if you buy a new car and you're worried about the car payment, you may actually dream about that car.

On the other hand, our dreams may be representative of our needs, fears, or desires. If you dream about dogs (in general, rather than your own dogs), you may be dreaming about the need for loyalty from someone or protection. If you dream about dogs playing, the dream may be reflecting your own social nature or mood. A dog alone in a dream may suggest your feeling of loneliness.

Of course, this is a very brief discourse on the significance of dreams. If you want to read more about interpreting your own dreams, see the resources in Appendix D: Resources.

When Your Dog Dreams

We know that dogs dream, but what do they dream about? The only way to find out is to ask your dog. If you were able to establish psychic communication with your dog, as I discussed in chapter 3, then you can ask him about his dreams, but note: Getting an accurate image of your dog's dreams is a delicate task. You don't want to distort the dream by your questions, and most importantly, you don't want to alarm your dog. After all, dreams are very normal, regardless of their content. You don't want your dog to worry.

To find out about your dog's dreams, practice your psychic communication. Make sure you can ask him questions, verbally, and receive his answers. Practice receiving his answers so that if you receive a visualization that is different or out of the ordinary, you won't doubt yourself.

Then, when you find your dog dreaming, sit down nearby and wait for him to wake up. Don't wake him; that could interrupt the flow of the dream and annoy him to boot. When he awakens, ask him if he remembers his dream. If he does, ask him what he saw, smelled, or heard. Most dogs seem to have dreams that use several senses, unlike our primarily visual dreams.

Write down the information he gives you, using his way of describing what he saw, smelled, or heard. Don't include any of your own thoughts.

Some commonly accepted dream interpretations include:

BEING CHASED WHILE RUNNING—This represents feeling stuck in a situation, unable to escape.

BIRDS—Birds represent freedom. A dog chasing a flying bird he cannot catch may be frustrated. A dog chasing a flying bird who suddenly takes to the air himself may be having an out-of-body experience, or may simply be enjoying the freedom.

CATS—Cats, sitting still and ignoring a dog, represent potential conflict. A fighting cat represents an ongoing conflict. A cat that is running away is leading the dog into trouble.

FEELING HEAVY—A heavy feeling usually represents a feeling of being overwhelmed and unable to find a way out from under burdens. It is associated with depression.

FOOD—Dogs who dream about food are usually satisfied with life, and are enjoying their situation.

INSECTS—Large flying insects represent a problem that the dog cannot solve without help. Ants represent anxiety.

RAIN—Rain may represent an issue that remains unsettled.

RUNNING FREE—Running free represents a feeling of freedom, liberation, or joy.

SUNSHINE—Sunny weather is always a positive sign and usually forecasts optimism and good fortune.

TREES—Trees tend to signify strength and determination, a powerful desire to prove oneself. It is not surprising that to a male dog they also represent a mark of territory, much like a fence post or a signpost.

WIND—Strong winds with sunshine simply suggest that things are moving quickly. Strong winds with rain mean a problem is escalating out of control.

Your dog may also have some ideas as to what his dreams mean. Perhaps he dreamed about a rabbit because he chased one a week before, and it was fun. He may have dreamed about food because he ate too much before going to sleep. Not all dreams have mysterious meanings; you'll have to communicate with your dog to find out.

Chapter 11

IS DEATH THE END?

Thirty days after we were married, my husband, Paul, received orders overseas. The U.S. Marine Corps wasn't particularly concerned about his status as a newlywed; in fact, a favorite Marine Corps comment was, "If the Marine Corps wanted you to have a wife, you would have been issued one."

Off he went to serve aboard ship, stopping in Japan and Okinawa. Finding myself alone, especially right after our wedding, was not a pleasant experience. I was an emotional mess and realized that I needed to do something concrete to ground myself. So I got a dog. I saw an ad in the newspaper about a litter of German Shepherd puppies that had been abandoned by a road in rural Poway. I went to see the puppies, fell in love right away, and took home Watachie.

Watachie roughly translates as "I, myself, me"—what I thought was an appropriate name for a sick, worm-infested, underfed puppy with a lot of attitude. Hundreds of dollars in vet bills later, Watachie began to overcome the effects of his rough start in life and quickly grew up to be a handsome, black and cream German Shepherd.

We went to dog training class where Watachie was the youngest dog in the group, but he graduated in first place. We competed in obedience trials where he often placed first or second and, in fact, we accumulated quite a trophy collection. He learned to pull a wagon, competed in Frisbee catch contests, herded sheep, and did everything I ever asked of him. As an adult, he even became a certified search and rescue dog with finds to his credit.

Watachie and I became great friends; I felt that we were literally soul mates. Unfortunately, at the age of seven, Watachie began suffering from a series of small strokes. Each stroke appeared unannounced, and each one did some damage. After a few months, the damage to Watachie's brain started to become apparent. He lost some memory and became fearful, not understanding what was happening in his head.

I took him to veterinarian after veterinarian, and even called a vet I knew three thousand miles away. There were no treatments for Watachie. His brain damage seemed to get increasingly severe over time. Physically, Watachie appeared fine. A photo I took of him the weekend before we lost him shows a handsome, stocky, athletic, and physically strong dog. However, when I looked into his eyes, I could see that the Watachie I knew and loved was gone and in his place was a frightened and confused dog. I took him to the vet's office, held his head, told him, "Good-bye," and let the vet give him a shot.

I cried for days. I felt guilty that I had killed my dog. I knew logically that I had done the right thing, but that logic didn't help me emotionally. Finally, I sat down, shook myself, and took a look at my own beliefs. Why was I so upset? Well, because I felt guilty and missed my dog, but don't I believe that we will meet again? Yes, I do, and I believe that strongly. So why was I upset? Because I missed my dog! Obviously, I was working in a vicious circle.

I started doing some research and talking to other dog owners. Of course, our beliefs differed, often in connection with our religious affiliations. Nonetheless, I found that most dog owners do believe they will see their dogs again, either in this lifetime or the next, or in an afterlife. As someone who had just lost a dog, I found these thoughts reassuring.

MANAGING AGING AND DEATH

My husband and I keep tortoises as well as our dogs, and many of our tortoises have a natural life span of seventy to one hundred years. Now, the tortoises are great fun and are very undemanding pets; however, I will never have a relationship with a tortoise like I have with my dogs. With all due respect for my tortoises, it seems very unfair that my dog may live fourteen years, while a tortoise lives one hundred.

Because I cannot change this very unfair fact, I have come to terms with the fact that I must just deal with it. I do so by treasuring the time I have with my dogs. Watachie was the first dog I had lost; all of the other dogs I had known well had belonged to my mother. Although those dogs tolerated us kids, they were not our dogs. Watachie, though, was my dog and losing him caused a hurt I had never felt before. I was determined that all future dogs would be loved and valued and enjoyed during their time with me, so that when it came time to lose them, I wouldn't feel so robbed and cheated.

That was a good thought, and loving and treasuring my dogs has certainly not been difficult, but nothing makes losing them any easier.

Michi, our second German Shepherd, also died too young—at the age of eight—and losing him was tough, too. Other dogs have followed, each of whom was able to live a long (for a dog), full life, each well loved through his or her lifetime, but all were missed horribly when it was their turn to leave us.

A DEAR OLD FRIEND

There is nothing quite like an old dog. A dog who has spent his lifetime with you may well know you better than you know yourself. He knows your moods, your likes and dislikes, and your sense of humor. An old dog may not be able to play or work as he once did, but he's a treasure nonetheless. An old dog should be loved and cared for as if he were the finest jewel—because he is.

Your Aging Dog

As your dog grows older, his body ages, slows down, and stiffens. Joints get creaky and don't work as well as they once did. Muscles atrophy, and he will find that he's not as strong as he was in his youth. His ability to see and hear diminish. Internal organs don't function as well, and liver, kidney, and heart diseases appear. Cancer, too, is a scourge of old dogs.

Your veterinarian, whether he practices traditional medicine or alternative medicine (or both), will be of tremendous help to you now. Regular visits will enable your vet to see aging problems as they begin, so that when medicine can help, it can be started early. Regular blood tests will keep you up-to-date as to the state of your dog's internal organs. Your vet, too, may suggest some things to help your old dog.

There are medicines to improve the function of the heart and kidneys. Your alternative vet may recommend some herbal or homeopathic remedies. Working with your vet (or vets) can be an expensive proposition, but it is always a good idea.

You can also help keep your old dog comfortable as he ages. Ursa, one of my Australian Shepherds, lived to fourteen and only had health problems in the last year of her life. Up until then, she was active (if a little slower over time), but I also worked to keep her healthy. She ate a very good natural diet that was appropriately supplemented, and she determined her activity level on a day-to-day basis. If she was stiff and sore, we took things slowly. If she was warm and limber, we did a little more.

"Treatments" for your aging dog come in a variety of forms. They include:

ACUPRESSURE/ACUPUNCTURE—Try acupressure or acupuncture for the effective relief of the discomfort of arthritis.

EXERCISE—Although exercise for an old dog is not the vigorous workout your dog probably enjoyed when he was younger, it is still important. Keep him moving, even if it's just a walk up and down the block. Not only is the exercise good for him, but he also needs to get out of the house. Let the neighbors and neighborhood kids say hi to him and let the new neighbor's puppy kiss him on the muzzle.

HERBAL—Gingko is very useful for helping keep an older dog mentally sharp, and at least in the early stages of senile dementia, it can help slow the process. Chamomile and peppermint can both soothe the older dog's sensitive stomach. Dandelion and hawthorn can help the kidneys' ability to remove wastes from the bloodstream.

HOMEOPATHIC—The flower essence olive stimulates the adrenal glands and keeps energy levels high. Hawthorn steadies and strengthens the heart, and as it does, it increases the blood flow.

MASSAGE—A daily massage will keep an older dog's blood flowing and will help alleviate some of the stiffness that comes with old age. It's great for lessening aches and pains. Your touch is also very important and is healing in itself.

NUTRITION—Feed a diet designed specifically for old dogs or a home-cooked diet. Aging dogs do not always digest food well, so add a little yogurt with live active cultures to the daily diet. Watch your dog's weight; older dogs often tend to put on weight as they exercise less, and the excess weight is hard on the body.

SUPPLEMENTS—Glucosamine and chondroitin help keep the joints healthy. A B-complex vitamin once per day helps a dog keep a positive attitude—the thiamin (B1) in B-complex is called the "morale" vitamin for just that reason. Kelp is an excellent source of minerals and is good for arthritis.

YOUR TIME—It is very easy to let the old dog relax and let life move on around him; however, don't forget about or ignore your old dog. Even though he can't go jogging with you, he still needs your time and companionship. He needs you to sit beside him, pet him, massage him; and talk to him. Even if you simply share memories with him, "Hey, Buck, do you remember when we went camping and you saw your first deer? That was a great trip." Continue to treasure each other's companionship.

When It's Time to Say Good-bye

Dogs rarely make saying good-bye easy. I have said good-bye to several treasured canine companions, and only three of them died naturally. For all the others, I had to make the decision as to when to let them go. It's always a very hard thing to do. Yet allowing a dog to die naturally is hard, too. So how do you decide?

Euthanasia, which in many dictionaries is defined as "the good death," is performed with an overdose of an anesthetic. The veterinarian gives the dog an injection, he goes to sleep, and his heart and breathing stop. It is usually very quiet, very calm, and peaceful. I am always there with my dogs (and cats) when they are euthanized, as I want them to be comfortable, to feel safe, and to know they are loved.

With my own pets, I try to wait until they indicate that it's time. When a dog is old, when his organs are failing, and he has no desire to continue, he will usually let you know. If he cannot psychically communicate with you, he will tell you by his attitude and actions. I knew it was time for Ursa when she refused to come in the house. She had lost bladder control and was very upset when she leaked in the house. I tried hard to reassure her it was no problem, but she was just as adamant that she wouldn't break housetraining. At the same time, she was tired. Her whole being emitted a sense of utter exhaustion. When I took her to the veterinarian and said good-bye, her eyes told me thank-you and she was gone.

Some people cannot make the decision, or carry through with the decision, to euthanize a well-loved pet. A friend of mine thinks that euthanasia is wrong, and her pets live until they die naturally. That is the right decision for her, and I respect that as long as the pet is not suffering. Unfortunately, natural death can be unpleasant, painful, and prolonged for an old, sick dog. If you decide that you would prefer to let your dog live until natural death claims him, work with your veterinarian to keep your dog comfortable and pain-free. That's the least you can do for him.

LOOK FOR THESE SIGNS

Dogs who are failing often show one or more of the following signs:
- *Breathing heavily or rapid breathing through the mouth*
- *Extreme weakness or exhaustion*
- *Lowered body temperature and refusal of warmth*
- *Mental confusion*
- *Refusal to eat or extreme thirst*
- *Staring off into space*

At the Moment of Physical Death

Many people have said that they know exactly when their dog died because they felt their dog's soul leave his physical body. It is often described as a "whoosh" or something like a small breeze.

I have to admit I have never had this experience. However, I know when my dogs (and cats) have died because I can feel it inside. I feel a certain emptiness, like there is a spot inside me that is now hollow. It's as if the dog's life force was attached to me in a certain spot, and when that life force is gone, I can feel it.

After Your Dog Dies

After your dog dies, you will cry, you may scream, and you may even get angry. Grieving is natural and it goes through many stages, of which crying, denial, anger, and acceptance are all a part. Don't try to stop the grieving process; it won't go away. Oh, you may bury it for a while but the embers will still smolder, and one day when your defenses are weak, it will reappear. Instead, let grief take its course.

As you grieve, avoid those people who don't understand. After losing Watachie, I almost lost my temper when a well-meaning (I suppose) acquaintance said, "Why are you so upset? It was only a dog." I swallowed my temper and told myself, "Obviously he has never loved and been loved by a dog." People who are not sensitive to your loss will not help your grieving process at all. Instead, spend time with people who understand. Of course, no one can make your dog young again; however, a hug or pat on the back and a soft, "I'm so sorry" can be very comforting.

Have you thought about what you want done with your dog's body? If you live in a rural area, you might be able to bury your dog at home. Because most cities and counties prohibit burying pets in the backyard, this is not an option for many people. You can have your dog buried in a pet cemetery, if there is one near you, or you can have your pet cremated. My husband and I have had our pets cremated, and we sprinkle our pets' ashes in the rose garden. We have a ceremony to say a final good-bye, and when the rose bushes bloom later, we can treasure our pets again. "Paul come look! Ursa's rosebush is blooming wonderfully this spring."

Ceremonies, of whatever kind you decide is right for you, give you a chance to bring closure to your grief. A ceremony gives you an opportunity to admit—to yourself and the world—that your dog is really gone. And that sense of closure is needed so that you can move on through your grief.

Your ceremony may be like mine. Perhaps you will sprinkle your pet's ashes under a tree or in a favorite meadow. You can invite some dog-loving friends over for coffee and share memories. You may take a walk where you and your dog liked to walk. It really doesn't matter what the ceremony is, you just need to perform it, and you need to view the ceremony as your last good-bye. With this ceremony, you are letting your dog go.

IS THAT ALL THERE IS?

When you let your dog's physical being pass, and you say your last farewell, is that really all there is? Is that the end? Will you no longer see him?

The doctrine of some religions provides answers to these questions. As I stated in chapter 4, the belief of many organized religions is that animals have no souls, and therefore are not admitted to heaven or to the hereafter. Personally, to me, if heaven is supposed to be the best of everything, the place where ultimate joy is achieved, then it won't be heaven if my dogs are not there.

That is my belief. What is yours? If you belong to an organized religion, you may want to talk to the minister or priest of your church about the role of animals and pets in your belief system, but don't be surprised if he doesn't support the sense that animals have a spiritual nature. If your dog is important to you and you feel he must be included in your belief system, super, do so. After all, who knows who has the "right" answer?

HE MAY BE BACK

Kathy lost her Doberman, King, a few years ago. King was Kathy's friend, companion, protector, and soul mate. He went everywhere with her, including to work, and their twelve years together were wonderful. When King died of cardiomyopathy, Kathy was devastated. She vowed to never again love a dog. I told her that was a natural response but to wait a while, she might change her mind.

Several months later Kathy called me and she had a funny sound to her voice. "Liz, I just brought home a new puppy," she said, "And I think it's King!" She continued by saying that she hadn't been looking for a dog but someone handed her this mixed-breed puppy. When she looked into the puppy's eyes, she said, "I know this dog." She didn't yet recognize him as King; she just had a feeling that she had met this dog before. However, when she took the puppy home and set him down on the floor, he immediately went to all of King's favorite places. She said she followed him as he went to each room, sniffed various things, checked out the dog bed and the dog toys, and then went to the door asking to go outside. She let him out and followed him. He went straight to King's favorite spots, relieved himself where King always went, and then asked to go back inside. When they sat down together, Kathy said it was if the puppy had said, "Okay, everything's accounted for and is where it should be."

Now, you could argue that the puppy simply followed King's scent and investigated those places that smelled strongly of King, and indeed, he may have done just that. But that's not what Kathy believes and no one will change her mind. She knows deep in her heart that King was reincarnated and that he came back to her.

Kathy isn't the only dog owner to feel this way. Many dog owners have marveled over the fact that their new dog Brownie seems to know things and do things that their old dog Jojo used to do. Some do put two and two together and figure out that hey, maybe Brownie used to be Jojo. Others don't make that connection and simply enjoy the coincidence.

Reincarnation is not a new belief, nor is it a New Age belief. People of many religions, including Hindus and Buddhists, have long believed that a soul is not just here for one short lifetime, but instead is here for many. Most Native American cultures, including the Cherokee, believe that people and animals will come back in one form or another and not necessarily in the same form. A man, for example, may come back as a bear or an elk, or even a much smaller animal such as a rabbit.

Many organized religions teach their followers that believers have an immortal soul. At birth, the immortal soul enters the body and remains in that body throughout the lifetime, leaving at the moment of death to journey to heaven. Does that concept sound familiar to you? If you said yes, then the idea of reincarnation shouldn't sound too strange. If the soul can enter and live in one body, why not more than one? Why can't the soul live several or many lifetimes?

Most cultures that believe in reincarnation also believe that life occurs for a reason, that we have lessons to learn during our time on earth, lessons to teach, or goals to accomplish. If those goals are achieved, we move on to the next level of existence after the death of that physical body. If the goals are not met, we will be back in the next lifetime to see if we can get it right.

Although many people feel that we are reincarnated in order to grow spiritually, others believe we share reincarnated lifetimes with our pets simply to relive our closeness to them. In other words, King came back to Kathy because he wanted to, because she missed him, and they had had a warm, loving relationship.

Diane Stein's *Natural Healing for Dogs & Cats,* quotes the psychic Laurel Steinhice: "Animals do reincarnate in tandem with their human companions. The closer the interspecies bonding, the more frequent the reincarnation is to occur. When your beloved companion lets you know she is considering leaving this body behind, it is a loving kindness to let her know you understand, and that you will welcome her into a new body, a new incarnation in which her spirit can continue to share a close bonding with you."

PAST LIVES

It is usually accepted by most believers of reincarnation that a baby (or puppy) comes into this world remembering his past lives. However, as the reality of this lifetime intrudes and produces its own memories, the memories of past lives fade. It is a rare individual who can retain those memories.

FINDING YOUR OWN ANSWERS

Until we have concrete proof that there is or is not something after death of the physical body, all we have are our beliefs.

You must look inside yourself and find the answers that comfort you. Personally, I firmly believe that physical death is not the end of my treasured canine and feline companions. I will see them again. When and where I see them is my secret; I have my beliefs. What are yours?

APPENDIX A: GLOSSARY OF TERMS

Acupoints—Points on the body where pressure is applied in the practice of acupressure or where needles are inserted in acupuncture.

Acupressure—A healing technique in which massage and pressure are used to promote healing, similar to acupuncture.

Acupuncture—An ancient Chinese healing art whereby specifically placed needles affect healing and change.

Aggression—Behavior that is threatening to another dog or a person; a type of socially unacceptable behavior. Protective behavior.

Allopathy—A method of medical practice that seeks to produce conditions unlike those produced by the disease treated.

Alternative—A method of medical practice or a drug that produces a healthful change in condition, which can be observed but not scientifically substantiated.

Analgesic—A pain-relieving substance.

Anaphylactic shock—A severe and sometimes fatal allergic reaction.

Anesthetic—Reduces painful sensitivity, locally or generally.

Anodyne—A pain reliever.

Antibacterial—Effective against bacteria.

Antibody—Molecules made by the body to fight antigens, toxins, or foreign substances.

Anti-inflammatory—Decreases swelling.

Antioxidant—Controls or eliminates free radicals or reduces cellular oxidation.

Antiparasitic—Expels, repels, kills, or inhibits reproduction of parasites.

Antiseptic—Stops putrification and infection.

Aromatic—Having a pleasing or stimulating smell.

Astringent—Causes tissues to contract.

Astrology—The science of the relationship of the stars, sun, and planets to an individual's affairs and characteristics.

Aura—The electromagnetic energy field that surrounds all living things. Often seen as colors.

Biotin—A water-soluble vitamin in the B-complex family.

Bitter tonic—A solution that stimulates digestive functions, first in the mouth, and then in the stomach and liver.

Capsaicin—The primary active ingredient of cayenne pepper.

Carcinogen—A substance that promotes the growth of cancer.

Chlorophyll—Green pigment in plants that allows them to photosynthesize.

Deciduous—A plant that loses leaves in the winter.

Decoction—An herbal preparation made by simmering plant material in water until maximum extraction is achieved.

Detergent—Cleansing, as to skin infections or abscesses.

Diuretic—Increases the flow of urine.

Emolient—Softens and soothes inflamed skin.

Flavonoid—A chemical compound found in some plants that is responsible for many medicinal actions. Usually found in red, yellow, or purple fruits.

Flower essence—Made from flower petals; also called flower remedies.

Homeopathy—The practice of administering highly diluted organic compounds for healing purposes. The goal of homeopathic medicine is to effect a desired response by stimulating body systems at a very low level, even at the molecular level.

Homeostasis—A maintained state of health in which the individual's mind, body, and spirit are all functioning together in balance.

Immuno-stimulant—Anything that strengthens the immune system; often an herb.

Infusion—A preparation made by pouring boiling water over an herb and allowing it to steep; a tea.

Medicinal action—The effect an herb or other substance has on the body.

Numerology—The science of numbers and their meanings.

Poultice—An herbal preparation made by combining mashed plant materials with a liquid (usually water) to make a paste.

Pro-biotics—Friendly bacteria or enzymes that support natural digestive functions.

Sedative—Causes sleep.

Signs—The signs of the zodiac, or astrological signs; often called sun signs; represent the position of the sun in the skies at the moment of birth.

Styptic—Stops bleeding.

Tincture—An herbal preparation made by soaking plant material in liquid (usually alcohol, glycerin, or vinegar) to extract the medicinal properties.

Tonic—A remedy that is invigorating and stimulating.

Vaccinosis—Illness resulting from vaccination.

APPENDIX B: REMEDIES FOR YOUR DOG

Although many people think that natural or alternative medicine may be simpler than modern medicine, which therapy to use isn't always an obvious choice. There are many options available.

SPECIFIC TREATMENTS FOR SPECIFIC PROBLEMS

Listed below are some remedies recommended by a variety of holistic professionals. Although these are effective remedies, you should select those that you're comfortable with and that you believe are the best choices for you and your dog.

This list of remedies is based upon the assumption that your dog is eating a good diet of quality food. Accordingly, a good diet is not included as a remedy unless it is of particular importance. It is also assumed that you and your dog have a good relationship, with good communication and understanding.

Each item is very brief. For more detailed information about each suggestion, see the main body of this book.

Abandoned Dogs, Adopted Dogs, and Rescued Dogs

NUTRITION/SUPPLEMENT—Add a B-complex vitamin to the diet.

HERBAL—St. John's Wort is nature's Prozac and is very good for calming nervous, anxious dogs.

HOMEOPATHIC—Flower essence pine eases the pain of rejection; while flower essence star-of-Bethlehem alleviates past fears. Rescue Remedy is always good for anxiety. Gorse helps ease grief.

ACUPRESSURE/MASSAGE—Massage daily; a gentle, whole-body massage. Touch is very healing.

OTHER THERAPIES—An amethyst gemstone on the dog's collar or hidden in his bed will elevate the dog's spirits. An aquamarine promotes peace and emphasizes courage.

Aggression

NUTRITION/SUPPLEMENTS—Make sure the dog is on a good diet that is high in protein and low in carbohydrates; meat should be the first ingredient and preferably the first two ingredients of any commercial food. Add a B-complex vitamin to the diet.

HERBAL—St. John's Wort is an herbal Prozac and works very well for many aggressive dogs.

HOMEOPATHIC—Flower essence holly helps a short-tempered dog become a little more accepting of the world around him. A combination of flower essences walnut, chestnut, beech, willow, and holly will help ease aggressive tendencies. Rescue Remedy is also usually effective when the dog is in a temper. Vine is good for overly dominant dogs.

AROMATIC—The scent of bergamot on your dog's collar, renewed every two to three hours, will ease aggressive tendencies.

ACUPRESSURE/MASSAGE—Massage gently over the entire body daily to utilize your healing touch. While you are massaging, make sure you repeat the ear stroke, gently running fingers and thumb from the base of the ear down the earflap to the tip.

OTHER THERAPIES—Good vigorous exercise is often very effective for letting aggressive dogs work off excess energy. A good run, a fast-paced game of catch-the-tennis-ball, or other strenuous exercise should be done daily. Emphasize leadership exercises and reinforcement of the standard obedience exercises. Aggression is probably the most taxing behavior of any dog, and many are given up because of it. Don't hesitate to call a professional trainer or behaviorist if you need help.

Aging

NUTRITION/SUPPLEMENTS—Feed either a diet specifically for older dogs or a home-cooked diet. Watch the dog's weight, as older dogs gain weight easily. Start the dog on glucosamine chondroitin to help keep joints healthy. Add a B-complex vitamin to the diet.

HOMEOPATHIC—Flower essence olive stimulates the adrenal glands and maintains energy levels, while hawthorn steadies and strengthens the heart and increases blood flow.

ACUPRESSURE/MASSAGE—A daily massage will help to maintain good circulation and aid in preventing stiffness. It will also reassure an old, confused dog.

OTHER THERAPIES—Appropriate daily exercise will help keep the dog limber and fit. An amethyst gemstone on the dog's collar or hidden in his bed will elevate the dog's spirits.

Allergies (Inhalant and Contact)

Note: See your veterinarian about allergy tests.

NUTRITION/SUPPLEMENTS—Feed a good quality, natural, commercial food or home-cooked food. Avoid giving your dog preservatives and additives to the best of your ability. Five hundred to 1,000 milligrams of vitamin C can help keep the system strong.

HERBAL—Keep the immune system strong by giving the dog echinacea throughout the allergy season. Also during that time, give your dog tea made from dried nettle; it is an excellent antihistamine. A poultice made from oatmeal is very calming and soothing for the skin. A wash made from calendula tea is also very soothing.

HOMEOPATHIC—A combination of flower essences walnut, olive, crab apple, and beech is very good for allergies.

ACUPRESSURE/MASSAGE—Massage your dog daily, making sure you hit the acupressure points for allergies. One point is on the outside of the elbow of the front leg, where the leg bends. The other is at the base of the skull, between the spine and the base of the ear on each side of the head.

Allergies (Food)

Note: See your veterinarian for allergy tests.

NUTRITION/SUPPLEMENTS—Feed a good quality food that does not contain ingredients causing the allergy. If feeding a commercial food, you may want to call the manufacturer for details.

HERBAL—Keep the immune system strong by giving the dog echinacea when inadvertently exposed.

HOMEOPATHIC—A combination of flower essences walnut, olive, crab apple, and beech is very good for allergies.

ACUPRESSURE/MASSAGE—Massage daily, making sure you hit the acupressure points for allergies. One is on the outside of the elbow of the front leg, where the leg bends. The other is at the base of the skull, between the spine and the base of the ear on each side of the head.

Anal Gland Problems

NUTRITION/SUPPLEMENTS—Feed a good quality food with plenty of fiber. Make sure the food is high in protein and low in carbohydrates (Meat should be the first ingredient and preferably the first two ingredients.) Add some flaxseed oil to the diet. Vitamins A and E often help keep anal glands functioning well.

OTHER THERAPIES—Adequate exercise will help keep muscles toned, allowing the anal muscles to squeeze the anal glands, expressing them. During grooming, express anal glands that are full or are prone to problems. When glands are inflamed, use a hot pack with red clover tea or calendula tea to loosen the fluid; then express them.

Arthritis

NUTRITION/SUPPLEMENTS—Feed a good quality diet with a minimum of preservatives and additives. Add glucosamine and chondroitin and vitamin C to the diet.

HERBAL—Alfalfa is excellent for easing the inflammation of arthritis. A feverfew tea is also effective in reducing arthritic pain. It dilates blood vessels and aids in healing.

HOMEOPATHIC—Arnica, zeel, and rhus tox are all good for arthritis.

ACUPRESSURE/MASSAGE—An all-body massage emphasizing strong circular motions will increase blood flow and loosen stiff muscles. A hot stone massage over the stiff joints is also effective.

OTHER THERAPIES—Heat therapy, using heat packs, is very good for loosening stiff joints. Exercise of an appropriate level will keep muscles toned and joints moving. A piece of copper hung from your dog's collar or tucked into his bed will ease arthritis.

Asthma

HOMEOPATHIC—Keep Rescue Remedy on hand; it will help calm the fear that accompanies asthma attacks.

ACUPRESSURE/MASSAGE—Massage the entire chest area, paying particular attention to the back muscles.

OTHER THERAPIES—Cold packs, using first aid packs or ice packs, will slow or ease wheezing. Keep the dog away from as many chemicals and fumes as possible.

Barking

HOMEOPATHIC—A combination of flower essences chestnut, cerato, heather, and vervain often help problem barkers. Add a B-complex vitamin to the diet.

ACUPRESSURE/MASSAGE—An entire body massage, emphasizing slow circular strokes, will calm an excited dog.

OTHER THERAPIES—Barking caused by boredom is often relieved by strenuous exercise every day. The dog also needs training to keep his mind occupied. Spend some time reviewing your dog's responses to commands; or teach him some new tricks. An amethyst gemstone on the dog's collar or hidden in his bed will help the dog accept training.

Bladder Control

NUTRITION/SUPPLEMENTS—Feed a good quality food, either commercial or homemade, and add yogurt to your dog's diet.

HOMEOPATHIC—Use a homeopathic remedy that combines alumina, gelsemium, plantago, causticum, and cantharis.

ACUPRESSURE/MASSAGE—Massage daily with emphasis on the bladder control acupressure points; they are: the outer edge of the outside toe on each rear paw, the inside of the rear leg just above the hock (the knee), and the rear leg just above the bend of the hock.

OTHER THERAPIES—Review the dog's housetraining just to make sure he understands the rules.

Bloat

NUTRITION/SUPPLEMENTS—Feed a good quality diet, either commercial or homemade, that does not produce gas. Add live active culture yogurt to the dog's diet to increase digestive action. Feed several smaller meals rather than one large meal.

HERBAL—Give your dog chamomile tea after each meal.

OTHER THERAPIES—To avoid bloat, do not exercise the dog strenuously right after eating. However, daily exercise will help keep the digestive system working well.

Boredom

HOMEOPATHIC—Flower essence wild oat helps relieves emotional needs resulting from boredom. Add a B-complex vitamin to the daily diet.

AROMATIC—Citrus oils create a sense of well-being, while peppermint acts as an emotional stimulant.

OTHER THERAPIES—Inadequate exercise is often a cause of backyard boredom. Training, playtimes, and environmental enrichment (take a long walk in the park) can all help to alleviate boredom. An amethyst gemstone on the dog's collar or hidden in his bed will help the dog accept training.

Cancer

Note: Consult with your veterinarian regarding all treatments.

NUTRITION/SUPPLEMENTS—A homemade diet tailored to your dog's specific needs will keep your dog well nourished. Add yogurt to the diet to keep the digestive tract working well. Add blue-green algae to the diet to increase absorption of minerals and trace elements.

HERBAL—Alfalfa is said to have strong anticancer properties as do comfrey and dill. A tea made from burdock, slippery elm, and rhubarb has anticancer properties. Keep the immune system strong; offer garlic, echinacea, and green tea daily.

HOMEOPATHIC—Cancerinum and nux vomica are both good for some types of cancer.

OTHER THERAPIES—An amethyst gemstone on the dog's collar or hidden in his bed will elevate the dog's spirits. Shark cartilage is showing promise as a treatment or preventive for some types of cancer.

Car Sickness

HERBAL—Ginger and peppermint are both very good for nausea.

HOMEOPATHIC—The remedy tabacum is good for motion sickness. A flower essence combination of walnut, chestnut, mimulus, and Rescue Remedy is often very effective.

AROMATIC—Peppermint oil helps to ease nausea. Basil and parsley can prevent motion sickness.

ACUPRESSURE/MASSAGE—An entire-body massage, emphasizing slow circular strokes, will calm an excited dog. The indentation on the back of the front legs, just above the paws, is the point to massage should your dog be nauseated.

Changes

NUTRITION/SUPPLEMENT—A B-complex vitamin will help the dog keep a positive attitude toward the changes in his life.

HOMEOPATHIC—Flower essence walnut helps dogs accept changes in their environment including moves, remodeling, and similar disruptions.

AROMATIC—Citrus oils create a sense of well-being.

ACUPRESSURE/MASSAGE—An entire-body massage, using slow circular strokes, will calm an excited dog.

OTHER THERAPIES—Aerobic exercise will use up some of the energy focused on the changes occurring around the dog. An amethyst gemstone on the dog's collar or hidden in his bed will elevate the dog's spirits if he's showing signs of depression.

Chewing

NUTRITION/SUPPLEMENTS—Offer the dog a multivitamin/mineral supplement. Make sure the dog has enough things of his own to chew on; however, don't offer too many toys—he will then think everything is his. Add a B-complex vitamin to the daily diet.

HOMEOPATHIC—The flower essence aspen is very good for dogs who are nervous and anxious. Chicory will help relieve jealousy, and vervain is good for pets who have too much energy.

ACUPRESSURE/MASSAGE—An entire-body massage, using slow circular strokes, will help to calm an excited dog.

OTHER THERAPIES—An amethyst gemstone on the dog's collar or hidden in his bed will help the dog accept training. Destructive behavior is often made worse by a lack of exercise. And so an easy method of deterring chewing is to simply go out and play with your dog. Emphasize leadership exercises and reinforcement of the standard obedience commands.

Circulatory System

HERBAL—Capsicum dilates blood vessels, improving blood circulation. Gingko has the same effect as capsicum, and it is also an anticoagulant. Hawthorn strengthens the circulatory system, steadies an erratic heartbeat, and dilates the blood vessels thereby increasing blood flow.

ACUPRESSURE/MASSAGE—A daily massage will help keep the blood flowing throughout the body.

Coat (Dry and Flaky)

Note: If treated dandruff does not improve, consult your veterinarian. This can be a symptom of parasites or other health problems.

NUTRITION/SUPPLEMENTS—Feed a good quality diet. Add some fatty acids to your dog's diet, such as flaxseed oil or fish oil.

OTHER THERAPIES—See your veterinarian to make sure there isn't an underlying health threat causing excessive flaking. After a good shampoo (I recommend Joy dishwashing soap), use vinegar to rinse the skin and coat; then rinse with water.

Coat (Oily or Smelly)

NUTRITION/SUPPLEMENTS—Make sure your dog is eating a good nutritious diet, and then add a mineral supplement. Kelp is a good source of minerals.

HERBAL—Burdock is good for restoring a healthy coat, especially oily coats.

OTHER THERAPIES—Shampoo with a cleanser made to cut through oil such as Joy dishwashing soap, followed by a vinegar rinse, and then a thorough water rinse.

Constipation

NUTRITION/SUPPLEMENTS—Add a teaspoon of olive oil or some flaxseed oil to your dog's food. Adding fiber to his food helps too.

HERBAL—Senna is a natural laxative, as is dandelion. Slippery elm is very good for the bowel, easing constipation without causing spasms of the colon.

HOMEOPATHIC—Aloe socotrina and nux vomica are both very good for relieving constipation and digestive upsets.

AROMATIC—Lavender relieves stress, including stress of the bowels.

ACUPRESSURE/MASSAGE—A daily all-body massage will stimulate the blood circulation, which, in turn, helps the digestive system. In addition, massage at the acupressure point for the bowels. Rub the outside of each back leg, just below the hock where the muscle attaches to the bone.

OTHER THERAPIES—Exercise will often get the bowels moving and keep them working normally. Soak a clear crystal quartz in your dog's water bowl, or put a clear crystal quartz in his bed.

Dehydration

Note: See your veterinarian to treat dehydration right away. Of course, when you get your dog home, you need to keep him hydrated.

NUTRITION/SUPPLEMENTS—Add some chicken broth (no salt added) to his drinking water so that he wants to drink more.

ACUPRESSURE/MASSAGE—Massage the acupressure point between the second and third vertebrae on either side of the spine.

Depression

NUTRITION/SUPPLEMENTS—Make sure the dog is eating a well-balanced diet. Add a B-complex vitamin to the daily diet.

HERBAL—St. John's Wort is a natural antidepressant. Oat tea is a good pick-me-up for dogs feeling a little down.

HOMEOPATHIC—Flower essence mustard helps to mitigate mood swings. Gentian and gorse are also good for depression.

AROMATIC—Citrus oils create a sense of well-being, and peppermint acts as an emotional stimulant.

ACUPRESSURE/MASSAGE—Touch is very healing; incorporate an all-body massage into your daily routine.

OTHER THERAPIES—Light therapy (increasing bright lights, sun-light, and UVA light) eases depression caused by shorter days and longer nights. Strenuous daily exercise is often used to combat depression. The color yellow helps lifts the spirits; try giving your dog a yellow blanket. An amethyst gemstone on the dog's collar or hidden in his bed should cheer him up. A carnelian gemstone tucked into your dog's bed promotes self-confidence and counteracts doubt and negative thoughts. Topaz relieves depression, worry, and other emotional strains.

Diabetes

Note: Discuss all treatments for diabetes with your veterinarian before taking any action.

NUTRITION/SUPPLEMENTS—Vanadium, a trace mineral, can make insulin more effective. Increase the fiber in your dog's diet to slow down digestion and thereby decrease the amount of insulin needed to process the food.

OTHER THERAPIES—Regular exercise is very important to keep a diabetic dog on an even keel.

Diarrhea

NUTRITION/SUPPLEMENTS—Make sure the diet is correct and the dog isn't allergic to any of the ingredients in the food. During bouts of diarrhea, feed bland foods such as rice and chicken and make sure your dog has plenty of fresh water.

HERBAL—A plantain-leaf tincture is very good for slowing down and stopping diarrhea. A combination of flower essences walnut, crab apple, olive, and Rescue Remedy will help.

HOMEOPATHIC—Nux vomica is soothing for the entire digestive tract and will also slow diarrhea.

AROMATIC—Cinnamon.

ACUPRESSURE/MASSAGE—Massage on the outside of the front leg at the elbow crease.

Digestive Disorders

NUTRITION/SUPPLEMENTS—Make sure your dog has no food allergies (have him tested by a professional), feed him well, and add a B-complex vitamin to his diet. Add a spoonful (small for small dog and large for a large dog) of live active culture yogurt to his food.

HERBAL—A tincture of calendula reduces inflammation of the digestive system. Dandelion tea has the same properties and will also stimulate the digestive tract. A fennel tea is very soothing yet stimulates digestion at the same time. Oregon grape tinctures have antimicrobial and anti-inflammatory properties. Parsley is excellent for helping dispel gas.

ACUPRESSURE/MASSAGE—Massage on the hind leg, just below the hock (or knee joint), on the outside of the leg.

Digging

NUTRITION/SUPPLEMENTS—Make sure your dog is eating a well-balanced diet complete with vitamins and minerals. Add a B-complex vitamin and a kelp supplement to the daily diet.

HOMEOPATHIC—Rescue Remedy is calming for a dog who is digging out of emotion.

ACUPRESSURE/MASSAGE—Provide an entire-body massage using slow circular strokes. It will soothe an excited dog.

OTHER THERAPIES—Destructive behaviors are often a result of inadequate exercise, so see to it that your dog gets a good workout every day. Try playing with a tennis ball in addition to the daily walks. To help a dog who is rejecting training, an amethyst gemstone on the dog's collar or hidden in his bed will help. Emphasize leadership exercises and reinforcement of the standard obedience training.

Dominant Personality

HOMEOPATHIC—Flower essence vine relieves the need to assert dominance. Add a B-complex vitamin to the daily diet.

AROMATIC—Add five drops of grapefruit oil, four drops of cypress, and two drops of geranium to a bowl of steaming hot water and encourage the dog to inhale it. Do not allow him to drink it; this is for breathing only.

ACUPRESSURE/MASSAGE—Incorporate an all-body massage into your daily routine.

OTHER THERAPIES—Don't hesitate to ask a professional trainer or behaviorist for help.

Ear Infections and Ear Mites

NUTRITION/SUPPLEMENTS—Vitamin C (between 500 and 1,000 milligrams) can help.

HERBAL—Oregon grape is a natural antibiotic and works well in the ears as a wash. Inca gold *(pau d'arco)* is also a natural antibiotic that kills fungi and bacteria. Mineral oil will smother mites.

OTHER THERAPIES—As a preventive, clean ears regularly with a cotton ball and ear cleaner, alcohol, vinegar, or witch hazel.

Epilepsy/Seizures

NUTRITION/SUPPLEMENTS—Make sure the dog is eating as natural a diet as possible, with few additives or preservatives. Supplement the diet with a B-complex vitamin, vitamin C, and a multivitamin/mineral supplement.

HOMEOPATHIC—Consult a veterinary homeopath; there are treatments available for specific types of seizures.

ACUPRESSURE/MASSAGE—Massage the dog daily to calm him and relieve stress.

OTHER THERAPIES—Purple is relaxing and soothing to a dog stressed by seizures.

Eye Irritation

NUTRITION/SUPPLEMENTS—Make sure your dog is eating a good balanced diet and add brewer's yeast to his meal, or if he's allergic to yeast, add a B-complex vitamin to his meal daily.

HERBAL—A goldenseal eyewash is very effective against conjunctivitis. The herb eyebright will ease irritated eyes.

HOMEOPATHIC—Arnica is good for eyes that are swollen and red. Belladonna is good for pinkeye. Pulsatilla is effective for conjunctivitis and euphrasia is good for eyes that are tearing.

ACUPRESSURE/MASSAGE—Use acupressure just above and at the corner of the eye to relieve conjunctivitis.

Fear

NUTRITION/SUPPLEMENTS—Add a B-complex vitamin to the daily diet.

HOMEOPATHIC—Use Rescue Remedy, a Bach flower remedy. Place drops directly in the dog's mouth and repeat at fifteen-minute intervals as long as the need is there. Try flower essence centaury for fear; and flower essence elm for anticipatory fear. Flower essence rockrose is very good for strong fears by building courage. A combination of the flower essences walnut, chestnut, mimulus, aspen, and rockrose is very effective.

AROMATIC—Lavender is soothing and eases stress.

ACUPRESSURE/MASSAGE—Give your dog an all-body massage, making sure to repeat the ear stroke several times throughout the massage.

OTHER THERAPIES—An aquamarine hung from your dog's collar or tucked into his bed promotes peace and emphasizes courage. An amethyst gemstone on the dog's collar or hidden in his bed will elevate his spirits. Emphasize leadership exercises and reinforce standard obedience training.

Fever

Note: A fever is not an illness of itself but instead is a symptom of another problem.

NUTRITION/SUPPLEMENTS—Make sure your dog is drinking enough. To prevent dehydration, add some low- or no-salt chicken broth to his drinking water. Vitamin C is good for illness and fever, and will help boost the immune system.

HERBAL—Strengthen the immune system with echinacea.

HOMEOPATHIC—Aconite (from the monkshood plant) and hepar sulph will both help reduce fevers. Rescue Remedy is good for the discomfort and stress associated with an illness.

ACUPRESSURE/MASSAGE—Massage your dog's neck where it meets the shoulder blades.

OTHER THERAPIES—Cold packs can ease a fever while other remedies are being absorbed by the body.

Fighting (Other Dogs)

NUTRITION/SUPPLEMENTS—Make sure the dog is eating a well-balanced food or homemade food complete with vitamins and minerals. Add a B-complex vitamin to the daily diet.

HERBAL—For a dog who is fighting over something specific, try St. John's Wort to relieve anxiety.

HOMEOPATHIC—A flower essence combination of walnut, chestnut, beach, willow, and holly should be given to both dogs, or to the aggressor. Rescue Remedy is also good to relieve the tension that causes a fight.

AROMATIC—Add five drops of grapefruit oil, four drops of cypress, and two drops of geranium to a bowl of steaming hot water and encourage the dog to inhale it. Do not allow him to drink it; this is for breathing only.

ACUPRESSURE/MASSAGE—An entire-body massage, emphasizing slow circular strokes, will calm an excited dog. Even if you can't (and shouldn't) massage your dog when he attempts to fight, make massage part of your daily routine.

OTHER THERAPIES—Don't hesitate to call a professional trainer or behaviorist for assistance.

Fleas

NUTRITION/SUPPLEMENTS—Add garlic, a B-complex vitamin, and brewer's yeast to the dog's daily diet.

HERBAL—Use cedar, eucalyptus, or pennyroyal oils in the dog's bed to repel fleas.

OTHER THERAPIES—Check for fleas regularly; talk to your veterinarian about flea preventives; and control fleas in the environment. Sprinkle borax in the carpet to dehydrate the fleas and their larvae.

Grief

NUTRITION/SUPPLEMENTS—Feed a good diet to support a dog who is undergoing emotional stress. Add a B-complex vitamin to the diet.

HERBAL—Echinacea can help keep the dog healthy while grieving.

HOMEOPATHIC—Flower essence gorse calms grief while allowing it to follow its natural course. A combination of flower essences star-of-Bethlehem, walnut, honeysuckle, chestnut, and gentian is very effective.

AROMATIC—Lavender is calming.

ACUPRESSURE/MASSAGE—Give your dog an all-body massage daily. Your touch is very healing.

OTHER THERAPIES—Vigorous daily exercise is a good way to combat depression. An amethyst gemstone on the dog's collar or hidden in his bed will elevate the dog's spirits.

Heart Problems

Note: Obviously, heart problems are serious. Be sure to consult with your veterinarian before treating your dog.

NUTRITION/SUPPLEMENTS—Make sure your dog is eating a good diet, and supplement it with brewer's yeast or if he's allergic to yeast, add a B-complex vitamin to his meal daily. Garlic, calcium, vitamin C, vitamin E, and fish oil supplements are also very good for a healthy heart. Cayenne is excellent for heart and circulatory problems, too.

HERBAL—Hawthorn strengthens the heartbeat.

HOMEOPATHIC—Flower essences star-of-Bethlehem and impatiens will reduce the emotional stress of heart disease. Other homeopathic remedies are available for specific heart defects. Consult with your homeopathic veterinarian.

AROMATIC—Rosemary.

ACUPRESSURE/MASSAGE—In case of cardiac arrest, massage just above the wrist joint of the front leg, toward the inside. Daily, give your dog an all-body massage to keep the blood flowing.

OTHER THERAPIES—Coenzyme Q10 helps keep the heart muscle strong. Good daily exercise is important to maintain physical and cardiac fitness. Let your veterinarian guide you as to the type of exercise that is best for a dog with a heart problem.

Heartworms

Note: Talk to your veterinarian about heartworm preventives.

NUTRITION/SUPPLEMENTS—Keep the heart healthy by feeding the dog a good diet and supplement with brewer's yeast, garlic, fish oil, and vitamins B-complex, C, and E.

OTHER REMEDIES—Coenzyme Q10 will help keep the heart strong.

Hip Dysplasia

NUTRITION/SUPPLEMENTS—Vitamins C and E will help reduce the inflammation of the overworked joints.

HERBAL—Glucosamine chondroitin can help keep the joints healthy. The herb boswellia will reduce the pain. Yucca is very healing.

HOMEOPATHIC—Arnica is very good for the pain and inflammation that accompanies hip dysplasia.

ACUPRESSURE/MASSAGE—A gentle massage all over the hip and back leg area will relax your dog. Include a massage of the pectineus muscle inside each thigh to loosen and lengthen that muscle.

OTHER THERAPIES—Vigorous daily exercise will keep your dog strong; however, let your veterinarian (and your dog) guide you as to what kind of exercise and how much is appropriate. Heat therapy will reduce the pain that can come with dysplasia and increase healing by bringing more blood to the area.

Hot Spots

HERBAL—Melaleuca (tea tree oil) can be very healing to hot spots, as can a calendula tea wash. Boric acid powder can dry a weepy hot spot.

OTHER THERAPIES—Wash hot spots with an antibacterial soap to reduce secondary infections.

Hyperactivity

NUTRITION/SUPPLEMENTS—Make sure the dog is eating a diet that is low in carbohydrates and high in protein. If you're feeding your dog a commercial food, meat should be the first ingredient and preferably the first two ingredients listed. Add a B-complex vitamin to the daily diet.

HOMEOPATHIC—Flower essence vervain calms dogs with chronic hyperactivity and high-energy behavior problems.

AROMATIC—Lavender is calming. Bergamot oil is quite effective for overactive dogs.

ACUPRESSURE/MASSAGE—An entire-body massage, using slow circular strokes, will calm an excited dog.

OTHER THERAPIES—Vigorous daily exercise will use up some of that excess energy. An amethyst gemstone on the dog's collar or hidden in his bed will help the dog accept training.

Immune System (Strengthening)

NUTRITION/SUPPLEMENTS—Feed a good diet, make sure your dog is getting a minimum of 5,000 IUs of vitamin A, and add a vitamin C tablet to his daily diet. Add a dash of apple cider vinegar to the food.

HERBAL—Echinacea is able to stimulate the immune system so that the body can fight off disease.

HOMEOPATHIC—A combination of the flower essences walnut, chestnut, olive, star-of-Bethlehem, and crab apple is strengthening for the immune system.

ACUPRESSURE/MASSAGE—In cases of a severe threat to the immune system, massage or use acupressure in the depression at the inside of the elbow on the front leg.

OTHER THERAPIES—In color therapy, the color green works to boost the immune system. Vigorous daily exercise is needed to help keep the body strong and fit. A piece of clear quartz, hung from your dog's collar or tucked into his bed, or held in your hand during a massage, helps promote healing. Green jasper is also a healing stone and works best when held in the hand during a massage.

Irritable Bowel Disease

NUTRITION/SUPPLEMENTS—Feed a good quality diet high in natural fibers, preferably a diet without preservatives and additives. Add some live active culture yogurt to the daily diet.

HERBAL—A fennel tea is soothing to the bowel and helps expel gas. Peppermint is one of the best herbs available for soothing an irritated digestive system. Plantain leaf tea and raspberry tea are both soothing to the digestive tract.

HOMEOPATHIC—Nux vomica is very soothing to the digestive system.

ACUPRESSURE/MASSAGE—To relieve gastric upset, massage at the mid-back, to either side of the spine, just past the shoulders toward the tail.

OTHER THERAPIES—Daily exercise is good for keeping all of the body's systems in order; it also helps the gastrointestinal tract, especially to prevent constipation.

Insect Bites and Stings

NUTRITION/SUPPLEMENTS—Supplement a good diet with garlic, fish oil, and B-complex vitamins to make your dog less attractive to insects.

HERBAL—Marshmallow root wash and nettle tea are both very soothing to flea-bitten, allergic skin. A wet black tea bag will draw the poisons out of the bite or sting.

HOMEOPATHIC—Flower essence agrimony eases the discomfort.

OTHER THERAPIES—In color therapy, the color blue cools and calms itching and inflammation.

Itching

NUTRITION/SUPPLEMENTS—Make sure the dog is eating a well-balanced diet with few (or no) preservatives or additives. Add a mineral supplement to the diet.

HERBAL—Both calendula tea and a wash made from marshmallow roots are soothing to irritated skin. Irritated, itching skin can also be treated with a sage poultice.

HOMEOPATHIC—Flower essence agrimony eases discomfort.

OTHER THERAPIES—Use the color blue to calm and cool itching and inflammation.

Jealousy

HOMEOPATHIC—The flower essences agrimony, aspen, beech, chicory, elm, and holly are all recommended for jealousy.

AROMATIC—Lavender oil is calming.

ACUPRESSURE/MASSAGE—Don't massage your dog while he is showing jealousy, but do make an all-body massage part of your daily routine. He will feel loved and more secure.

OTHER THERAPIES—An amethyst gemstone on the dog's collar or hidden in his bed will elevate the dog's spirits. Training and behavior identification techniques can be very halpful in boosting a dog's self-esteem and thwarting feelings of jealousy. Don't hesitate to call a professional trainer or behaviorist for help.

Jumping Up (on People)

NUTRITION/SUPPLEMENTS—Feed an all natural food high in meat protein and supplement with extra minerals.

HERBAL—St. John's Wort to ease excitability.

HOMEOPATHIC—Silica.

ACUPRESSURE/MASSAGE—An entire body massage, using slow circular strokes, will calm an excited dog.

OTHER THERAPIES—An amethyst gemstone on the dog's collar or hidden in his bed will help the dog accept training. Emphasize leadership exercises and reinforce standard obedience training. Don't hesitate to call a professional trainer or behaviorist for help.

Lethargy

NUTRITION/SUPPLEMENTS—Feed an all natural diet supplemented with B-complex vitamins, minerals, and garlic.

HERBAL—A daily supplement of ginseng will give a lethargic dog more pep.

ACUPRESSURE/MASSAGE—Make an all-body massage part of your daily routine; get that blood flowing.

OTHER THERAPIES—Vigorous daily exercise will get a dog's endorphins moving throughout his system, easing lethargy. An amethyst gemstone on the dog's collar or hidden in his bed will elevate the dog's spirits.

Motherhood (Gestation, Lactation)

NUTRITION/SUPPLEMENTS—Feed a good quality, natural diet supplemented with vitamins and minerals.

HERBAL—Red clover increases estrogen production. A dill tea will increase milk production. Raspberry tea is very soothing to dogs coming into season who may be under the weather.

HOMEOPATHIC—Flower essence honeysuckle for mothers who feel tired or overwhelmed and flower essence mustard for hormonal imbalances. A combination of flower essences red chestnut, walnut, larch, gentian, olive, and Rescue Remedy is very good for the new mother.

ACUPRESSURE/MASSAGE—A daily all-body massage will reassure her that you are there for her and will help her combat stress. An amethyst gemstone on the dog's collar or hidden in her bed will elevate the dog's spirits.

Muscle Soreness

HOMEOPATHIC—Arnica (made from leopard's bane).

ACUPRESSURE/MASSAGE—Massage the entire body gently and be sure to incorporate the specific strokes for muscle soreness, including kneading dough and the long stroke.

OTHER THERAPIES—Heat therapy, using heat packs, eases stiffness and opens blood vessels, allowing better circulation and healing.

Nausea

NUTRITION/SUPPLEMENTS—Put the dog on a fast for twenty-four hours after vomiting. If the dog is nauseated but hasn't vomited, feed a bland diet.

HERBAL—Peppermint is wonderful for calming an upset stomach, or try dill tea.

HOMEOPATHIC—Ipecacuaha (made from ipec root).

Noise Sensitivity

HERBAL—Chamomile tea is very soothing.

HOMEOPATHIC—Flower essence aspen calms anticipatory fears; flower essence rockrose calms strong fears by building courage.

OTHER THERAPIES—Don't hesitate to call a professional trainer or behaviorist for help. The color blue is very calming; install a blue light bulb where your dog likes to rest. Place an aquamarine in an amulet for his collar, or hide one beneath his bed to promote peacefulness.

Obesity

NUTRITION/SUPPLEMENTS—Feed a good quality diet that is high in protein, low in carbohydrates, and low in fats. Supplement with a multivitamin/mineral tablet. Eliminate high calorie treats.

ACUPRESSURE/MASSAGE—Give your dog an all-body massage daily, emphasizing the stimulating long body strokes.

OTHER THERAPIES—Daily exercise is very important to help increase weight loss. Tailor the exercise to the dog's fitness level and increase the time or rigor of the exercise as the dog's ability increases.

Pain

HERBAL—Calendula salve is wonderful to relieve the pain of open wounds. Capsicum has anti-inflammatory and analgesic properties.

HOMEOPATHIC—Ruta (rue) helps alleviate the pain of sprains, strains, and broken bones.

OTHER THERAPIES—Cold packs will reduce swelling and ease pain.

Separation Anxiety

NUTRITION/SUPPLEMENTS—Feed a good quality diet and add a B-complex vitamin to it.

HOMEOPATHIC—Try Rescue Remedy, a Bach flower remedy. Place several drops in the dog's mouth thirty minutes and again fifteen minutes before you leave; also put several drops in the dog's water. Flower essence chicory.

AROMATIC—Add five drops of grapefruit oil, four drops of cypress, and two drops of geranium to a bowl of steaming hot water and encourage the dog to inhale it. Do not allow him to drink it; this is for breathing only.

ACUPRESSURE/MASSAGE—An entire-body massage, emphasizing slow circular strokes, will calm an excited dog and comfort him. An amethyst gemstone on the dog's collar or hidden in his bed will elevate the dog's spirits. Don't hesitate to call a professional trainer or behaviorist for help.

Shedding (Excessive)

NUTRITION/SUPPLEMENTS—Supplement a good quality diet with kelp, flaxseed oil, and fish oil.

OTHER THERAPIES—Brush the coat well; brush again; then bathe and brush again. Bathing loosens the remaining dead hairs.

Sleeping Problems

HERBAL—Chamomile tea is one of the best sleep remedies available. It is effective and safe.

ACUPRESSURE/MASSAGE—An all-body massage using slow circular strokes is very relaxing.

OTHER THERAPIES—In color therapy, the color purple is relaxing and aids in sleep. Exercise helps tire the body, making sleep more likely.

Stressful Situation

NUTRITION/SUPPLEMENTS—Feed a good quality diet and add a B-complex vitamin to it.

HERBAL—If the danger is ongoing, supplement the diet with echinacea to help keep the immune system healthy.

HOMEOPATHIC—Flower essence aspen.

Submissive Urination

HOMEOPATHIC—Flower essence centaury.

AROMATIC—Add five drops of grapefruit oil, four drops of cypress, and two drops of geranium to a bowl of steaming hot water and encourage the dog to inhale it. The mixture is for inhaling only; do not allow your dog to drink it.

ACUPRESSURE/MASSAGE—Massage your dog's entire body, using predominantly slow circular strokes. This will reassure an insecure dog. An amethyst gemstone on the dog's collar or hidden in his bed will elevate the dog's spirits and help him accept training.

Swelling (From an Injury)

OTHER THERAPIES—Cold packs will ease the swelling following an injury. After twenty-four hours, use a heat pack to promote healing.

Teething

HERBAL—A chamomile extract rubbed on a puppy's gums will ease the discomfort of teething. Aloe vera juice is also very good for relieving the pain.

HOMEOPATHIC—Ulmus fulva will ease inflammation. For anxiety accompanying teething, try Rescue Remedy.

ACUPRESSURE/MASSAGE—Gently massage the gums where the teeth are coming in.

Training (Behavior Modification Training)

HOMEOPATHIC—Flower essence chestnut enhances memory. A combination of flower essences walnut, chestnut, crab apple, clematis, and impatiens is very good for dogs in training; it helps acceptance and learning.

AROMATIC—Add five drops of grapefruit oil, four drops of cypress, and two drops of geranium to a bowl of steaming hot water and encourage the dog to inhale it; this is for breathing only.

OTHER THERAPIES—Vigorous daily exercise is a great stress reliever, keeping mind and body fit. An amethyst gemstone on the dog's collar or hidden in his bed will help the dog accept training.

Training (Competition Training)

HOMEOPATHIC—Flower essence crab apple aids self-esteem and flower essence honeysuckle is good for overexertion. A combination of flower essences walnut, chestnut, crab apple, clematis, and impatiens helps the learning process. Elm helps the dog cope with overwhelming activities.

AROMATIC—Add five drops of grapefruit oil, four drops of cypress, and two drops of geranium to a bowl of steaming hot water and encourage the dog to inhale it. Do not allow him to drink it; this is for breathing only.

OTHER THERAPIES—Exercise will go far to keep a dog's mind and body fit. An amethyst gemstone on the dog's collar or hidden in his bed will help the dog accept training.

Training (Obedience Training, Service Training, Hard-Working Dogs)

HOMEOPATHIC—Try flower essence cerato to improve concentration and learning while flower essence oak alleviates stress and builds perseverance and stamina. A combination of flower essences walnut, chestnut, crab apple, clematis, and impatiens is very good for dogs undergoing training; it helps acceptance and learning.

AROMATIC—Add five drops of grapefruit oil, four drops of cypress, and two drops of geranium to a bowl of steaming hot water and encourage the dog to inhale it. Do not allow him to drink it; this is for breathing only.

OTHER THERAPIES—Vigorous daily exercise is a great stress reliever, keeping mind and body fit. An amethyst gemstone on the dog's collar or hidden in his bed will help the dog accept training. A bloodstone is an excellent stone for working dogs; it emphasizes courage and calmness. Garnet is the stone of strength for working dogs; it is a very strong stone and conveys strength to the dogs who wear it.

Upper Respiratory Distress

HERBAL—Licorice is an expectorant, while at the same time it soothes and protects the mucous membranes.

HOMEOPATHIC—Try gelsemium (made from yellow jasmine).

AROMATIC—Add three drops lemon oil, two drops thyme oil, two drops of tea tree oil, and one drop eucalyptus oil to a bowl of steaming water. Let the dog inhale it. Do not let him drink it; this is for inhaling only. If the dog is coughing, add a dab of Vicks Vaporub to the hot water mixture.

ACUPRESSURE/MASSAGE—Massage just under the shoulder blade, on the side, midway on the second rib.

OTHER THERAPIES—In color therapy, the color orange stimulates the respiratory system.

Vomiting

NUTRITION/SUPPLEMENTS—Put the dog on a fast for twenty-four hours, then put on a bland diet—such as chicken and rice—for forty-eight hours.

HERBAL—Peppermint and chamomile are both very soothing to an upset stomach.

HOMEOPATHIC—Try nux vomica and Rescue Remedy.

ACUPRESSURE/MASSAGE—Massage on the outside of the rear legs, just below the hock.

Worms

Note: Be sure to see your veterinarian for guidance. Don't hesitate to talk to your veterinarian about conventional therapies; internal parasites can be a serious problem.

NUTRITION/SUPPLEMENTS—Add some wheat or oat bran to your dog's diet.

HERBAL—Wormwood and black walnut are natural wormers; note that the latter must be used with care, as it can be quite harmful to your dog if improperly administered. Parsley has antiparasitic properties.

Wounds

NUTRITION/SUPPLEMENTS—Make sure the dog is eating well so that his body has the nutrients to heal the wound. Garlic is a wonderful antibacterial supplement.

HERBAL—Licorice is an anti-inflammatory. An arnica salve opens blood vessels and speeds healing. A calendula salve will relieve the pain and swelling of a wound and will also speed healing. Similarly, a comfrey salve or ointment is effective and also has anti-inflammatory properties. Yucca is excellent for healing wounds.

HOMEOPATHIC—Arnica is often very helpful for wounds with bruising.

OTHER THERAPIES—Bad wounds often respond well to magnet therapy, which is effective in relieving pain and in increasing the blood circulation for better healing.

APPENDIX C: THE SIGNIFICANCE OF COLOR

Color is such a powerful force in our lives. Our homes and offices are decorated with color. Even the stores where we shop use color to entice us to stop and browse. Our traffic signs, intersection lights, and building identification signs are all color-coded. So much in our lives is affected by color, yet often we don't even notice it. Unless, of course, something is the wrong color—we would certainly notice that!

Red

Red is a strong, powerful color—the color of a warrior. In healing, red stimulates the sensory nervous system. In astrology, red is the color of Aries, and in Chinese astrology, it's one of the colors of the tiger and the rooster. In numerology, red is associated with the number nine. In an aura, red symbolizes physical strength and activity; reds are leaders and teachers.

Yellow

Yellow lifts the spirits and is good for alleviating depression. In healing, yellow stimulates the lymph system. Yellow is the color for Gemini, and in Chinese astrology, it is one of the colors for the snake and the monkey. In numerology, it is one of the colors for the number one. Yellow signifies joyfulness in an aura. Although yellows may seem impatient and pushy to some, to others they simply live life to the fullest.

Orange

Orange, the mixture of red and yellow, is a warm color. In healing, orange stimulates the respiratory system and eases spasms and cramps.

In Chinese astrology, orange is one of the colors for the rooster and the tiger. In numerology, it is one of the colors for the number one. In an aura, orange represents physical extremes. Oranges are explorers and athletes.

Green

Green is the color of nature—of growing, living things. In healing, green is a very soothing color; it brings the body into balance and strengthens the immune system. In Chinese astrology, light green is one of the colors for the hare, while dark, forest green is one of the colors for the dragon. In astrology, Taurus favors emerald green. In numerology, several numbers are associated with green, including two, six, and seven. In an aura, green represents an intellectual quality.

Blue

Blue is a cool color, and its coolness is good for inflamed and itching skin. It is also effective as a mild sedative. In astrology, sky blue is the color of Virgo. In Chinese astrology, light blue is one of the colors of the rat, and medium blue is one of the colors of the pig. In numerology, the numbers four and six are both associated with blue. In an aura, blues symbolize sensitivity and intuitiveness.

Purple

Purple is a relaxing color and aids in sleep. It lowers blood pressure, reduces the heart rate, lowers the body temperature, and calms emotions. In Chinese astrology, the ox favors violet while the goat likes purple. In numerology, the number three is associated with purple. Those who are psychic, spiritual, and intelligent are likely to have a purple aura.

Brown and Earth Tones

Colors in the gold and brown family, in all their various shades, represent the earth. These are centering and calming colors. In Chinese astrology, the horse, monkey, and dog all favor browns and related earth tones. The monkey and dog also favor gold as does the dragon. The astrological sun sign Leo is associated with gold, and in numerology, gold is one of the colors for the number one. In an aura, earth tones are associated with being grounded, practical, and logical.

Black, Gray, and Silver

Black has been called the absence of all other color or the combination of all colors. In any event, black is often labeled a negative or depressing color. Black is, however, a very warm, protective color. In Chinese astrology, it is the powerful color of both the dragon and the snake. In numerology, black is the color for the number eight. Silver, a diluted black, is the color for the astrological sun sign Cancer. In numerology, silver is the color for the number five.

APPENDIX D: RESOURCES

Animal Communicators and Psychics

Sharon Callahan
530-926-1245
www.anaflora.com

Anita Curtis
610-327-3820
www.anitacurtis.com

Gail De Sciose
212-388-7319

Anastacia Gourley
413-548-9806

Carol Gurney
818-597-1154

Dawn Hayman
315-737-9339
www.springfarmcares.org

Lydia Hiby
818-365-4647
www.lydiahiby.com

Deb Jones
310-305-1552

Samantha Khury
310-374-6812

Betty Lewis
603-673-3263

Judy Meyer
505-820-7387

Penelope Smith
415-663-1247

Kate Brower Solisti
505-984-8876

Laurel Steinhice
615-356-4280

Aromatherapy

Oshadhi USA, 1340 G Industrial Avenue, Petaluma, CA 94952

Dog Therapy Organizations

Delta Society, 289 Perimeter Road East, Renton, VA 98055-1329
800-869-6898

Foundation for Pet Provided Therapy, P.O. Box 6308, Oceanside, CA 92058
www.fppt.org

Dog Training and Obedience

Association of Pet Dog Trainers
www.familyinternet.com/pet/apdt

National Association of Dog Obedience Instructors
www.kimberly.uidaho.edu//nadoi

Gems, Metals, and Stones

Boji Inc., 4682 Shaw Boulevard, Westminster, CO 80030

Everett Buss, P.O. Box 221, Crestone, CO 81131

Heaven and Earth, P.O. Box 224, Marshfield, VT 05658
800-942-9423

Isis, 5701 East Colfax Avenue, Denver, CO 80220

Marguerite Elsbeth, P.O. Box 1535, Pena Blanca, NM 87041
505-465-0806

Pegasus Products, Inc., P.O. Box 228, Boulder, CO 80306
800-527-6104

Wegner Crystal Warehouse, 4013 West Magnolia Boulevard,
Burbank, CA 91505
(Walk-in sales only)

The Pyramid Collection

800-333-4220

www.pyramidcollection.com

Herbs, Herbal Research, and Flowers

Animal Apawthecary, P.O. Box 212, Conner, MT 59827

Bach, Ellen, USA, P.O. Box 320, Woodmere, NY 11598

800-433-7523

Boericke & Tafel, Inc., 2381 Circadian Way, Santa Rosa, CA 95407

707-571-8202

Boiron-Borneman, 1208 Amosland Road, Norwood, PA 19074

800-258-8823

Canadian Herb Society, Van Dusen Botanical Garden, 5251 Oak Street, Vancouver, British Columbia, Canada V6M 4H1

Coyote Moon Herbs, P.O. Box 312, Gainesville, FL 32602

904-377-0765

Flower Essence Services, P.O. Box 1769, Nevada City, CA 95959

800-548-0075

Flower Essence Society, P.O. Box 459, Nevada City, CA 95959

Frontier Cooperative Herbs, P.O. Box 299, Norway, CA 52318

800-365-4372

Greenhope Farms Flower Essences, P.O. Box 125, Meriden, NH 03770

603-469-3662

Healing Herbs for Pets
888-775-PETS

Herb Research Foundation, 1007 Pearl Street, Suite 200, Boulder, CO 80302
303-449-2265

Iris Herbal Products, P.O. Box 160, San Cristobal, NM 87564
505-586-1802

ITM Herb Products, 2017 Southeast Hawthorne, Portland, OR 97214
800-544-7404

Longevity Pure Medicine, 9595 Wilshire Boulevard, Suite 706, Beverly Hills, CA
90212
213-273-7423

The Source, 2501 71st Street, North Bergen, NJ 07047

Holistic and Alternative Veterinarians

American Holistic Veterinary Medical Association
2214 Old Emmorton Road, Bel Air, MD 21015
410-569-0795
www.altvetmmed.com/ahhvmadir

Holistic and Herbal Veterinarians

Ihor Basko, DVM, 4160 Waiapa Road, Kilauea, HI 96754
808-828-1330

Jeffrey Judkins, DVM, 1431 SE 23rd Avenue, Portland, OR 97214
503-233-2332

Douglas Lemire, DVM, P.O. Box 40521, Santa Barbara, CA 93140
805-565-3985

Deborah Mallu, DVM, HC 30, Box 849, Sedona, AZ 86336
520-282-5651

Susan Wynn, DVM, 1080 North Cobb Parkway, Marietta, GA 30062
770-424-6303

Homeopathy Resources

Arnica, Inc., 144 East Garry Avenue, Santa Ana, CA 92707

Dr. Goodpet, P.O. Box 4547, Inglewood, CA 90309
800-222-9932

Hahnemann Pharmacy, 1940 4th Street, San Rafael, CA 94901
510-527-3003

Hanson Homeopathic Herbal Medicine, 4540 Southside Boulevard, #5,
Jacksonville, FL 32216-5458
904-641-6301

Homeopathic Educational Services, 2124 Kittredge Street, Berkeley, CA 94704
800-359-9051

Homeopathy Overnight, RR 1, Box 818, Kingfield, ME 04947
800-276-4223

National Center for Homeopathy, 801 North Fairfax Street, Suite 306, Alexandria,
VA 22314
703-548-7790

Standard Homeopathic Company, 154 West 131st Street, Los Angeles, CA 90061

Magnets

Animal Magnets

www.animalmagnets.net

Magnetic Field Therapy, IBS Systems, 4754 East Flamingo Road #453, Las Vegas, NV 89121

Magnets Heal, Magnet Therapy Products, Denver, CO 80209

303-722-1434

www.magnetsheal.com

Magnetic Wellness Products, 3500 Parkdale Avenue, Building A, Baltimore, MD 21211

Massage and Touch

American Massage Therapy Association, 820 Davis Street, Suite 100, Evanston, IL 60201

Linda Tellington-Jones, TEAM and Touch Training, P.O. Box 3793, Santa Fe, NM 87501

Nutrition and Supplements

California Natural, 1101 South Winchester Boulevard, Suite J225, San Jose, CA 95128

L & H Vitamins, 37-10 Crescent Street, Long Island City, NY 11101

800-221-1152

Merritt Naturals, P.O. Box 532, Rumson, NJ 07760

888-463-7748

www.merrittnaturals.com

Natural Animal Nutrition, 2109 Emmorton Park Drive, Edgewood, MD 21040

Natural Pet Care Company, 8050 Lake City Way, Northeast, Seattle, WA 98115
800-962-8266

Nutrition Now, Inc., 6350 Northeast Campus Drive, Vancouver, WA 98661

Nutri Pet Research
800-360-3300

Prozyme Products, 6600 North Lincoln Avenue, Lincolnwood, IL 60645

Robert Abady Dog Food Company, Nutra-vet Research Corporation, 201 Smith Street, Poughkeepsie, NY 12601

Solid Gold Health Products and Dog Food, 14883 North Cuyamaca Street, El Cajon, CA 92020

Vitamin Shoppe, 4700 Westside Avenue, North Bergen, NJ 07047
800-223-1216

Poison Hotline

Toxicology Hotline for Animals, University of Illinois
800-548-2423 (credit cards) or 900-680-0000 (phone bill)

Therapeutic Lights

Light Treatment and Biological Rhythms, P.O. Box 478, Wilsonville, OR 97070

SunBox Company, 19127 Orbit Drive, Gaithersburg, MD 20879

Veterinary Acupuncturists

American Academy of Veterinary Acupuncturists, P.O. Box 419, Hygiene, CO 80533-0419

Center for Veterinary Acupuncture

Dr. Maria Glinski, DVM, 1405 W. Silver Spring Drive, Glendale, WI 53209

800-680-2282

International Veterinary Acupuncture Association

Meridith Snader, DVM, 2140 Conestoga Road, Chester Springs, PA 19425

215-827-7245

or P.O. Box 1478, Longmont, CO 80502

303-682-1167

Veterinary Homeopathy

Academy of Veterinary Homeopathy, 751 Northeast 168th Street, North Miami, FL 33162

International Association for Veterinary Homeopathy

Susan Wynn

334 Knollwood Lane, Woodstock, GA 30188

770-424-6303

National Center for Homeopathy, 801 North Fairfax, Suite 306, Alexandria, VA 22314-1757

703-548-7790

References and Additional Reading

Adams, Janine. *You Can Talk to Your Animals*. New York: Howell Book House, 2000.

Anderson, Ken. *Where to Find It in the Bible*. Nashville, TN: Thomas Nelson Publishers, 1996.

Ball, Pamela. *The Complete Dream Dictionary: A Practical Guide to Interpreting Dreams*. Edison, NJ: Book Sales, Inc, 2000.

Bardens, Dennis. *Psychic Animals*. New York: Barnes & Noble Books, 1987.

Boone, J. Allen. *Kinship with All Life*. San Francisco: HarperSanFrancisco, 1954.

Brennan, Mary L., D.V.M. *The Natural Dog: A Complete Giude for Caring Owners.* New York: A Plume Book, Penguin Books, 1994.

Boorstein, Sylvia. *That's Funny, You Don't Look Buddhist*. San Francisco: HarperSan-Francisco, 1997.

Bowers, Barbara. *What Color Is Your Aura?* New York: Pocket Books, 1989.

Caduto, Michael J., and Joseph Bruchac. *Native American Animal Stories.* Golden, CO: Fulcrum Publishing, 1992.

Craze, Richard. *Chinese Astrology*. Hauppauge, NY: Barron's Educational Series, 1999.

Cryptozoological Society of London. *A Natural History of the Unnatural World.* New York: St. Martin's Press, 1999.

Cunningham, Scott. *Crystal, Gem & Metal Magic.* St. Paul, MN: Llewellyn Publications, 1999.

De Long, Douglas. *Ancient Teachings for Beginners.* St. Paul, MN: Llewellyn Publications, 2000.

Dunbar, Ian. *Dog Behavior: An Owner's Guide to a Happy Healthy Pet.* New York: Howell Book House, 1998.

Eason, Cassandra. *Discover Your Past Lives*. Berkshire, England: Foulsham, 1996.

Elsbeth, Marguerite. *Crystal Medicine.* St. Paul, MN: Llewellyn Publications, 1998.

Garfield, Frank, and Rhondda Stewart-Garfield. *Dreams*. Sydney, Australia: Barnes & Noble Books, 1998.

Gerwick-Brodeur, Madeline, and Lisa Lenard. *The Pocket Idiot's Guide to Horoscopes.* New York: Alpha Books, 1999.

Hammerschlag, Carl A., M.D. *The Dancing Healers.* San Francisco: HarperSan-Francisco, 1988.

Hoffman, Mathew, ed. *Dogspeak.* Emmaus, PA: Rodale Press, 1999.

Hutchens, Alma R. *Indian Herbalogy of North America.* Boston & London: Shambhala Publications, 1973.

Kreiisler, Kristin von. *The Compassion of Animals.* Roseville, CA: Prima Publishing, 1999.

Lilly, Simon. *Crystal Healing.* Boston: Element Books, Bridgewater Book Company, 2000.

Meyer, Judy. *The Animal Connection: A Guide to Intuitive Communication with Your Pet.* New York: A Plume Book; Penguin Books, 2000.

Mooney, James. *The Myths of the Cherokee.* New York: Dover Publications, 1995.

Morgan, Diane. *The Best Guide to Eastern Philosophy and Religion.* Los Angeles: Renaissance Books, 2001.

Palika, Liz. *The Complete Idiot's Guide to Raising a Puppy.* New York: Alpha Books, 1999.

———. *The Consumer's Guide to Dog Food.* New York: Howell Book House, 1997.

Pitcairn, Richard, D.V.M., and Susan Hubble Pitcairn. *Dr. Pitcairn's Complete Guide to Natural Health for Dogs and Cats.* Emmaus, PA: Rodale Press, 1995.

Puotinen, C. J. *The Encyclopedia of Natural Pet Care.* New Canaan, CT: Keats Publishing, 1998.

Quammen, David. *The Flight of the Iguana.* New York: A Touchstone Book, Simon & Schuster, 1988.

Randour, Mary Lou. *Animal Grace.* Novato, CA: New World Library, 2000.

Robinson, Jonathan. *The Complete Idiot's Guide to Awakening Your Spirituality.* New York: Alpha Books, 2000.

Russell, Stephen. *Barefoot Doctor's Guide to the Tao.* New York: Times Books, 1998.

Ryan, Terry. *The Toolbox for Remodeling Your Problem Dog.* New York: Howell Book House, 1998.

Schoen, Allen M., D.V.M. *Kindred Spirits: How the Remarkable Bond Between Humans and Animals Can Change the Way We Live.* New York: Random House, 2001.

Shojai, Amy, and the editors of *Prevention for Pets. New Choices in Natural Healing for Dogs and Cats.* Emmaus, PA: Rodale Press, 1999.

Stein, Diane. *Natural Health for Dogs and Cats.* Freedom, CA: The Crossing Press, 1993.

Stein, Diane. *The Natural Remedy Book for Dogs and Cats.* Freedom, CA: The Crossing Press, 1994.

Suzuki, D. T. *Zen Buddhism.* New York: Grove Press, 1964.

Thurston, Mary E. *The Lost History of the Canine Race.* Kansas City, MO: Andrews and McMeel, 1996.

Tilford, Gregory, and Mary Wulff-Tilford. *Herbs for Pets.* Irvine, CA: Bow Tie Press, 1999.

Volhard, Wendy, and Kerry Brown, D.V.M. *Holistic Guide for a Healthy Dog,* 2nd ed. New York: Howell Book House, 2000.

Watts, Alan. *What is Tao?* Novato, CA: New World Library, 2000.

Whitaker, Hazel. *Numerology.* New York: Barnes & Noble Books, 1998.

———. *Develop Your Psychic Ability.* New York: Barnes & Noble Books, 1998.

———. *Fortune Telling.* New York: Barnes & Noble Books, 1999.

INDEX